MODERNISATION OF BUDDHISM CONTRIBUTIONS OF AMBEDKAR AND DALAI LAMA-XIV

MODERNISATION OF BUDDHISM
CONTRIBUTIONS OF AMBEDKAR AND DALAI LAMA-XIV

DR. LELLA KARUNYAKARA

GYAN PUBLISHING HOUSE
New Delhi-110002

MODERNISATION OF BUDDHISM: CONTRIBUTIONS OF AMBEDKAR AND DALAI LAMA-XIV

(History, Religion, Social Sciences)

Rs. 695

ISBN: 81-212-0813-0

Published in 2002 in India by
Gyan Publishing House
5, Ansari Road
New Delhi 110 002
Phones: 3261060, 3282060, Fax: 3285914
e-mail: gyanbook@vsnl.com
visit our website at: http://www.gyanbooks.com

Laser Typeset at Alphabet, Delhi
Printed at Mehra Offset Printers, New Delhi.

DEDICATED TO

PARENTS	:	Lella Arogyam & Rahel
Sister	:	L. Vijaya & L. Jayasree
Wife	:	Indu Bala
Son	:	Lella Sharan

Contents

Preface

The Modern History of Buddhism is the history of Revival of Buddhism. The most important factor which has been instrumental for the revival of Buddhism is modernisation of this religion. Modernisation is a continuous process. So the revival of Buddhism continues. Modernisation is a social paradigm, which represents social attitudes or programmes dedicated to supporting what is perceived as modern. Modernisation is a kind of change, and certainly positive change. It is a social change because it brings change in the social attitudes of the people. Social attitudes are largely influenced by religion. To bring change in the social attitudes of the people, religious philosophy must involve the people in social programmes which in turn brings change in the social system. Thus there is a need to modernise religion with such a social programme and social philosophy that could compel to face with contemporary problems of the society. Modernisation of Buddhism involves newer interpretations of the Dhamma of the Buddha to suit the needs and to face challenges posed by the modern society. Change in the religious values and beliefs is an outcome of the new interpretations of the religious philosophy from the point of view of the necessities of contemporary society or social groups. The religious values and beliefs are generally based on the social philosophy of religious system. If a religious philosophy is interpreted in accordance with the needs of particular social groups or society in general, the religion itself gets involved in the process of modernisation. This is the basic source for the survival of any religion in the changing situations to withstand newer challenges. Ambedkar and the Dalai Lama XIV contributed to the modernisation of Buddhism on the lines mentioned above. The purpose of modernisation of Buddhism for them is to establish the society of justice, equality and democratic.

The question is: Does Dhamma of the Buddha need to be modernised? If the answer is in negative it is a negation of the very fundamentals of philosophy of the Buddha. Gautama Buddha allowed his followers to question everything until they get satisfactory answer and that answer must have of social utility.

The work is a valuable contribution to the Buddhist thought and not just an addition to the existing literature on Buddhism. It has raised the relevance of the religion to modern man in the context of social utility. The work certainly entice interest among both academics and lay readers. It is highly useful for the western followers of the Dhamma to know more about intricacies faced by the Buddhist society in modern India. The book may also be useful to students of Buddhism, Ambedkar thought and History of Dalits.

I wish to express my deep sense of gratitude to Prof. (Dr.) Dawa Norbu, Jawaharlal Nehru University, New Delhi, Hon'ble fellow, University of Durham (U.K.) and author of internationally acclaimed works, for his guidance and for sharing his in-depth knowledge and vast experience, who was instrumental in giving a good shape for this work.

I am very much grateful to D.C. Ahir, author of several books on Ambedkar and Buddhism and Prof. (Dr.). D. Kantowsky, Faculty of Sociology, University of Konstanz, Germany, for their apt suggestions, which made me to go deep into the study.

I am very indebted to authors, whose works I have consulted. I am thankful to the Library staff of J.N.U., Delhi University, Tibetan Library, Delhi, Dr. Babasaheb Ambedkar Institute of Social Sciences, MHOW, Madhya Pradesh, Tibetan Works and Archives and Information Office of H.H. Dalai Lama, Dharamsala, Himachal Pradesh.

I would also like to acknowledge the services of Thangaraj for the efficient and good typing of the manuscript.

Lucknow
14th April, 2002

Dr. Lella Karunyakara

One

Methodology in Buddhist History

Historian of India traditionally faces difficulties since he started studying India in a historical perspective to identify different cultural traditions, outside the Hindu cultural system. It was indeed, first highlighted by the Anglican Western historians. B.R. Ambedkar was the first Indian historian to discuss indigenous cultural traditions and social values in his own historical context. He applied a different approach to study Indian history, particularly from the point of view of Dalit - Bahujan Buddhist tradition.

Nativity or local identities form the basis of Ambedkarite approaches of historical thought. Social identity of individual or group in indigenous context is the core part of the methodology. In this work the word 'Dalit' is used as synonym of indigenous. There is a strong historical justification to mean 'Dalit' for indigenous. There has been a broad cultural stream from Indus civilization to the age of the Buddha and to the modern Dalit-Bahujan movements. Apart from this, for a social historian to clearly identify the roots of indigenous history, tradition and symbols, there is a need to adopt proper terminology. The emergence of strong Dalit movements at social and political levels compels social scientists to study Dalit history in a positive historical context. Dalitism to mean as a historical term, encompasses all the alternative cultural thoughts i.e., Charvaka, Buddhism, Kabir, Phuley, Periyar on one side, Sikkhism, Indian Islam and Indian Christianity on the other side, with Ambedkarism as a connecting reference. Ambedkarism is the core thought of Dalitism that consists of all 'bahujan' thought streams. Today it is popularly called as 'Dalit-bahujan' thought. Indigenous culture is hence projected as an alternative culture by Dalit-Bahujan academics. The non-Brahminical and the anti-Brahminical streams are identified with Dalit identity academically. This methodology has been broadly applied in the present study. And effort has been made to reconstruct and to redefine indigenous non-Hindu Brahminical Aryan culture as a 'Dalit-bahujan' or broadly Dalit culture.

Positive success of Dalit movements at different levels convinced traditional academic lobby to see reason with Ambedkarite point of view, to study social dynamics that influenced Indian history. Dalit the indigenous people, the people belong to non-Hindu-Brahmin Aryan culture and identified with the different historical streams that produced Indus culture, Charavaka-Lokayata, Gautam Buddha, Asoka, Kanishka, Harsh Vardhana, Kabir, Ravidas, Chokkamela, Jyotiba Phuley, Ramaswami Naicker, Bhimrao Ambedkar and also Sikkhism, Indian Islam and Indian Christianity. The projection of Jesus Christ as the Dalit Christ by Dalit Christians (like Black Christ for Blacks in America) broadly belongs to indigenous Dalit-Ambedkar cultural scheme. Apart from identifying indigenous cultural system with Dalits, the social dynamics of Indian society have been studied not only in the Buddhist context and also in the Christian and Indian Islamic value systems, since Dalit cultural system broadly provides space for all of them.

There have always been two broad cultural streams that moulded the course of Indian history, identified with indigenous cultural traditions and Aryan believes and values respectively. The two, too contradictory to combine, too difficult to synthesize, too irrational to treat equal. Budhism is the basis for the former and Hinduism for the latter. The religious behaviour that offered by these two dominant identities is the point to be examined to understand the relevance of the very idea of modernising religion.

The sociological study of religious behaviour rests upon the assumption that religious behaviour is social behaviour. What is studied is human beings as they behave in regard to religion and in turn its effect on society or social interaction and social relations. So religious behaviour has concrete effects in this world, even though some of it may be directed to what is believed to be another world. Sociologically, religion is viewed as a part of culture and is frequently referred to as one of the major social institutions. The social scientist is concerned with empirical phenomena, not metaphysical phenomena. The study is made on these lines while evaluating the contributions of Ambedkar and the Dalai Lama-XIV to the modernisation of Buddhist philosophy and practice.

Every society has already developed the blueprint it expects its members to follow in their religious behaviour. Indeed, every society applies great effort to see that the blueprint is followed rather closely. While it is true that new religions and religious innovations do develop, it is also true that most of a man's religious behaviour was outlined and planned for him long before he was born. It is certainly a part of the culture of his group.

Religion is entirely man made invention. That is, human beings are involved in the formation of religious concepts and practices. The meaning of these religious concepts are social products and part of one's own culture. 'Meaning', indeed, emerges in the process of social interaction. This can be a result of consensus or manipulative religious mechanism of the dominant group. Even though social meanings mostly emerge out of manipulations of the dominant group, in course of time they gain, wider acceptability since the lack of awareness about the functioning of social system with given social meanings among the socially exploited groups in the society.

It should be recognised that social meanings do much more than merely provide labels or titles or names for different social groups as well as individuals. Social meanings also provide plans of actions. These plans of action can be both secular and religious but actions are social. Once the social actions are given religious sanction, the influence of social action becomes religious. In other words the religious social actions are more effective in influencing the social interaction.

When an individual is labelled as a criminal or an untouchable, low, mean, or impure etc., he doesn't carry just a label but social identity. Apart from that, it also provides whole society the instructions as to how one should treat this person, or how one should interact with him.

Suppose, in a secular society, criminal or untouchable sort of definitions carry the class discrimination on the basis of rich and poor, where there is no religious sanction to these identities. But in a religious society, i.e., giving religious sanction to social identities like untouchable on the basis of birth, the religion has to take whole responsibility for the compartamentalised social divisions within its society.

In fact human behaviour is mostly a procedure of reacting to things and people to which the individual has already applied a label. The reactions are patterned by the plans of actions, incorporated in one's own definitions. So it is the definitions that people carry around in their heads which primarily determine human behaviour.

Thus, it is important to recognise in this connection, that these definitions are real to the individual who accepts them. In fact, it can properly be maintained that they are the only 'reality' the individual knows. They are the reality in the individual's life, whether or not these definitions really correspond to the reality. It is so because of social acceptability and religious sanction.

New words and new definitions are constantly being injected into the culture. Most people simply adopt the labels, concepts and definitions which are a part of their religion as well as culture. However, history had produced great men like the Buddha in 6thc.B.C., the Ashoka (3rdc.B.C.) and in modern history men like Ambedkar and the Dalai Lama-XIV to question some of the meanings, definitions and concepts provided by the traditional religions and societies. They modernised human thought with humanity and rationality as their basis.

Values or moral definitions matter in the social relations. Goodness or badness is not an innate quality of anything but is rather strictly a matter of human definition. Since values are definitional in nature it is easy to understand why one does not usually obtain easy agreement on value questions. Because something may be good today and bad tomorrow. A practice may be good for one group and bad for another. For example according to Manu, a true Hindu should practice untouchability and should follow caste hierarchy. Even though such treatment is unacceptable to the untouchables.

Religious behaviour can be meaningfully studied only at the social level. A fruitful approach to the study of religion is through an analysis of society. This is the approach which has been adopted by Ambedkar and the Dalai Lama-XIV in their evaluation of the role of religion in general and Buddhism in particular.

Religion doesn't play the same role in all stable societies. This is because we have different religions with different philosophies and social purposes. The social utility of these religions differs from each other particularly in the context of philosophical dichotomy of Hindu and non-Hindu religions.

Specific religions have come and gone, have changed very slowly or very rapidly, but so far as we know, religion has always been present in the society. It has to accept the fact that religion exists and effects human behaviour. Once we accept this fact, we also accept the fact that the religious belief is not simply the acceptance of an idea, it is an attitude in human behaviour in relation to each other.

These beliefs influence on the decision of an individual in identifying common motive, like what is moral and what is immoral, what is good and what is bad to himself and his social group, the group of believers who share common religious beliefs and practices, also share common values; they accept common definitions as to what is good and what is bad.

Social values are a necessary element of religion, because religion consists of definitions as to how man should relate himself to man. Religion in fact influences the decisions, which decides the direction of society or evolution of society. In other words, religion involves in what type of society should be evolving.

Religious behaviour is intricately related to his other behaviour i.e., economic, familial and political. Religion doesn't exist in isolation, nor does man's religious behaviour occur in social isolation. In any form of social organisation, religion is one of the important variables to be considered.

In a stable society, the major religion provides interpretations favourable to the dominant groups and to the maintenance of the *statusquo*, particularly in Hindu society. The essence of any stratification pattern is inequality. Thus, in India individuals at different social levels have unequal chances, among other things, of getting an education, of becoming Prime Minister of India, of ending up in prison, of living to a ripe old age.

The patterns of differential rewards and punishments developed by the groups are similarly reflected in its religious definitions. Thus, when a group develops a particular stratification pattern which becomes well established in the culture, it will in the process usually also develop moral definitions describing the system as good and just and asserting that the criteria utilised in differently distributing the rewards of the society are moral ones.

However, if such definitions turn out to be inconsistent due to the rise of contradictory definitions of other religion or religions in the same society, they become disruptive factors, which contribute to the disorganisation of the society. The Hindu society in India faced the same problem at different levels in the historical periods due to the revival and modernisation of Buddhism.

When Hindu society came in contact with Islam and Christianity, it had faced the same problem of disintegration of its society. With Ambedkar's effort to revive and modernise Buddhism, the Hindu society is once again finding it difficult to face the challenge posed by modern Buddhism, which does not endorse any stratification system or unequal reward system. It is interesting to study the problems faced by Hindu society whenever it faced new religious beliefs from different religions. This is because Hinduism stands entirely different from other religions on the question of stratification and reward system, since it has a unique stratification pattern based on caste, which is not existing in any other religion.

Religious endorsement of the general principle of stratification is possibly most clearly exhibited in the definitions by religious groups as to the 'life after death'. The stratifications of the after life are typically defined as being determined by divine wisdom, and as therefore unquestionably moral and just. A common belief concerning this afterlife is that those with certain qualifications will be assigned to particular strata for all eternity; they will, in other words, be consigned to different castes, such as heaven and hell, in a system without vertical mobility and will remain in these castes forever.

The whole matter of caste is obviously an important one to any society, which stratifies along caste lines. Such societies have decided that individuals born within a particular group in that society inherit particular treatment and must be required to retain their group identification and the treatment which goes with it throughout their entire life. The society structures to its various interaction patterns so that the caste identification is generally recognised and taken into account by these special patterns of treatment in all forms of social interaction.

Individuals born into the caste are expected to find friends within their group, marry within that group, worship within that group, and die still carrying that group identification. Society sets up the necessary social machinery to enforce such expectations, usually in the conviction that the preservation of the caste identity is essential for the welfare of the larger group. If a society makes it difficult for an individual ever to lose a particular label or identification, it does so on grounds, which it considers extremely important. Society reinforces caste distinctions with religious sanctification and make them morally justifiable.

Thus, in India, where upper - lower caste lines have been institutionalised, we find that religious definitions provide moral approval for maintaining these caste lines. The situation in India is, an intricately complex one, evidencing great variability. Patterns vary from region to region and even from town to town within regions, with religion endorsing differing and contradictory patterns to provide moral justification for the local position. In many cases justification is secured for both sides form the same religion (read as Hinduism) and from the same set of scriptures.

So, in any pattern of differential rewards and punishments utilised by a society, religion is an integral part. It is involved in the moral definitions by which the system is evaluated, and religious factors may also be taken into account in the differential system itself. Social stratification comes about when norms and values are developed by the group and are arranged into some hierarchical pattern. Religious endorsement to top level norms and values reinforce justification on stratification patterns. Stratification patterns including the religious dimensions therefore, tend to be woven into the large social system in such a way that relative overall harmony is obtained.

It can be seen that religion provides the oxygen for stratification. Any action of an individual or social group is influenced by a belief system. And the belief systems can be used in the both directions, positively or negatively, depending on one's social interest.

The need of modern society is an ideal religious philosophy with practical solutions to the problems faced by man. What is needed is a philosophy that aims at abolishing stratification. Religion's role should be evaluated and all religious definitions which support discriminatory practices should be abolished.

Indeed, it would seem to be humanly impossible to abolish discriminatory or differential practices. Social stratification patterns are a universal phenomenon, and that although great differences exist therein from one group to another and from one time to another, religion in its various forms has characteristically provided moral definitions for all such patterns, so as to give them moral meaning for the human beings affected by them. However differential response patterns can also be found in human relations. These response patterns are to be justified with religious philosophy. This is what exactly termed as modernisation of religion in this study.

The term modernistation represents social attitudes or organised programmes dedicated to supporting what is perceived as modern. It is inappropriate to refer to the modernisation of a religion unless we mean as part of a self-conscious, perhaps largely social programme. The concepts of modernity and religion identify the broad range of religious response to intense and self-conscious social change in the contemporary world. Modernisation is a kind of social change, which suppose to be positive. This sort of change is possible, if change occurs in the social attitude of people. Since social attitudes are largely influenced by religion (i.e., religious philosophy), there is a need to modernise religion altogether. Religion must be equipped with modern and innovative techniques so as to confront contemporary problems.

Social and economic changes are involved in modernisation process. To gain socio-economic change there is a need of change in religious values and beliefs. This is the main aim of both Ambedkar and the Dalai Lama, to modernise and paternise Buddhism. They felt mental attitude could be changed with the change in the religious-beliefs. And in turn the change could be brought in social and economic attitudes of an individual.

However, "it should be noted at the outset that the sociological concept of modernisation does not refer simply to becoming current or up to date but rather specifies particular contents and process of societal changes in the course of national development. The modernity in philosophical and epistemological discussions refers to the perspective that there is one true descriptive and explanatory model that reflects the actual world".[1] Hence both Ambedkar and the Dalai Lama interpreted the Buddhist philosophy in such a way that they not only modernised the Buddhism to make it current or up to date but evolved Buddhist model that reflects the actual world. The Buddhist belief system, which they have succeeded to build up is to call it in Weberian terms a "rational-law", which could be used to initiate the process of societal changes for national development.

Much of the world is now engaged in an unprecedented process of social change that seeks to govern itself by rational policy planning. Modernisation operates rather through a transformation of institutions that can only be accomplished by the transformation of individuals - the painfully complex process which epitomised as 'a change of Heart. Contemporary thinkers recognised that economic development is a high priority objective of every modernising society. Indeed it is not the only motivation for modernisation.

Satisfaction of life is the real priority objective of both rich and poor. It is not that rich man or economically, industrially highly developed societies like the west, have no problems at all. The major problem, today, the modern society is facing is that of 'rising violent human attitude'. This disturbs the peace and stability of the human life. May be to some extent, man sees his life with material development. But he obviously feels unsatisfied with his work and life, since, economic motivation without touch of humanity doesn't provide the ultimate satisfaction.

So modernisation of a society depends not necessarily on economic or industrial development but also on positive social attitudes of people. This change could be achieved only with change in their religious belief system. Religious philosophy of a society should suffice the 'Humanity' as ultimate goal to be achieved by any individual in all spheres of life. It could be possible only with change in religious goals.

If the religious goals, again, contradicting reality or the wordily problems and finding ambiguous answers from supernatural powers, and satisfying both exploiters and exploited to maintain *status quo* of the system, they are not going to solve the problems faced by the modern society.

The transformation of a society is a question with moral and religious implications. Development depends not only on men's notions of what is possible, but also on their notions of what is good, and on the dynamics of their pursuit of what they deem good, the force of their motivations and the quality of their acting.

The question posed by the modern society is that what course will men choose. This depends on what kind of social value system the society has. Obviously, social system derives its necessity from economic considerations. However it gets wider acceptability only with the support of religious ideology. Ultimately it is the ideology of religions, which determined the kind of society.

Hence, modernisation of a religion means, the modernisation of a society. Because modernisation is a kind of social change related to the religious ideology.

The current and future development of any society, depends and will continue to depend on what men in that particular society think and feel and choose, and with what quality they act. In fact these are questions which are determined by the kind of religious ideology.

What any country, not on paper but at heart, chooses to be, and how devotedly it pursues that choice, will finally determine its future. The questions of human behaviour at this level are religious questions. So the modernisation of a society involves the modernisation ot its religious life.

It means social system is influenced by the religious ideology and to bring a needed change in the social values there is a need of a change in the religious beliefs. To bring this change, one needs to modernise the religious philosophy. Generally, it is the responsibility of the intellectuals of a society to provide the contour of ideas within the limits of which that society acts. Most of the populace in each case act within the ideational framework of a traditional culture.

The intellectuals of any society are by definition those who formulate and nourish that society's ideology, they are the custodians and extrapolators of its dominant ideas and values. During sixth century B.C., it was Gautama Buddha who undertook this intellectual task. And he modernized the notion of religion and formulated new meaning of religion by emphasizing 'Humanism'.

The birth of Buddhism, itself a product of the process of modernisation of religion. So, Buddhism, one can put it as 'religious modernity'. The philosophy of Buddhism is symbolised with modernism. Buddhism was the first religious philosophy that propagated the principle of 'service to humanity' than to God and rituals and religion is for man and man is not for religion. It humanised the institution of religion and the concept of God. This is the innovation which has born in the history of religions, six hundred years before the birth of Christ. And even to present modern society, this looks new, modern and innovative.

This has brought revolution in the thought of religion. It changed the criteria to decide the identity of religion. It promulgated new values, ethics for human society. It proved that religion could also be secular. These are the features, which have brought special place to Buddhism among all the religions.

Gautama Buddha can be called as the first one, who modernised the very thought of religion. Apart form its metaphysical difference, Buddhism has become important, due to its 'Ethics and social order'. The ancient canonical teachings set the Buddhist notion of the good society in definite contrast to pre-existing Brahmanic views on caste and sacrifice. For example, in the Pali *Agganna Sutta* the Buddha described the devolution of the present world system and human society in such a way that the Brahmanic grounding of the social hierarchy in ontological and hereditary distinctions was definitively undercut.

In the famous *sigalovada Sutta* the Buddha commended the suspension of traditional Brahmanic rituals for the maintenance of proper order in the world, and urged their replacement by the cultivation of proper relationships between parents and children, teachers and students, husbands and their dependents, friends and companions, masters and workers, and religious teachers and ordinary practitioners.

The ancient Buddhist canons also established the basis for Buddhist ideals of morally regulated sacral kingship that came to play a crucial role in the Buddhist tradition. For example, in the *Agganna Sutta* the primordial devolution of human society was checked by the decision of the people to appoint a king i.e., *maha sammata*, the great elect, who was given responsibility for establishing justice and adjudicating quarrels. Other *suttas* presented similar religio-ethical figures, such as the '*cakravartin*' the mythical monarch, who set in motion the wheel of dhamma and went on to establish his royal dominion over all the earth; and the Dhammaraja, the dhamma - king, who established prosperity, justice, and peace in his realm.

The next important phase in the history of modernisation of Buddhism could be found with the major turning point in the development of the Buddhist social ethic, during the reign of an important Indian monarch named Asoka, who was a Buddhist and a sponsor and interpreter of the dhamma. Asoka's *Dhamma* can be called in other way as the new form of Buddhism. His inscription display his conception of the 'true *dhamma*' consisting of basic social morality supported by ritual celebrations and simple forms of meditational practice. Asoka held that his people could not really be happy unless they led a highly moral life. Morality was an essential condition for true happiness.

Some historians, of the opinion that Asoka picked up some of the great principles of ethics from various religions and these principles collectively were styled as Dhamma. Asoka's Dhamma for them, therefore, does not mean any religious system. Nor does it mean Buddhism. However, they could not succeed to prove, their argument, since they able to provide the list of neither ethical principles nor the religions, which were said to be adopted by Asoka to frame his Dhamma. It is interesting to note that, almost all of them are from Hindu background and their interest seemed to be, to down play the importance of Buddhism in the life of Asoka.

Asoka's Dhamma is modernised Buddhism, at that particular historical point of period. His Dhamma is undoubtedly the Dhamma of the Buddha. He contributed to the modernisation of Buddhism, to make Buddha-Dhamma, more adaptable ethical-religious system to the society of his age. It was an effort to keep Buddhist tradition in the contemporary value system.

Asoka-*Dhamma* consists of well-known principles of morality, like *Daya* (mercy), *danam* (charity), *satyam* (truthfulness), *saucham* (inner and outer purity), and *madave* (Gentleness). It does not have any dogmas, rituals and ceremonies. The *Dhamma* of Asoka has two aspects namely, the doctrinal and practical. The practical aspect was emphasised more. He exhorted the people to acquire virtues like charity, mercy, truthfulness, etc. The doctrinal aspect consists of *ahimsa* (non-violence), belief in *swarga* (heaven) etc.

One can conclude that, next to the Buddha, Asoka was the earliest teacher of religious humanity and universal morality. Asoka did not in fact enunciate any new principles in his *Dhamma.* What he did was that he defined, preached and published universal morality of Buddhism. Probably, this was the first attempt at greater level to modernise Buddhism in the history of early Buddhist India.

As Buddhism developed and spread, its ideal of a society regulated in accordance with *Dharma* was realised in a variety of forms. In Theravada societies, religious social order took the form and made an emphasis on maintenance of the purity hence spiritual authority of the *sangha*; on the king as a unique *Bodhisattva* figure responsible for protecting the sangha and for maintaining religious order and justice within his realm; and on the responsibility of the lay people to follow the five basic precepts and to cultivate the virtue of giving.

In *Mahayana* and *Vajrayana* societies, the relations between Buddhist ideals and actual social structures were more problematic. Generally, however, religious order in these situations took form around a single figure, usually a monarch but occasionally (as in Tibet) a monk. This figure, because of his status as a pre-eminent *Bodhisattva* or living Buddha, tended to be the primary locus of concentrated religious authority.

Buddhist social ideals were articulated in one way by those who were integrated into the established regimes, in quite another way by those who sought to overthrow established authorities. Conservative social visions that legitimated and guided the exercise of authority by those already in power have been the norm in Buddhist history. But revolutionary versions of the Buddhist social ethic were also developed in countries all across Asia.

Many of these anti-establishment expressions of Buddhist social ideals were connected with expectations of the imminent coming of the future Buddha- *Maitreya.* This *Bodhisattva,* often identified with the leaders of revolutionary groups espousing socio-political change, for example, Ambedkar and Dalai Lama XIV; who are expected to establish on earth a new social dispensation in which prosperity, justice, and steriological opportunity would abound for all classes of people.

Ambedkar's tirade against Hindu socio-political system and his adaption of Buddhist ethical system as a means to bring change in the Indian society, represented anti-establishment expressions of Buddhist social ideals. His efforts to modernise Buddhism had resulted into formation of radical versions of the Buddhist social ethics. That's why he became modern *Bodhisattva.*

Ambedkar's interpretation can be seen mainly in the concepts of God, atman, karma, re-birth and *dukkha* (suffering). Ambedkar denied the existence of God. Whereas the Buddha on these questions apparently maintained silence. Ambedkar's Buddha is certain and explicit. Ambedkar rejected the existence of atman. He rejected the belief in samsara i.e. transmigration of the soul, belief in moksha or salvation of the soul. He also rejected belief of karma and refused to acknowledge it as the determination of man's position in present life. He replaced the fatalistic view of karma with the scientific view of karma.

According to this scientific view, re-birth as a concept applies only to the natural components of a being. When the body dies, the four elements disperse and live on. While any psychological or spiritual dimension to the concept of rebirth is denied, karma as moral law is acknowledged. It is operative only within one's present life and the general moral order. He interpreted the Buddha's gospel as essentially social. So the traditional Buddhist vision of *dukkha* is omitted and suffering is interpreted as a social phenomenon. Man's misery is not just because of desire but is the result of man's inequity to man. Man's suffering is because of social and economic injustice.

Ambedkar stressed a rational, humanitarian egalitarian Buddhism, drawn chiefly from Pali texts. Hindu beliefs and practices and any supernatural Buddhist ideas were eliminated from the Buddhism propounded by Ambedkar.

The more recent efforts to modernise Buddhism have come from Tenzin Gyatso, the Dalai Lama XIV. Historians have held the view that the institution of Dalai Lama represented the ideology of established authority and the conservative social visions. However, the present Dalai Lama has initiated the process of making the Buddhist institution as an anti-establishment expression.

He gives utmost importance to democracy and made his intention public to establish modern democratic system on the basis of Buddhist social ideals in the free Tibet. His politico-religious leadership has immensely contributed to the evolution of modern thought at both the political and religious levels.

The Dalai Lama's main contribution lies in the principles, like universal brotherhood, compassion and world peace. For him, all human beings are members of human family. Love and compassion is the essence of religion. And peaceful co-existence is the only way for the modern nations to survive without violence. Non-violence is the core of his philosophy. He urged his audiences to forget their sectarian differences and tolerate each other for the good of the survival of human society. He asked Buddhists to adopt western science and technology while preserving their own moral and religious values. He is, however, principally a religious revolutionary.

Both Ambedkar and the Dalai Lama differ in their approaches in modernising the Buddhism, due to their different cultural backgrounds. Ambedkar was born in Hindu society and being an untouchable he had experience the negative side of the Hindu social system. So his approach towards Buddhism was very much a reflection of his experience as an untouchable.

The relevance of religion, as he felt that, for the welfare of humanity but not to satisfy any supernatural power or not to aim at supernatural world. His main emphasis was on the ethical values of the social system of a religion. In fact, the origin of Buddhism can be traced in the same context.

Hence Ambedkar concentrated on the two tasks, to modernise Buddhism. One is to understand Buddhism in Hindu social context and the other one is to make Buddhism a relevant for modern society. In both the tasks, he followed the ideals laid by the Buddha.

In other words whatever new angles, he provided to study the Buddhist philosophy are not different from the basic philosophy of the Buddha. However, he modernised the Buddhism and made it more relevant to modern society.

He differentiated Hinduism with rest of the religions on the question of socio-ethical system. He kept Buddhism under the category of non-theistic religion, making it a different one from rest of the major religions. This is the basis of his approach for the study of Buddhism.

The Dalai Lama XIV, born in a humble peasant family, in Tibet and the first Dalai Lama who has spent a major part of his life in India. Chinese occupation of Tibet made him, to be more realistic in his approach towards society and religion. Hence, the main emphasis in his philosophy is the concept of non-violence, and peaceful co-existence.

In this background, the Dalai Lama, incorporated in his philosophy, the principles like universal brotherhood, compassion, and world peace. He modernised the Buddhism with these principles and made it capable of giving solutions to the problems faced by post-industrial societies. His efforts to propagate Buddhism in western countries, as an answer to the modern problems, and at the same time his emphasis on the relevance of co-existence of all religions, have brought a new meaning to the ideals of the Buddha.

Ambedkar felt the idea of all religions are equally good, is a wrong belief. He is of the opinion that religion is an institution or an influence like all social influences and institutions it may help or it may harm a society, which is in its grip.

The Dalai Lama is of the view that all the religions have closer understanding and he holds that the essence of the messages of all religions is love, mercy, tolerance and forgiveness. He also believed that, religious unity is sure to bring about world peace because the basic aim of all religions is to make man good and mentally tension free.

This contradiction between their interpretations is certainly because of their different cultural backgrounds. The Dalai Lama trying to harmonize between varied religious philosophies, where as Ambedkar finds it difficult since his social goal is to establish rationalised belief system. The Dalai Lama is making his views in the general religious environment, whereas Ambedkar moulded his ideas in the context of Hindu social system. The other area, where the Dalai Lama differs from Ambedkar is over the question of existence of God. For Ambedkar God is not an essential element of a religion. In his view the religion of the savage society had no idea of god and felt that the idea of God is not integral of religion. Whereas the Dalai Lama believes in the existence of several gods. He feels that Buddhism consist of many gods and the Buddha could be visualised in many forms.

However, there are many views, which are in agreement with the both of them. Both Ambedkar and the Dalai Lama underlined the congruity between Buddhism and modernity and emphasized the role of exercise of individual judgement, in order to free Buddhism from rigid interpretations and render it adaptable to the demands of modern society without compromising its fundamental principles. They believed that the change in religious beliefs could bring, change in social relations. For which, they first made an attempt to re-define the meaning of religion and then modernise the Buddhism according to it.

For them, religious modernisation refers to those processes of democratization of religious structure, secularization and rationalisation of religious culture and humanisation of religious philosophy, which enhance the capability, effectiveness and efficiency of performance of a society's religious system. They maintained that religion as morality is of its very substance. In other words, the religious problem is not a speculative one in which the religious object is validated primarily at the metaphysical level, it is a practical problem, pertaining wholly to men's ethical nature.

The rationalism, which this implies there fore necessitates a critique of traditional beliefs and institutions in anticipation of a more positive statement of what, a genuinely rational religion must involve. Such insistence on the need for distinguishing between the essential and non-essential—reason and conscience, social utility providing the criteria — is to become the guiding principle of all forms of liberal religion or modernised religion. Hence both of them represent modern social visions and the social justice forces, who sought to overthrow the established non-democratic socio-political traditions.

There is a great deal of continuity between the historical development of Buddhism and the current responses and innovations. Thus, the civilisational, and cultural patterns continue to exert a predominant influence in the evolution of Buddhist tradition. Buddhist modernism is better understood when placed within its present historical context. Modernism evolved in an attempt to establish the ability of Buddhism to face the new challenge.

The goal of Buddhist modernism is to make Buddhism relevant and responsive in the context of modern society. Its message is that Buddhists can live, engage, and contribute actively to the modern world while remaining faithful to their religion. Its ultimate objective is to provide Buddhist societies with an indigenous ideology of development, and could become the basis of a rational, modern society. At minimum, modernist thinkers wanted to provide Buddhists with criteria by which the process of change resulting from the impact of an alien culture should be controlled and filtered.

In Buddhist terms modernised society connotes, the society, which has welfare of the mankind as its fundamental motive for social change by rational planning. It makes a rational formula for the transfer of institutions both economic and social for "Bahujan Sukhya", (welfare of many).

The Buddha as an innovator, offered systematic critiques to the older values and redefined the meaning of existence and the nature of man and society within a more universal, transcendent framework, which became the basis for new cultural re-construction.

The Buddha's thought has been modified with time and re-defined to make solutions for the contemporary problems. This process has been carried out by many personalities at different historical times i.e., Asoka's Dhamma; in modern period Ambedkar's Buddhism and the Dalai Lama XIV's Modern Tibetan Buddhism.

Reference

1. Armer, Michael J., John Katsillis, "Modernization Theory", Encyclopaedia of Sociology, ed., by Edgar F. Borgatta, Max Millan Publishing Company, New York, 1992, p. 1300.

Two

Emergence of Buddhism in the Context of Contesting Philosophies and Social Conditions in Ancient India

The Buddhism of the Buddha[1], during the 2500 years of its existence, has survived both as glory and downfall among the fierce encounters it met with other faiths and philosophies, not only in India, but also in other parts of the world. The first encounter, when Buddhism itself came into existence on Indian horizon in 6th century B.C., came up with Vedism, the cult of Vedas, which is said to constitute the driving force of ancient Aryan culture and civilisation.

The rituals and sacrifices of Vedic religion gradually developed into a bloody cult that created a community of priests who preached worship of gods for individual gains. The art of imprecation was considerably in practice. The Vedas also refer to a particular social system based on the four-fold classification of human beings–the Brahmins, the Kshatriyas, the Vaishyas, and the Shudras–known as *Varna vyavastha*. That social stratification later turned into a tyranny of casteism and untouchability. The classification was not natural, it was arbitrarily developed for the supremacy of certain classes. Subsequently, the so-called higher classes, particularly the Brahmins, were the beneficiaries from the Vedic rituals and the lower castes driven by them into a mass of serfs; they were condemned to live as sub-human beings.

It was the Buddha who, for the first time, opposed the social system, dogmatism and priesthood of Vedic cult. The Buddha created a new social order based on the equality of men, fraternity and universal brotherhood. It was he, who first denounced the worthlessness sacrifice of animals to Gods, and taught men the value of social service. It was he who emancipated men from the thraldom of Vedic religion. It was he, again, who released men from the iron heel of confederacy of priests. And it was he who first told men to exercise reason and not meekly to follow the dogma of Vedic religion.

It is said that the Buddha liberated man from the domination of priests, from the idea of institutionalized mediation between man and God, and from the spiritual and liturgical dogmatism of priesthood. By rejecting the caste system, the Buddha became the greatest social reformer of his age. His teachings were directed to all men, and not to a given caste or group. He opposed the blood sacrifice of animals which was characteristic of Brahmanism.[2]

It was Buddhism's successful revolt against Vedism and Brahmanism. The subsequent course of history favoured the Buddhist transformation of socio-religious life. It was the liberalism and humanism of Buddhism, whose influence went far beyond the spheres of religion and philosophy, that contributed to the disruption of Vedic religious social pattern and ushered in a classless society.[3] It happened after Buddhism had been officially propagated during the Mauryan period. It was indeed Ashoka, with his humanitarian Mission, who preached the universal *Dhamma*.

Importance of Philosophy

The indestructible foundation of the whole of human life is its philosophy. It is an effective weapon against religious fanaticism and superstition. It provides a life throughout, like showing the correct way of solving human problems that agitates men's minds. Philosophy is imbued with utmost faith in the human intellect, in the power of knowledge, in man's ability to fathom all the secrets of the world around him, and to create an order of justice based on reason and love.

Social environment is a sort of an order; it consists of varied customs, traditions, beliefs, and types of organisation, which exist within the social group in which men are socialised. It is the order of social institutions. The sociological imperatives of social environment are such that they can be understood and be manipulated by men; they are not given by some unseen power. Though they are not of the individual's making, yet they exert an influence upon them which is compelling. The social environment is an infinitely ideological universe of meanings unified into rich systems of language, science, religion, philosophy, laws, ethics, etc., and includes the totality of the best actions of mankind.

A philosophy, which does not present a global outlook, is decidedly lacking in comprehensive understanding. It is incomplete, unworthy to practice. A correct comprehensive understanding then becomes the essential basis of all philosophies of human interest. In the absence of a correct world understanding, natural events would dominate human life thereby creating several interruptions in the course of progress and prosperity. Man's philosophical insight is both a "process of self expression and of penetration into the environment about him".[4] A better understanding of the world is necessary in everyday living and this is given by philosophical insight. It is a philosophy only when it presents a better understanding of world. Buddhism got the opportunity to performs all these functions.

Hindu Thought

In other words, Brahmanic Hindu theistic thoughts: Vedic, and Upanishadic. Dalit Materialistic thoughts: *Sankhya* and *Lokayata* philosophies lack systemic coherence in relation to Buddhist philosophy. Although Buddhism was a continuity of the broader Dalit tradition, it opposed to pure materialistic thoughts.

The *Purusa Sukta*, hymn in the Rig Veda, refers to the origin of different classes (*varnas*) by the Supreme God. For the prosperity of the world, the creator, from his mouth, arms, thighs and feet, created the Brahmins, the Kshatriyas, the Vaishyas and the Shudras, respectively. These four classes are called as '*chaturvarna*' as an ideal organization of society. It was elaborated in rigid rules in the Brahmanic period, and later, by *Manu-smriti*. There was division of occupations among these classes.

The occupation of the Brahmins was learning, teaching and the performance of religious rites. The occupation of Kshatriyas was fighting. Trade was assigned to the Vaishyas. The occupation of the Shudras was service of the three superior classes. As a rule, one class could not transgress the occupation of the other. The Shudra, because he was on the lowest step of the social ladder, was denied the rights to education and arms. These two rights were also denied to the women of all classes as the Hindu Shastras (religious books) state.

In the Hindu society, a man's life was divided into four stages: The first was called *Brahmacharya*; its object was study and education. The second was the stage of *Grahasth*, which meant a married life. The third was *Vanaprastha* the object of which was to familiarize a man with the life of a hermit, i.e., serving the family ties. And the fourth was the stage of *Sanyasa*. Its chief object was to enable the man to go in search of God and seek union with him. The first and the last stages were not open to the shudras and women. And no mention was made in the Hindu scriptures about the Untouchables, since they were not under varna or caste system. They were outcastes–*Jativihin*. The subsequent course of history witnessed them as the untouchable castes, because of their Buddhist background and for their commitment to create alternative religious—cultural system that threatened Hindu Brahminic religious set-up.

The core idea of Hindu philosophy is the theory of *Karma*. The birth of a man is the result of his past Karmas done in previous life. It is one of the main subject of the theory of transmigration of soul, which means that what a man is in this life is wholly due to his previous Karmas (deeds) done in the former life.

There was an emphasis on sacrifice in the Hindu rituals. The increasing dominance of the idea of sacrifice helped to raise the position of the priests. These priests declared that only the due performance of Vedic sacrifices and observance of religious rites and ceremonies and the offering of gifts to Brahmins could have salvation of the soul or deliverance from harm ruin or loss. The result was that priesthood became a profession and a hereditary one. The priest who possessed the Vedic lore became the accredited intermediary between gods and men and the dispensers of the divine grace.

In brief, the ancient Hindu period was marked by the observance of caste and the ashramas, emphasis on sacrifice, the eternity of the Vedas, the supremacy of the priest and a belief in past karma and transmigration of an individual's soul.

On the question of authorship of Upanishads, divergent views are projected. It is popularly believed that the authors of Upanishads belonged to different cultural backgrounds and belief. Hence some of the Upanishads (i.e., Dalit Upanishads) opposed to the Vedic thought, questioned divine origin of the Vedas. They denied the efficacy attributed to sacrifices, to funeral oblations, and gifts to the priests, which were the fundamentals of brahmanic philosophy. Some other Upanishads, which were probably written by organized groups, adopted essence of Vedic teaching. The Brahmanic Upanishads are said to form concluding portions of Vedas, and are called as *Vedanta* (the end of the Vedas). The central thesis of these Hindu Upanishads is that *Brahma* is the ultimate reality, which is spiritual and that *Atman* is the same as *Brahma*. The *Brahma* is eternal and unchanging principle. Historical authentication about the origin of the Brahma could be identified with Brahmin as a priest, and as (self-claimed) supreme human being on earth attached with the supreme god Brahma.

The Hindu Upanishad philosophy regards '*Brahma*' as the 'ultimate reality'. In some of the advanced speculations of the Upanishads, it came to mean the pure knower or the pure consciousness. Thus, according to the idealistic outlook that finally emerged in the Upanishads, the ultimate reality is pure consciousness. The corollary, is that the material world normally experienced has no intrinsic reality of its own.[5] This was the starting point of all idealistic philosophies which came in sharp conflict with the materialistic ideas of ancient Dalit thought.

In the Hindu Upanishads, there is also the conception of the Lord of *Karman*, who administers the law and gives reward according to one's past deeds. He is *Isvara*, the *Apara Brahman*, and the dispenser of justice.[6] The core idea of *Vendanta* i.e., *Karma* theory, is justified by Hindu Upanishadic thought. The Karmic belief propagated that by doing service to Brahmans the Shudras could improve their status in the next birth. And the Lord of Karman of Hindu Upanishadic thought in fact justifies the exploitative nature of belief system under the grab of providing higher status to lower rungs in the next life. This is only to make suppressed people not to revolt against the brahmanical social order that is the basis of the whole Hindu culture. Hence, for the deprived communities the Lord of *Karman*–the *Apara Brahman*, could only dispense injustice.

Materialistic Ideas

Apart from Vedic and Upanishadic philosophies, there were also materialistic ideas in Ancient Indian thought. The first school of thought that professed 'materialism' was *Charavaka* philosophy, also known as the *Lokayata-darsana*, belonged to the earliest Dalit materialistic tradition.

The fundamental feature of the *Lokayata* materialism is its theory of *'deha-vada'*: the view that self is nothing but the body. Consciousness is a function of the body. Consciousness does not inherit in the particles of matter. When these particles come or evolve themselves to be arranged, they show signs of life. Life and consciousness are identical. Man's thinking power ceases to function when the dissolution of physical body takes place. Consequently, there remains no consciousness after the body has perished. Hence there is nothing to transmigrate. In other words, the *Lokayata* materialism holds that mind is only a form or product of body. The ultimate reality is matter.[7]

A thing unperceivable by sense organs is not acceptable to Charavakas. They recognise four elements of existence: earth, water, air and fire. The ether does not exist, because it is perceivable. In the same way, there is no immortality of soul and no existence of God. Hence the *Lokayata* knows nothing apart from nature, the material world.

Sankhya philosophy of Kapil was another Ancient Dalit materialistic thought. His philosophy is based on three principles: First, every true statement must be supported by proof. The second principle of his philosophy relates to causality; creation and its cause. Kapil denied the theory that there was a being that created the Universe. *Prakriti* is the material cause of the world, not God, because there is no God. The total material Universe is the effect of *Prakriti*. There is no God to create the universe. It is a self-evolved world. Only a definite product can be produced from a definite material; and only a specific material can yield a specific result.

The third principle relates to the existence of three constituents and their interaction. The process of development of the unevolved (*Prakriti*) is through the activities of three constituents (gunas) of which it is made up: *'Sattva'*, which corresponds to what we call as light in nature, which reveals and causes pleasure to man; *'Raja'* is that which impels and moves, what produces activity; and *'Tamas'* is heavy and puts under restraint, it produces the state of indifference or inactivity.

These three constituents act essentially in close relation; but they overpower and support one another and intermingle with one another. They are like the constituents of a lamp, the flame, the oil and the wick. When these three constituents (gunas) are in perfect balance, none overpowering the other, the Universe appears static (a*chetan)* and ceases to evolve. When they are not in balance, one overpowers the other, the universe becomes dynamic (*Sachetan*) and evolution begins. Kapil said the constituents become unbalanced, due to disturbance in the balance of the three gunas and the disturbance was due to the presence of *Dukkha* (suffering), i.e., disequilibrium in the original nature of the gunas.

The *Prakriti*, as conceived in *Sankhya* philosophy, is not only complex and all pervasive; it also evolves or undergoes change perpetually. Naturally the things that develop out of it are also conceived as sharing in its fluid character.[8] The whole of the physical Universe emanates from it; and, since it is conceived as ultimate and independent; the explanation so far may be characterized as naturalistic.[9]

Buddhism as an Opposition to Hinduism

The above brief description of Vedantic, Upanishadic, *Charvaka* and *Sankhya* philosophies enable us to have a comparative understanding about the Buddhist thought. The Buddhist philosophy is a discovery, in a sense that it was a result of inquiry and investigation into the conditions of human habitation on earth and understanding of the working of human instincts, with which, man was born. And moulding of his instincts and dispositions man has formed as a result of history and tradition which, works to his detriment.[10]

The non-Buddhist philosophies in ancient India had their own limitations. They could not give correct world-view and so could not offer a solution to social conflicts of the human society. They were all engaged in speculation and imagination about the origin of the universe. They did not apply their thoughts to the problems to society, whereas Buddha did it.

In the Vedic hymns, the Buddha saw nothing that was morally elevating. Similarly, he did not find anything in the philosophical ideas of the Vedic philosophies. Their theories were mere speculations, which were neither logical nor factual. Their contributions to philosophy created no world outlook, no social values necessary for human happiness. However, Buddhism did not arise somewhere in isolated environment of Indian philosophical thought. Certainly it lied its foundations on already existed thoughts of Dalit traditions and Gautama Buddha modified and rationalised theme. Buddha's thought inherited all the best elements of the earliest Dalit materialist philosophies which preceded it, which although the Buddha did not accept as a whole. Buddhism was not a simple continuation of previous Dalit philosophical ideas. It was fundamentally a new discovery, a new philosophy that enriched Dalit tradition of philosophical thought.

The Buddha rejected the Hindu philosophy as a whole. He repudiated its thesis that the Vedas were infallible and their authority could never be questioned. In his opinion, everything must be open to re-examination and re-consideration in order to know the truth. Infallibility of the Vedas meant complete denial of freedom of thought. He was equally opposed to the Brahmanic priesthood and the way in which sacrifices were performed. For him, there was no virtue in false sacrifice.

The most repugnant theory, the Buddha thought, was the theory of *Chatturvarna*. It did not appear him, 'natural organization'. Its class composition was compulsory and arbitrary. It was a society made to order.

It intensified class-conflict, because it was based on, in Ambedkar's words 'graded inequality'. Inequality exists in every society in some or other form; but the Inequality preached by Hinduism was its official doctrine. The Hindu philosophy did not believe in equality. Far from producing harmony, graded inequality produced in Hindu society an ascending scale of hatred and a descending scale of contempt, which has been a perpetual source of social conflict. This social order did not serve the interests of all, much less did it advance the welfare of all. Indeed, it was deliberately designed to make many serve the interests of a few. In it man was made to serve a class of self-styled supermen. It was calculated to suppress and exploit the weak and to keep them in a state of complete subjugation.[11] For these reason, the Buddha condemned the theory of *varna vyavastha*. It is the root of Indian caste system and still it is keeping the people divided into rigid social groups like enemies.

The Buddha vehemently opposed the Hindu law of Karma,

because this law was aimed to cut down the very spirit of revolt. It misdirected the people by saying that no one was responsible for the suffering of man except he himself. Revolt could not alter the state of suffering; for suffering was fixed by his past Karma as his lot in this life. Hinduism preached a retributive theory of Karma that was opposed to the human way of life. By preaching the ideal of *Chaturvarna*, Hinduism divided the people into four rigid classes on the one hand, and on the other, it isolated the individual from social effects by giving a false theory of Karma. That is why the Buddha rejected the whole philosophy of Hinduism.

It is said that the Buddha was influenced by the teachings of Upanishads. It is not true. There is a fundamental difference between Buddhism and Upanishadic philosophy. The Buddha did not believe that '*Brahma* was a reality'. There was no proof for its existence. It was sheer speculation. And also Brahma does not serve the interests of all sections of society.

'How can anything be reality about which no one knows anything?', asked the Buddha. Therefore, he had no second opinion in rejecting the Upanishads and their ideas as being based on pure imagination. The philosophy of Upanishads was purely idealistic – 'world denying speculative superstructure', in which the Buddha had no interest. This was a philosophy basically opposed to idealism of Upanishads. He propounded a theory of 'dynamic realism' which believed in the changing character of reality itself, whereas the *Brahman*, as the ultimate reality, was regarded as an 'unchanging principle'. The Upanishadic stand being basically wrong, its idealistic outlook became an obstacle in the way of people's dynamic thinking. Perhaps, it can be said that the Buddha was influenced by Dalit Upanishadic thought that opposes the existence of Brahman, the Supreme being.

The *Lokayata* philosophy too could not attract the Buddha. In fact, the Buddha recognised the materiality and knowability of the world; he did not believe in rituals, Soul and Godship; yet he opposed to the pleasure-seeking activities preached by the ancient materialists. Moreover, there was not a mature and comprehensive global outlook in the philosophy of *Lokayata*.

Of all the philosophers, the Buddha was greatly impressed

by the doctrines of Kapil. He realized that some of his ideas were reasonable; but the integral view of ultimate reality has been muddled in it, as a result of dualistic thinking. The notion of 'perpetual change' and the idea of natural law (*Svabhava-vada*) are also vitiated by this separation. Buddha accepted only three things from the philosophy of Kapil: (i) that reality must be based on proof; (ii) that there was no logical (factual) basis for the presumption that God exists and He created the world; and (iii) that there is *Dukkha* in the world.

The non-Buddhist philosophy believed in the understanding and explanation of the origins of the world, the existence of God, the immortality of Soul, the number of elements, etc. It was philosophy of contemplative, inactive and passive nature, which inevitably led to a denial of reforming the social practice, the material conditions, of life. The philosophers spent most of their time either in defence of idealism or materialism each of whom, therefore, was involved in an extremist attitude.

The Buddha could not accept a view like one based on any extremism, either idealism or materialism. He thought sensible participation and intervention in human life so as to change it, to reform it in order to make this world worth living. The Buddhist philosophy believed in the transformation of the material world and the reformation of human mind. It did not cling to worthless traditional sterile and speculative ideas, unrelated to human interests. It avoided philosophical extremism, speculative idealism and enervating materialism. It always stood for a change, if it was necessary. The Buddha rejected the ideas, which did not satisfy his reason. Thus arose a new philosophy, which moulded the subsequent course of world-history.

The Buddha was a practical reformer. He was primarily an ethical teacher, not a metaphysician. He avoided discussing fruitless controversies regarding the a*tman* (Soul) and the *Brahma*, which were dominant in the arguments of intellectuals in his time. He avoided the metaphysical questions like, whether the soul was different from the body, whether it survived death, whether the world was finite or infinite, eternal or non-eternal, etc. Discussion of problems for the solution of which there is not sufficient evidence leads only to different partial views like the conflicting one-sided accounts of an elephant given by different blind persons who touch its different parts.[12]

Instead of discussing metaphysical questions, which are ethically useless and intellectually uncertain, the Buddha always tried to enlighten persons on the most important questions of sorrow, its origin, its cessation and the path leading to its cessation. He addressed himself to the worldly problems. In Buddha's own words, "this does profit, has to do with fundamentals of religion, and tends to aversion, absence of passion, cessation, quiescence, knowledge, supreme wisdom and *nirvana*". [13] The Buddha said that the world is full of sorrows and people suffer on account of desires. If desires are conquered, nirvana will be attained.

The Vedic and Brahmanical Upanishadic philosophies did not do justice to those people who were appraised and exploited. More and more they ran counter to both the developments of science and progressive social movements. They aroused the protest of conscientious, honest-minded social scientists and philosophers, as indeed of all those who put the interests of the people foremost and a radiant future for mankind above themselves. In ancient India, it was the Buddhist philosophy, which guided the people in this direction and showed a real way for social emancipation. Today the people of Asia are realizing the value of Buddhism and the increasing attention is being paid also in the west for Buddhist thought.

References

1. Since many interpretations of the Buddhist philosophy are in circulation among the schools of Buddhism all over the world, the phrase is used to mean original Buddhism i.e., Dhamma originally told by the Buddha himself.
2. Wijewardhena, D. O., *The Revolt in the Temple*, Colombo, 1963, p. 76.
3. Mukherjee, Radha Kamal, *The Culture and Art of India*, London, 1959, p. 90.
4. Alston, W.P., and Brandt, R.B., ed., *Problems of Philosophy*, Boston, 1975, p. 6.
5. Chattopadhyay, D. *Indian Philosophy*, Delhi, 1964, p. 75.
6. Dutt, N., *Early Monastic Buddhism*, Delhi, 1960, p. 19.
7. Shastri D. R., *A Short History of Indian Materialism Sensationalism and Hedonism*, Calcutta, 1957, pp. 17-20.

8. Hariyana, M., *The Essentials of Indian Philosophy*, London, 1951, p. 109.
9. *Ibid*, p. 113.
10. Ambedkar B.R., *The Buddha and His Dhamma*, Bombay, 1957, pp. 217-218.
11. *Ibid.*
12. Rhys Davids, T. W., tr. *Dialogues of Buddha*, I. London, 1950, pp. 187-88.
13. *Majjhma-nikaya-sutta*, 63, H.C., Warren, Buddhism in Translations, Harvard, First Print, 1922, p. 122.

Three

A Historical Survey of Buddhist Revival in India

Modernisation of Buddhism is a part of the revival process. It is analysed that revival leads to modernisation and modernisation contributes to revival. A brief discussion on the Buddhist revival in modern India is necessary to understand the social and religious elements that constitute the modernisation process. The revival can mainly be attributed to Ambedkar and Dalai Lama in modern India.

The revival phenomenon initiated by Ambedkar indeed has modernised the philosophy and culture of Buddhism. What is the historical necessity to revive Buddhism in India and in what way the revival is related to modernisation? What is the social and philosophical context in which Ambedkar revived and modernised the Buddhism? This chapter aims to answer all these queries. The second part of this chapter is aimed to discuss on the contribution of the Dalai Lama XIV to the Buddhist revival and its relation to the historical necessity of modernisation of Buddhist religion and philosophy in the Tibetan Buddhist context.

It is believed that ancient India was dominantly a Buddhist society. The minority condition of the Buddhist population in modern India force us to question the history of Hindu dominance. Undoubtedly a critical study of Hindu religion provides required answers to understand the historical necessity for the revival of Buddhism and its modernisation. The study of Hindu religion involves the study of its aims and ideals to find out the social utility of its philosophy.

Aims and Ideals of Hinduism

Religion is an institution or an influence and like all social influences and institutions, it may help or it may harm a society, which is in its grip. Indeed, religion is a social force. As every religion has its historical necessity in its birth, growth and presence, each religion needs to be understood and analysed differently.

Inquiry into the aims and ideals of a religion is necessary to understand the utility of its presence in the society. It is not for judging right and wrong or to decide true and good religion. It is to find out the content of social utility and justice in the aims and ideals of a religion. The main concern here is to evaluate aims and ideals of Hinduism to relocate the importance of Buddhist ideals in the Hindu dominated Indian society. The inquiry cannot be ignored under the argument that religion is of no importance or that all religions are good. It cannot be avoided by saying that although religions are many they are equally good. Because, the ideal of a religion may be non-existent in the sense that it is something which is constructed. But although non-existent, it is real. For an ideal it has full operative force which is inherent in every ideal of a religion.

Ambedkar applied the test of justice and the test of utility to judge the philosophy of Hinduism.[1] Justice is simply another name for liberty, equality and fraternity. It is in this sense Ambedkar used justice as a criterion to judge Hinduism. *Varna*[2] (caste) system of Hinduism divided society into many grades. It can be said that Hinduism does not recognise equality since it supports the scheme that places Brahmin, Kshatriya, Vaishya and Shudra in descending order. The Untouchables[3] at the lowest, reserved to serve the higher orders. This inequality in status is a permanent social relationship among the classes to be observed to be enforced at all times in all places and for all purposes.

System of slavery, marriage and Rule of Law can be taken as a few examples to examine Hindu religious social system. Manu[4] confined slavery to the Shudras. Only Shudras could be made slaves of the three caste Hindus.[5] But the caste Hindus could not be the slaves of the Shudras. Indeed in the ancient Indian society not only Shudras happened to become slaves but members of the other three castes also become slaves. However, the successors of Manu namely Narada[6] and Yajnavalkya[7] enacted a new rule that forbades slavery to disturb the Varna purity. In other words, a Brahmin may become the slave of another Brahmin but he shall not be the slave of a person of another *Varna*. On the other hand a Brahmin may hold as his slave anyone belonging to the four *Varnas*. That means a Shudra can hold a Shudra and an untouchable can hold only an untouchable as his slave.

The second example that needs to be dealt with is marriage. Manu gave injunction that each caste to marry within one's own caste. His law is opposed to inter *Varna* marriage. Rule of Law is another example to show how anxious Manu was to preserve the rule of inequality. Rule of Law is generally understood to mean equality before law. But a true Hindu criminal jurisprudence knows only an irrational system of punishment. Manu's Hindu Penal Code prescribes inequality of punishment for the same offence.

Manu Smriti: VIII. 279.

> "With whatever member a low-born man shall assault or hurt a superior, even that member of his must be slit, or cut more or less in proportion to the injury; this is an ordinance of Manu".

VIII. 380.

> "Never shall the king slay a Brahman, though convicted of all possible crimes; let him banish the offender from his realm, but with all his property secure, and his body unhurt".

Inequality designed not merely to punish the offender but to protect also the dignity and to maintain the baseness of the parties coming to a Court of Law to seek justice in other words to maintain the social inequality on which whole Hindu scheme is founded.

Manu has also ordained Religious inequality. By birth one can become a member of his caste but he cannot be a member of Hindu religion unless he is initiated. This initiation is effected by the investitute of a person with the socalled sacred thread.

Manu Smriti: II. 36.

> "In the eight year from the conception of a Brahman, in the eleventh from that of a Kshatriya, and in the twelth from that of a Vaisya, let the father invest the child with the mark of his caste".

II. 37.

> "Should a Brahman, or his father for him, be desirous of his advancement in sacred knowledge; a Kshatriya, of

extending his power; or a Vaisya of engaging in mercantile business; the investitute may be made in the fifth, sixth, or eigth years respectively".

II. 38.

"The ceremony of investitute hallowed by the *Gayatri*[8] must not be delayed, in the case of a priest, beyond the sixteenth year; nor in that of a soldier, beyond the twenty second; nor in that of a merchant, beyond the twenty fourth".

II. 39.

"After that, all youths of these three classes, who have not been invested at the proper time, become vratyas, or outcastes, degraded from the Gayatri, and condemned by the virtuous".

Manu prohibited the Shudras and Untouchables to become Hindus. He did not allow them to wear sacred thread. Even if a Shudra (backward caste) or an untouchable wears sacred thread he cannot become a Hindu, since according to Manu's Hindu law sacred thread is reserved only for the three higher Varnas. This shows that originally Backward castes and Untouchables were Buddhists. Later on they were forced to become lower varnas in the Hindu social system without being initiating them into Hindu religion.[9]

Thus in Hinduism we find both social inequality and religious inequality imbedded in its philosophy. Everyone is not equal before God. Even Gods in Hindu scriptures maintain *jati Dharma*. *Brahma* — Brahmin; *Vishnu* - Kshatriya; *Shiva* - Vaishya; — the trinity represents three higher Varnas. *Saraswathi*, wife of *Brahma* is as Brahmin and entrusted the role of learning-duty of Brahmin is learning; *Lakshmi*, wife of Vishnu is a Kshatriya and Goddess of wealth. Concept of *Lakshmi* developed, when the ancient Indian society was started emerging into a feudal state. More than the coins, land was regarded as the most important variable of wealth. *Lakshmi* bestowed wealth to Kshatriya castes in the form of land. Even today the most educated caste of Hindu society is Brahmin and highly wealthy caste in terms of possession of agricultural lands is Kshatriya (i.e. Thakurs, etc.,) In the beginning, Vaishyas were cattle breeders and worshipped *Shiva* the *pasupala*, later on they switched over to business and became traders when the society reached the stage of surplus income. Being the commercial class they started worshipping *Lakshmi* for wealth, when coins were symbolised with the wealth. Portrayal of *Lakshmi* with hand full of flowing coins is not an ancient image.

Other important Gods are *Rama* and *Krishna*.[10] The story of *Ramayana* supports the Varna dharma and to protect *Varna* purity *Rama* killed *Shambuk* a shudra. *Krishna* in *Gita* emphasises to maintain Varna dharma by all the castes. Unfortunately the Dharma which propagated in the name of Hindu religion, according to Ambedkar[11] is a denial of equality and injustice both social as well as religious and it is a degradation of human personality.

Manu's Hinduism is the only divine law in the ancient world that has denied the common man the right to knowledge. There is concept of liberty in the ideal Hindu society. It is the only society that has been guilty of closing to the generality of its people the study of the books of its religion. It has been guilty of prohibiting the mass of its people from acquiring knowledge. It is the only society that has declared that any attempt made by the common man to acquire knowledge shall be punishable as a crime. All this resulted into the emergence of illiterate and ignorant society. The fact of prohibiting the masses (Backward castes and untouchables) from the access to education and acquiring knowledge corroborate the fact that lower *Varnas* were non-Hindus (i.e., Buddhists). Therefore, there is no liberty for the masses in Hindu society in the matters of right to decent life, right to education, right to teaching, right to dining (with other castes) and right to marry (irrespective of caste) and also in other matters. Thus Hinduism, far from encouraging spread of knowledge, in the words of Ambedkar is a "gospel of darkness".[12]

On the question of Fraternity in Hindu ideal scheme of society, it can be said that the hierarchical character of the caste system doesn't allow the feeling of fraternity to grow among the members of the society. The caste system is a system of gradation in which every caste except the highest and the lowest has a priority and precedence over some other castes.

There is no fraternity among Hindus can be ascertained from the fact that there were innumerable caste wars in the ancient Hindu society. Indeed, the contemporary society is also witnessing conflict among various caste groups. In Hindu scriptures, there were several instances of caste wars particularly between Kshatriya and Brahmin.

There was a conflict between king *Vena* and the Brahmins;[13] King *Pururavas* and the Brahmins;[14] King *Nahusha* and the Brahmins;[15] King *Nimi* and the Brahmins;[16] King *Sumukha* and the Brahmins.[17] There were references to the slaughter of the Brahmins by the Kshatriyas. The story of *Vishvamitra*[18] and the slaughter of the *Bhrigus* the Brahmin priests by the Kshatriyas the descendants of King *Kritrvirya.*[19] There was also a reference to the slaughter of the Kshatriyas by the Brahmins. *Parsuram* the son of a Brahman vowed to destroy the whole Kshatriya race and executed his threat by killing first Arjun's sons and their followers.[20] It was the proud boast of the Brahmin *Parsuram* that he exterminated the Kshatriyas twenty one times.

Caste war is not restricted to ancient Hindu society only. It has been present all along. It even destroyed the *Maratha*[21] empire at the beginning of the British Raj in India. The absence of subscription of social ethics to human relations in the Hindu philosophy perpetuated a society meant for not only caste conflicts within but also religious hatred with others. There were several instances of indigenous people fighting with *Aryan* castes — *Dasyu* — *Aryan* conflicts and *Indra* role in *Rigveda;*[22] Brihadrata's assassination.[23] *Pushyamitra Sunga* (187-151 BC) was a great persecutor of Buddhists who were predominantly Dalits.[24] The *Huna* King *Mihirakula,* also killed hundreds of Buddhists who were Dalits. The Shivate Brahman King *Shashanka* of *Gauda* was also hostile to Dalit Buddhists. The Tibetan historians records Kumarila's enmity against Buddhists who might be dalits.[27] Harshavardhana[28] (A.D. 606-647) the last Buddhist king executed large number of Brahmins who made an attempt to assassinate him for his Buddhist activities.[29]

It must not be supposed that these caste-religious wars were like ordinary wars which are a temporary phenomena which come and go and which leave no permanent chasms to divide the people of the different nations.[30] In India the caste-religious war is a permanent phenomenon which is silently but surely working its way. It is a grain in the life and it has become genius of the Hindus.[31]

Caste conflicts between Dalits and others; recent Babri Masjid demolition at Ayodhya; Hindu attacks on Dalit and Tribal christians and the christians like Australian Missionary Graham Steins who are working among the weaker sections to provide health and education testify the continuity of historical phenomenon of caste - religious wars in Hindu dominated Indian society.[32] It is Hinduism and its philosophy that is categorically responsible for it.[33]

There is no sharing among Hindus of joys and sorrows involved in the vital facts of life. Everything is separate and exclusive. The Hindu is separate and exclusive all through his life. Joys and sorrows of one caste are not the joys and sorrows of another. One caste has hardly concern with other castes. Even charity has become caste bound. For example Brahmin charity for Brahmins and Vaishya charity for Vaishyas only. Thus one Hindu will share nothing with another Hindu while they are alive. But they will be separated and exclusive even when they are dead. Some Hindus bury their dead. Some Hindus burn their dead. But those bury will not share the same cemetery. Each will appropriate a part of the cemetery to bury its dead. Those who burn will not burn at the same burning place. If they do, each will have a separate funeral pan. Even death has caste. Lower castes are not allowed to bury their dead bodies in the same cemetery. Caste continues even after the death.

Hinduism teaches not to inter dine, not to inter marry and to associate. Thus the philosophy of Hinduism is a direct denial of fraternity. In the words of Ambedkar, "Hinduism is inimical to equality, antagonistic to liberty and opposed to fraternity".[34] In his opinion inequality is a part of Hindu religious doctrine adopted and conscientiously preached as a sacred dogma, It is an official creed and nobody is ashamed to profess it openly. Inequality for the Hindus is a divinely prescribed way of life as a religious doctrine and as prescribed way of life, it has become incarnate in Hindu society and is shaped and moulded by it in its thoughts and in its doings. Indeed inequality can be said the soul of Hinduism.[35]

From the point of view of social unity also Hinduism doesn't stand as religion. Caste philosophy of Hinduism makes Hinduism not useful to society as a religion. Caste system purely as a form of social organisation stands condemned because the Hinduism has been unable to form a common front. As a producer's organisation it stands discredited, since its technique never advanced beyond that of the primitive man. As a scheme of distribution it has miserably failed since it has produced appalling inequality of wealth, immense wealth side by side extreme poverty. Ambedkar makes the following conclusions[36] on the caste philosophy of Hinduism:

(1) Hinduism as a system of caste divides Labourers;
(2) disassociates work from interest;
(3) disconnects intelligence from manual labour;
(4) divitalises by denying to him the right to cultivate vital interest; and
(5) prevents mobilization. Caste system is not merely division of labour. The most important thesis of Ambedkar on the caste philosophy of Hinduism is *'Caste is a division of labourers'*. Even Karl Marx unable to understand Hindu social system which is unique in itself. Marx talked of class struggle on the basis of division of labour. Hindu system offers caste struggle on the basis of division of labourers.

The most unfortunate fact of the caste system of Hindu society is that it dissociates intelligence from work and creates contempt for labour. There is no dignity of labour in it. A Brahmin who is permitted to cultivate his intellect is not permitted to labour, indeed is taught to look down upon labour. While the Shudra (Backward caste) who is required to labour is not permitted to cultivate his intelligence. Caste devitalises a man.

Caste in Hindu society prevents mobilisation. Occasions like national tragedy due to natural calamities force the society to mobilise all its resources to one end. For instance, there were several reports that Hindu Government and Hindu organisations involved in the relief measures to the earth quake victims in Gujarat, were discriminating against lower caste, Muslim and Christian victims.[37] Ancient India was the best example to test the fact that caste prevents mobilisation. To take a catastrophy like war, society must mobilize all its resources for militarisation. Indeed the destiny of a defeat, which has been the lot of India throughout history, is due to caste. Caste prevented general mobilisation. Indian wars have been mostly wars of single battles or single campaigns. This was due to the fact that once the Kshatriyas fell everything fell. Shudras (Backward Castes) who formed the large majority of the country were disarmed. This was also a major cause for the failure of Indian mutiny against British rule in 1857.

Even present India faces the problem of illiteracy. Since the ages Hindu system prevented shudras (Backward castes) from getting education. There cannot be a more degrading system of social organisation than Hindu Varna. As History bears ample evidence it is the system which deadens, paralyses and cripples the people from helpful activity. The three classes, Brahmins, Kshatriyas and Vaishyas although not very happy in their mutual relationship managed to work by compromise. The Brahmin flattered the Kshatriya and both let the Vaishya live in order to be able to live upon him. But the three agreed to beat down the Shudra. He was not allowed to acquire wealth. He was prohibited from acquiring knowledge. He was prohibited from bearing arms. In Modern India, when Backward Castes trying to get into system through job reservation, caste Hindus started privatising the state machinery. They privatised primary education, so that it becomes dearer to the poor Backward Caste masses, so that knowledge systems can be monopolised forever.

The Trayavarnikas helped themselves mutually against Backward Caste masses at different times. There is no code of laws more infamous regarding social rights than the Hindu Laws of Manu. Any instance from anywhere of social injustice must pale before it. There have been social revolutions in other countries of the world. Unfortunately history of India has never witnessed any social revolution. The Indian mass of people tolerated patiently the social evils to which they have been subjugated. In Europe, the strong have never contrived to make the weak helpless against exploitation so shamelessly as was the case in India among the Hindus. Social war has been raging between the strong and the weak far more violently in Europe that it has ever been in India. Yet the weak in Europe has had in him freedom of military services his physical weapon, in suffrage his political weapon and in education his moral weapon. Three weapons for emancipation were never withheld by the strong from the weak in Europe. All these weapons were however denied to the masses in Hindu society.

There is only one period in Indian history which is a period of, in Ambedkar words, 'freedom' greatness and glory'.[38] That is the period of the Mourya Empire — the great Buddhist kings. At all other times the country suffered from defeat and darkness. But the Mourya period was a period when Hindu Varna was completely annihilated, when the Shudras (Backward Castes), who constituted the mass of the people came into their own and became the rulers of the country. Ambedkar puts it that the period of defeat and darkness is the period when Hinduism flourished to the damnation of the greater part of the people of the country.[39] Under Hindu system Backward Caste masses were condemned to be lowly and not knowing the way of escape and not having the means of escape, they became reconciled to eternal servitudes which they accepted as their inescapable fate. Since they could receive no education, they could not think out or know the way to their salvation.

On these counts Ambedkar regarded aims and ideals of Hinduism, neither satisfy the test of social utility or test of individual justice. He propagated Buddhism to the masses of India in the context of failure of Hinduism to provide true humane religious values to the Indian society.

Destruction of Buddhism by Hindu Kings

One argument says that, Buddhism had natural death but for others 'it was murdered'. Ambedkar says, "Buddhism in its material form disappeared ... but as a spiritual force it still exists."[40] Yet it is obvious that in some or other form Buddhism disappeared. The destruction of Buddhism can be attributed mainly to the hostility of Hindu Kings and brahmanical forces. Lalmini Joshi in his work, *Studies in Buddhistic Culture of India,*[41] points to evidence of the fact of brahmanical hostility to Buddhism teaching and unwillingness to share royal patronage and cultural influence with Buddhist monks. The *Manava Sastra* of Manu and Kautilya's *Artha Sastra* afford plenty of evidence of this kind of attitude.

Taranath, the Tibetan historian describes the Brahmin ruler, Pushyamitra Singa[42] was a great persecutor of Buddhism. He waged a cruel war against the helpless Buddhist monks and announced a prize of 100 gold coins for each head of a monk. He destroyed and burnt the *Viharas* from Pataliputra to Sakala.[43]

Several instances of persecution occur in the sixth-seventh centuries A.D. The Huna King Mihirkula, who was a worshipper of Shiva, killed hundreds of Buddhists. In Kashmir he overthrew stupas destroyed the Sangharamas, nearly sixteen hundred foundations and put to death nine hundred kotis [44] of lay adherents of Buddhism.[45] The shivate Brahmana King Shashanka of Gauda cut off the Bodh tree at Bodh Gaya, where the Buddha had attained enlightenment and removed Buddha image from a temple east of the Bodhi-tree and replaced it by Shiva Linga.[46] The Tibetan historians records Kumarila's enmity against Buddhists who instigated King Sudhaman of Ujjain to exterminate the Buddhists.[47] The persecution and horrifying of Buddhists by Brahmanical rulers both in north and south is far from unknown in the pages of Indian History.

The Brahmins appropriated the Buddhist shrines in due course and replaced the Buddhist images with those of Brahmin God and Goddesses. The great Maha Bodhi temple at Bodhgaya the seat of the Buddha's enlightenment is still under the domination of Hindus, even though they paid so far little attention to the Buddha, the falsely called Vishnu Avatara. Balaji temple at Tirupati-Tirumala, Puri Jagannath temple and many more were all Buddhist Viharas. When Cunningham discovered Kusinara in 1860-61 the sacred spot where the Buddha had entered in Mahaparinibbana, he found that the cremation stupa had been converted into the temple and the top of it stood the shrine of Rambhara Bhavani.[48]

In Andhara, the Caityas of Chezrala and Ter are now Siva and Vishnu temples. The temple of Madhava at Salkusa opposite Gauhati in Assam was once a sacred shrine of Buddhist.[49]

Sankaracharya is also said to have founded his Sringerimath in Kerala on the site of the Buddhist Vihara.[50] The temple for Amareswara was constructed upon the Buddhist stupa in Amaravati on the right bank of the river Krishna in Andhra Pradesh.[51] All these took place roughly between 6th and 8th A.D. By the twelfth century A.D., Buddhism became practically extinct in India.

British conquest of India although helped to know more about Buddhism academically due to some of the Britishers who were interested in Buddhism and involved in researching it out, indeed actual revival started only with Ambedkar that too after independence.

Revival before Ambedkar

W. W. Hunter in his Indian Empire says, "The revival of Buddhism is always a possibility in India.... The life and teaching of the Buddha are also beginning to exercise a new influence on religious thought in Europe and America. As that teaching becomes more accurately known to the western world, it will be divested of the mystical pretensions with which certain of its modern professors have obscured it. Buddhism will stand forth as the embodiment of the eternal verity that as a man sows he will reap; associated with the personal duties of mastery over self and kindness to all men; and quickened into a popular religion by the example of a noble and beautiful life. A revival of Buddhism, I repeat, is one of the present possibilities in India".[52]

In the South India, the revival of Buddhism was started by a reputed Tamil Dalit Scholar C. Iyodhi Doss who was a crusader against untouchability in Hindu society. He propagated the fact that the famous Tirukkural[53] is a Buddhist work and authored by an untouchable who was a Buddhist, and from the palm leaf manuscript of Asvaghosha[54] he proved that Pariahs were once Buddhists. In 1990, Pandit Doss started the South India Sakya Buddhist Association[55] with its headquarters at Madras (Chennai). He wrote Buddharathu Adivedan (Buddha's ancient religion). It was at his request that British Government of Madras Presidency separated Buddhists from others in the Census of 1910. He converted thousands of Dalits to Buddhism and died in 1914.

P. Lakshmi Narasu was another Tamil Buddhist scholar. His famous work *Essence of Buddhism* (1907) is even today a scholarly reference book on Buddhist philosophy. He converted many Dalits to Buddhism.

In Northern India Angarika Dharmapala[56] who worked for the revival of Buddhism in pre-Ambedkar period. In 1891 he established Mahabodhi Society at Calcutta and started publication of the Maha Bodhi Journal in 1892. He represented Buddhism at the World Parliament of Religions held at Chicago in 1893. His Chicago speech is popularly called as 'World's debt to Buddha' and was hailed as one of the most popular Speakers of that Assembly.

This is a brief background of the history of Indian Buddhists and the Hindu social context in which Ambedkar oriented his thought and action to revive and modernise Buddhism.

Ambedkar and Revival

'The depressed classes must leave the Hindu fold and join some other religion that gives social and religious equality to them... choose any religion that gives you equality of status and of treatment'.[57] This was the resolution which was unanimously passed at the *Yeola Conference*, Nasik, in September 1935, by about ten thousand untouchables. Ambedkar declared in this conference: "Unfortunately, I was born a Hindu untouchable, it was beyond my power to prevent that, but it is within my power to refuse to live under ignoble and humiliating conditions. I solemnly assure you that I will not die a Hindu".[58] Interestingly, the resolution of Yeola conference urged the depressed classes not to spend money and man power fruitlessly and to stop the fight to enter into Hindu society. It asked the Dalits to consider their society separate from the Hindu society and organise the former to obtain for it an independent and respectable place in the country. The resolution forbades Dalits to take part in any Hindu festivals, Raths, Melas, Worships and other similar occasions.[59]

M. K. Gandhi accused the untouchables for dividing Hindu society by their Yeola resolution. He felt that religion is not like a house or a clock, which can be changed at will. It is a more integral part of one's own self than one's body. "I am convinced that a change of religion by Ambedkar and those who passed the resolution will not serve the cause which they have at their heart".[60] In his reply, Ambedkar refuted all charges made by Gandhi. He felt that it is right that religion is essential but for a man the religion of his ancestor is not essential who finds that the same religion is opposed to his needs and is an obstacle in the way of his welfare and progress.[61]

Ambedkar viewed the change of religion for Dalits as a means of liberation and path to freedom. For him, just as Swaraj (independence) is necessary for India, so also is change of religion necessary for the Dalits; because the underlying motive in both the movements is the desire for freedom.[62] He had prepared his followers psychologically for a conversion from Hinduism from 1935 onwards. However, his conversion took place quite late, on October 14, 1956. The oldest Bhikku then in India, Mahasthavira Chandramani of Myanmar, came to Nagpur for the conversion ceremony and initiated Ambedkar into Buddhism.

Along with Ambedkar three lakh and eighty thousand people embraced Buddhism.[63] On the day of his conversion, Ambedkar founded the *Bharathiya Buddha Mahasabha* (Buddhist Society of India) with the object of propagating the Dhamma, especially among the Dalits and Backward Castes. In his speech on the occasion of conversion he said: "This conversion has given me enormous satisfaction and pleasure unimaginable. I feel as if I have been liberated from hell".[64] About the motive behind the conversion movement, Ambedkar said, "We are making efforts to reach Manhood". He was very clear in his intension to convert the downtrodden masses of India to Buddhism, He wanted to achieve basic human values in the religion of Indian masses.

Ambedkar laid a path of liberation to the Dalit-backward masses of Indian society. He made it clear that the Buddha's message was equality. He introduced Dhamma Diksha ceremony for the people to become lay Buddhists. His rationalised Buddhism can be seen in his twenty-two 'Buddhist Oaths'[65] which constituted part of the conversion ritual:

1. I will not regard Brahma, Vishnu and Mahesh as Gods nor will I worship them.
2. I will not regard Rama and Krishna as Gods nor will I worship them.

3. I will not accept Hindu Deities like Gauri, Ganapati, etc. nor will I worship them.
4. I do not believe that God had taken birth or incarnation in any form.
5. I do not believe that Lord Buddha was the incarnation of Vishnu. I believe this propaganda as mischievous and false.
6. I will never perform any *Shraadha*[66] nor will I offer any *pinda*.[67]
7. I will never act against the tenets of Buddhism.
8. I will never get any SAMSKAAR performed by Brahmins.
9. I believe in the principle that all are equal.
10. I will try to establish equality.
11. I will follow the Eight-fold path of Lord Buddha.
12. I will follow all the Ten Paramitas of the Dhamma.
13. I will have compassion on all living beings and will try to look after them.
14. I will not lie.
15. I will not commit theft.
16. I will not indulge in lust or sexual transgression.
17. I will not take any liquor or drink that causes intoxication.
18. I will try to mould my life in accordance with the Buddhist preachings, based on enlightenment, precept and compassion.
19. I embrace today the Buddha Dhamma discarding the Hindu Religion which is detrimental to the emancipation of human beings and which believes in inequality and regards human beings other than the Brahmins as low born.
20. This is my firm belief that the Buddha Dhamma is the best religion.
21. I believe that today I am taking New-birth.
22. I solemnly take oath that from today onwards I will act according to the Buddha DHAMMA.

In less than two months after his Diksha Ambedkar attained Mahaparinirvana on 6 December 1956. Thus he died a Buddhist and before his death set in motion a movement that soon involved over three million people. Ten days after the death of Ambedkar, another huge ceremony was held in Bombay in which Ananda Kausalyayana, a Buddhist monk initiated thousands to Buddhism. Indeed these massive conversions mainly affected the Dalits. Their conversion however made the authority of Babasaheb Ambedkar unquestioned for them. His followers called him a 'Second Buddha' and described the 'Nagpur Diksha' as a new 'Dharmachakra-parivartana'.[68]

Later on many conversions took place at various places, especially, in Delhi, Ajmer, Lucknow and Bombay, (Mumbai). In south conversions took place at places like Madras (Chennai), Vellore, Bangalore, Hubli and the Kolar Gold Fields. Within two years after the conversion, the Dalit Buddhist population was 20 million.[69]

Dr. Zakir Hussain rightly called Ambedkar as the founder of New Buddhism in modern India.[70] Ambedkar conversion gave Buddhism a respectable place in the history of independent India although it is not much practiced in Indian society. Ambedkar made Buddhist symbols like the wheel on the Indian flag and the lion pillar as symbols of independent India. The importance of conversion for Dalits can be understood from the address given by Ambedkar in 1936 in a conference in Bombay.

> "Religion is for man; man is not for religion.
> If you want to gain self-respect, change your religion.
> If you want to create a cooperating society, change your religion.
> If you want power, change your religion.
> If you want equality, change your religion.
> If you want independence, change your religion.
> If you want to make that world in which you live, happy, change your religion...."[71]

The present question is not untouchability alone. The untouchables had been Buddhists who had been pushed aside from society when they fiercely clung to their religion, while there was a resurgence of Brahmanical Hinduism in ancient India. The untouchables were indigenous Indians who followed Buddhism. Ambedkar's change of religion is 'a come back to home' Buddhism.

The Dalai Lama XIV — Revival of Tibetan Buddhism in India[72]

Tenzin Gyatso, the 14th Dalai Lama lives in Dharamsala in a northern Indian state. He heads a strong spiritual presence of about more than 100,000 Tibetan exiles in India. Indeed the Dalai Lama and his people cannot work with missionary zeal to propagate Buddhism in India. His exile status is a greater limitation. As the temporal and spiritual sovereign of Tibet, the Dalai Lama faces two basic problems in exile. The national liberation of Tibet and the preservation of the great cultural heritage to which he and his people proudly belong. Despite the tremendous difficulties that he faces as an exile, the Dalai Lama has done much in both fields. However, naturally his interests have been more of spiritual nature and in this respect he has done much in promoting and preserving Tibetan culture.[73]

The most significant event in the history of the Dalai Lama's contribution for the revival of Buddhism in India was that he initiated over 1,000 Indians to Buddhism at Ramlila Ground in Delhi on 11th March 1973. The Dalai Lama for the first time involved in leading the legacy of Ambedkar by initiating the larger number of Ambedkarites into Buddhism. On this occasion, explaining the Diksha in Tibetan, the Dalai Lama said all beings are equal. The entire ceremony was held in Pali recited by him and repeated thrice by those embracing Buddhism. They also repeated a 22-point pledge laid down by Ambedkar for the initiation ceremony. They also made slogans like 'Victory to Ambedkar and victory to His Holiness the Dalai Lama'.[74]

The Dalai Lama participation in Buddhist leaders conference to lead Buddhist restoration was another significant development in the history of revival of Buddhism in Modern India. The conference was held in Darjeeling from 24th to 25 May 1975. Over 200 delegates, scholars and political leaders, attended it from India, Nepal and Bhutan. On the occasion the Dalai Lama addressed 20,000 crowd. At the conference the leaders decided to support the restoration and upliftment of Buddhism on different parts of Asia and Tibet under the spiritual leadership of the Dalai Lama.[75]

With a view to promote Buddhist studies the conference resolved to seek the introduction of postgraduate Buddhist studies in the institute of Tibetology at Gangtok, Sikkim and Nalanda

Mahavihar. It also resolved to set up a Buddhist research centre at Darjeeling and another at Lumbini in Nepal and to seek government grants for them. The Buddhist leaders who participated in the conference resolved to support the restoration and upliftment of Buddhism in different parts of Asia and Tibet under the spiritual leadership of the Dalai Lama.[76]

The All India frontier Buddha Maha Sabha organised a Buddhist conference on religion, education and culture on 18th September 1978 with the blessings of the Dalai Lama. The three major points deliberated in the conference were: (1) The development of Buddhist education and research in the world; (2) promotion of cultural contacts among world Buddhists; and (3) the role of Buddhism in the advancement of human values.

The All Frontier Buddha Maha Sabha was formed on 11th January, 1974 by the Buddhist leaders and followers of Buddhism form the frontier states of India with a view to preserve, strengthen and develop the Buddhist culture and thought, art and literature, morals and manners'.[78] The Mahasabha also aimed at working for the Scheduled Castes, Scheduled Tribes and Backward Classes of the frontier areas. According to its published aims and objectives,[79] it wanted to bring together the Buddhists of all sects and shades of opinion, traditional Buddhists and Modern Buddhists, living in border areas and in all parts of the mainland of India.

Apart from all these efforts to preserve Buddhist culture, the Dalai Lama also made short visits to Tibetan and other Buddhist dominated areas to give sermons and also to see the welfare of Buddhists in India. He even participated in so many discussions with prominent personalities to put forward the Buddhist point to view. Sometimes he himself organised teaching classes to develop interest among Indians about Buddhism.

Under the guidance of the Dalai Lama, number of institutions and organisations are started with the aim of preserving Buddhist culture in India. These are namely:[80] (1) Indo-Tibetan cultural Institute, Kalimpong; (2) The Institute of Higher Tibetan Studies (IHTS), Sarnath; (3) Library of Tibetan Works and Archives, Dharamsala; (4) Tibet House, New Delhi; (5) Tibetan Music, Dance and Drama Society, Dharamsala; (6) Tibetan Young Buddhist Association, Dharamsala.

Though the Dalai Lama never tried to show missionary zeal in spreading Buddhism in India, he propagated Buddha Dhamma for all humankind, of all religious denominations to build a society based on peace and co-existence. He modernised Mahayanism more than an ordinary religion and he gave it the status of 'Dhamma'. Although the Buddhist revival under his leadership is not as successful as of Ambedkar in terms of increasing the number of Buddhists, it has contributed to the modernisation of Buddhism i.e., understanding Buddhism in the world context and particularly its relevance in post industrial societies.

Revival movements under the guidance of Ambedkar and the Dalai Lama thus contributed to the Modernisation of Buddhism and made it more acceptable to the modern society. Indeed they made a new chapter in the history of Buddhism.

References

1. Ambedkar, B. R., *Philosophy of Hinduism*, (Comp)., Vasant Moon, Dr. Babasaheb Ambedkar Writings And Speeches, Vol. 3, Education Department, Governement of Maharashtra, 1987, pp. 24-25.
2. Varna means colour, howsoever synonym of jati (Caste). In the beginning it was a discriminative system based on colour later acquired caste meaning. In the contemporary society Varna connotes caste. Generally, Westerners get confused Caste system with racial system. They equate casteism with racism. The basic difference between the two is that casteism is supported by a religion and the racism doesn't have any divine approval. In other words casteism is not only a social but also a religious discrimination. For instance, lower castes are not allowed even today to enter into the some of the Hindu temples. Indeed, lower castes' Gods are different - *Pochamma, Mysamma, Karumariamma* etc. and do not find place among the caste Hindu Gods. Socially speaking casteism is a form of racism. However, Culturally it is different from racism. Casteism is a basis of Hindu religion.
3. Ambedkar called them *Ati-shudra*.
4. Manu, the ancient Hindu law giver, whose work *Manava Dharma Shastra* popularly known as Manu Smriti codifies Hindu laws to perpetuate inequality in Hindu religious social system.
5. Caste Hindus are Brahmin, Kshatriya and Vaishya. Shudras are modern Backward Castes in other words Bahujans.
6. Narada Smriti.
7. Yajnavalkya Smriti.
8. Gayatri is a Mantra or an invocation of special spiritual efficacy.
9. Manu lived about 200 A.D., Manu Smriti might have composed 800 years after the death of the Gautama Buddha.

10. Read Ambedkar Riddle of Rama and Krishna in his Riddle of Hinduism
11. Ambedkar, B.R., *op. cit.*, p. 36.
12. *Ibid.*, p. 44.
13. Mahabharat gives numerous references to Kshatriya - Brahman conflicts.
14. *Adiparva* of the Mahabharat.
15. *Udyogaparva* of the Mahabharat.
16. Vishnupuran.
17. Manu Smriti.
18. Ramayana.
19. *Adiparva* of the Mahabharat.
20. The story is told in several places in the Mahabharat.
21. Marathas were *Shudra* Kings. *Shivaji* was the founder of *Maratha* empire.
22. Indra was Chief God of Vedic Aryans, who was also called as *Purandhara*, the breaker of forts of indigenous people (i.e., Daityas etc). *Aryan* army led by *Indra* destroyed *Hariyuppa* (*Harappa*) the city of Indus civilization.
23. His Brahmin Minister *Pushyamitra Sunga* treacherously killed *Brihadrata* the last Mouryan ruler.
24. Vaidya, P.L.(ed.), Divyavadana, Text No.20, Darbhanga, 1959, p. 282.
25. Watters, Thomas (tr.) edited by T.W. Rhysdavids and S.W. Bushell, on *Yuan - Chwang's Travel in India*, Vol. I, Delhi, 1961, pp. 288-289.
26. Watters, Thomas., *op. cit.*, p. 243.
27. Elliot, T.S., *Hinduism and Buddhism*, Vol. II, London, 1957. p. 6.
28. Harsha could be called as the last Dalit Buddhist emperor.
29. *Hsuan Tsang* attended a grand Buddhist assembly convened by *Harsha* at Kanauj to widely publicize the doctrines of *Mahyana*. Hsuan Tsang initiated the discussion in the conference and challenged the audience to refute his arguments that resulted into his theological rivals particularly Brahmins to conspire to take the pilgrim's life. Harsh threatened to behead anybody causing the least hour to *Hsuan Tsang*. This provocated the Brahmins to make an attempt to assassinate Harsha. Detailed reading can be had from T. Watters, *op. cit.*
30. For Ambedkar, India is not a single nation. It is an amalgamation of different nations. He equates different castes and religious groups with nations. He finds common bond between them neither socially nor religiously.
31. Ambedkar, B.R., *op. cit.*, p. 64.
32. School of Ambedkar historical thought sees a method in the madness of Hindutva attacks. Unfortunately established schools of history look at this caste-religious attacks as momentary phenomenon. For Ambedkarite school every communal attack on minorities has caste connotation. Hindu attacks generally aimed at weaker sections of other religions and their localities.
33. Ambedkar, B.R., *op. cit.*, p. 64.
34. *Ibid.*, p. 66
35. *Ibid.*
36. *Ibid.*, p. 67.
37. Earthquake that struck Gujarat on 26th January 2001 was the biggest and most devastating one in 50 year.

38. Ambedkar, B.R., *op. cit.*, p. 71.
39. *Ibid.*
40. Sattar, Abdul., S., "Dr. Ambedkar's Contribution to Buddhism" (Religion and Philosophy), Paper presented in the National Seminar on the Life, Mssion, Contributions and Relevance of Babasaheb Dr. B. R. Ambedkar, Centenary Cell, New Delhi, 1991, p. 43.
41. Joshi, Lalmini, *Studies in the Buddhistic culture of India*, Delhi, 1977, PP. 394-401.
42. *Pushyamitra assassinated* Brihadrita *of* Maurya *dynasty* and ruled between 187-151 BC, under whom Manu the Hindu lawgiver wrote infamous Manu Smriti.
43. Vaidya, P. L. (ed.), *Divyavadana*, Text no. 20, Darbhanga, 1959, p. 282.
44. 1 Koti is equal to 10 million.
45. Walters, Thomas (tr.), edited by T.W. Rhysdavids and S.W. Bushell *Yuan - chwang's Travel in India*, Vol. I, Delhi, 1961, pp. 288-289.
46. *Ibid.*, P. 243.
47. Elliot, T.S., *Hinduism and Buddhism*, Vol. II, London, 1957, p. 6.
48. Ramteke, D. L., *Revival of Buddhism in Modern India*, New Delhi, 1983, p. 32.
49. *Ibid.*
50. *Ibid.*
51. Rao, Padma, K., *Women and Caste in India, Nidubrolu*, 1983, P. 39.
52. W. W. Hunter, *Indian Empire*, London, 1893, p. 240, requoted in *Ambedkar and The neo-Buddhist Movement* edited by T. S. Wilkinson and M.M. Thomas, The Christian Literature Society, Madras, 1972, pp. 14-15.
53. Tirukkural of Tiruvalluvar belonged to not later than the 10th C. A. D. and pariah or untouchable by caste. It explains the old Samkhya philosophy in 1330 poetical aphorisms dealing with the three chief desires of the human heart, wealth, pleasure and virtue
54. Asvaghosha (2nd C.A.D.) was one of the founders of Mahayana Buddhism and wrote the *Buddha Charita* which is a biography of the Buddha.
55. Later it was changed to South India Buddhist Association with branches all over the state.
56. Original name is David Hewavitharne, a Sri Lankan Christian.
57. Wilkinson, T. S., and Thomas, M. M., *op. cit.*, pp. 3 & 28.
58. Ramteke, D. C., *op. cit.*, p. 122.
59. *Ibid.*
60. Gandhi's paper *The Harijan*, 15 October 1935.
61. The Times of India, 16 October 1935. Ramteke discussed in his book. *op. cit.*, p. 122.
62. Ramteke, D. L., *op. cit.*, p. 124.
63. Ambedkar in his letter to D. Valisinha, the General Secretary of the Maha Bodhi Society, Calcutta on 30th October 1956. Appeared under the title 'Dr. B. R. Ambedkar's Testatment' in *The Maha Bodhi*, May 1957, p. 226. Stated in Wilkinson, *op. cit.*, p. 31.
64. Ambedkar, Speech at Nagpur on 15th October 1956. Quoted in Wilkinson, *op. cit.*, p. 31.
65. Zelliot, Eleanor, *From Untouchable To Dalit*, Manohar Publications, New

Delhi, 1992, p. 215. In the page 216, a note states: This Enlgish version of the 22 oaths has been taken, without correction, from a pamphlet published by the Buddhist Society of India, New Delhi, no date.

66. A Ceremony after the death of the man in Hinduism.
67. Handful rice offered in the name of the deceased.
68. Macy, Joanna Rogers and Zelliot, Eleanor, "Tradition and innovation in contemporary Indian Buddhism," *Studies in History of Buddhism,* (ed.) by A.K. Narain, Delhi, 1980, p. 134.
69. Shastry, S.N., "Revival of Buddhism in India", *The Maha Bodhi,* Calcutta, Feb. 1959, p. 67.
70. Ramchand, "Relevance of Philosophy of Dr. Ambedkar for Human rights," a paper presented on Ambedkar, Centenary Cell, *op. cit.*, p. 54.
71. Zelliot, Eleanor, *op. cit.*, p. 192.
72. For more on same topic refer L. Kenadi's *Revival of Buddhism in Modern India: The Role of Ambedkar and the Dalai Lama XIV* (1995).
73. Norbu, Dawa, "The Democratic Dalai Lama", *Tibetan Review,* New Delhi, July, 1973, p. 13.
74. *Tibetan Review,* March 1973, p. 5.
75. *Ibid.*, July - August, 1995, p. 7.
76. *Ibid.*
77. *Ibid.*, September, 1978, p. 7.
78. *Ibid.*, August, 1978, p. 9.
79. *Ibid.*
80. Read L. Kenadi, *op. cit.*

Four

Ambedkar and Buddhism of the Buddha

In twentieth century it was Ambedkar, who set the process of Modernisation of Buddhism; Modernisation of Buddhism was an effort aimed at bringing social transformation in the Indian Society; as a part of it he felt that, three steps appear to be quite necessary: *First*: To produce a Buddhist Bible; *Second*: to make changes in the aims and objects of the 'Bhikku Sangh'; *Third*: to set up a world Buddhist Mission.[1]

Despite having a vast literature, Ambedkar felt that Buddhism's disadvantage vis-à-vis other religions was that it lacked a handy gospel[2]; a book which one could carry in person and read. And therefore, he felt the need for having a Buddhist Bible[3] that is his, 'The Buddha and His *Dhamma*'. The Buddhist Bible encompasses the life and personality of the Buddha and presents an analytical exposition of the *Dhamma* (Buddhism). It is a book meant to be the gospel, for his Buddhist followers, contains his interpretation of Buddhism and the principles which guided him in his work'.[4] In this treatise, Ambedkar has endeavoured to re-interpret the *Dhamma* in order to show that Buddhism can amply meet the needs of the modern world.

Parivraja

Ambedkar raises four important Questions in his Buddhist Bible. The first problem relates to the main event in the life of the Buddha, namely *Parivraja*.[5] A.L. Basham opines, the traditional story of the Buddha, like those of most saints and heroes of ancient days, has suffered much at the hands of higher criticism. The story of his birth and early life appears only in the later books of the Buddhist scriptures and many of the references to him in those parts of the canon which purport to give his teachings are by no means reliable".[6] Traditionalist are of the belief that Buddha took *Parivraja* because he saw a dead person, a sick person and an old person. It is an absurd answer. These are common events occurring by hundreds and the Buddha could not have failed to come across them earlier, because at the time of his *Parivraja* he was twenty-nine years old. Ambedkar gives a rational reason according to the historical importance of the Gautama Buddha.

During the time of Sidhartha Gautama, there was an atmosphere of war, social conflict and political change. He was born in the family of King Suddhodana of Kapilavastu in northern India, whose men came into clash with the neighbouring state of Koliyas, on the question of distribution of water of river Rohini. The military chief proposed a violent war against the Koliyas for setting the water dispute. Sidhartha, as a member of the military *sangha*, protested against the proposal of war so vigorously that his protest resulted in his exile. However, finally the war was averted and matter of water dispute was settled peacefully. The war had ended in peace.

The problem of war is essentially a problem of conflict. It is only a part of a larger problem (i.e. of universal struggle for survival and existence). This conflict is going on not only between Kings, nations, but also between householders, between father and son, between sister and brother, between companions. The conflict between nation is occasional. But the conflict between classes is constant and perpetual. It is this, which is the root of all sorrow and suffering in the world.

The Buddha left his home an account of war. But he could not go back home despite the war between the Sakyas and Koliyas had ended. Now his problem had become wider. He had to find a solution for this problem of social conflict. Ambedkar finds that, the Buddha left his home to find an answer for the question of social conflict, which is the root of all sorrow and suffering in the world[7]. The enlightenment of the Buddha at Gaya was the final answer. It was to find a solution to the basic problem of the human society i.e. social conflict.

Four Noble Truths

The other problems, which are discussed by Ambedkar in his work, related to philosophy of the Buddha. These are (1) Four Noble Truths (2) Doctrines of Soul, of Karma and Re-birth; (3) Object of Bhikkhu. A.L. Basham's views on the authenticity of traditionalist writings are in support with Ambedkar. In the words of Basham, "Even the 'Sermon of the Turning of the wheel of the Law', which is said to be the first sermon preached after the Buddha's enlightenment, and which is the basic teaching of all Buddhist sects, is of dubious authenticity, and in the form in which we have it is not among the earliest parts of the canon".[8] *Dhammacakkapavattana Sutta* (Sermon of the Turning of the wheel of the Law), which the Buddha is said to have preached to his first five disciples called as *Panchavargiya Bhikkhus*, at Varanasi. This contains the 'four Noble Truths' and the 'Middle Path' that consists of the 'Eight fold Path', which are accepted as basic categories by all Buddhist sects. *Samyutta Nikaya*, thus, says, "Once the Master was at Varanasi, at the deer park called *Isipatana*. There the master addressed the five monks:

"There are two ends not to be served by a wanderer. What are those two? The pursuit of desires and of the pleasure which springs from desires, which is base, common, leading to rebirth, ignoble and unprofitable; and the pursuit of pain and hardship, which is grievous, ignoble and unprofitable. The Middle way of the Tathagata[9] avoids both these ends; it is enlightened, it brings clear vision, it makes for wisdom, and leads to peace, insight, full wisdom and Nirvana. What is this Middle Way? It is the Noble Eight fold Path - Right Views, Right Resolve, Right Speech, Right Conduct, Right Livelihood, Right Effort, Right Recollection and Right Meditation. This is the Middle way.

"And this is the Noble Truth of sorrow (dukkha). Birth is sorrow, age is sorrow, disease is sorrow, death is sorrow, contact with the unpleasant is sorrow, separation from the pleasant is sorrow, every wish unfulfilled is sorrow - in short all the five components of individuality are sorrow.

"And this is the noble Truth of the Arising of Sorrow (dukkha samudaya). [It arises from] thirst, which leads to rebirth, which brings delight and passion, and seeks pleasure now here, now there the thirst for sensual pleasure, the thirst for continued life, the thirst for power.

"And this is the Noble Truth of the stopping of sorrow (dukkha nirodha). It is the complete stopping of that thirst so that no passion remains, leaving it, being emancipated from it, being released from it, giving no place to it.

"And this is the Noble Truth of the Way which leads to the stopping of sorrow (dukkha nirodha marga). It is the Noble Eight fold Path - Right Views, Right Resolves, Right Speech, Right Conduct, Right Livelihood, Right Effort, Right Recollection and Right Meditation."[10]

In other words, Life in the world is full of suffering; there is a cause for this suffering; it is possible to stop suffering; there is a path, which leads to the cessation of suffering. Four Aryan Truths put forwarded by the traditionalists indeed don't form part of the original teachings of the Buddha. This formula cuts at the root of Buddhism. If life is sorrow, death is sorrow and re-birth is sorrow, then there is an end of everything. Neither religion nor philosophy can help a man to achieve happiness in the world. If there is no escape from sorrow, then what can religion do, what can Buddha do to relieve man from such sorrow, which is ever there in birth itself? The four Aryan Truths are a great stumbling block in the way of non-Buddhists accepting the gospel of Buddhism. The four Aryan Truths deny hope to man. They make the gospel of the Buddha a gospel of pessimism. *Dukkha* in its original sense given to it by Kapila means unrest, commotion. Initially it had a metaphysical meaning. Later on it acquired the meaning of suffering and sorrow. Unrest brings sorrow and suffering. Soon *Dukkha* acquired the meaning of sorrow and suffering from social and economic causes. For the Buddha poverty was a cause of sorrow.[11] The Buddha's conception of *Dukkha* is material can be known from a sermon: Buddha says.....

"Monks, is poverty a woeful thing for a worldly wanton?"

"Surely, Lord".

"And when a man is poor, needy, in straits, he gets into debt, and is that woeful too?"

"Surely, Lord".

"And when he gets into debt, he borrows, and is that woeful too?"

"Surely, Lord".

"and when the bill falls due, he pays not and they press him; is that woeful too?"

"Surely, Lord".

"And when pressed, he pays not and they beset him is that woeful too?"

"Surely, Lord".

"And when beset, he pays not and they bind him; is; is that woeful too?"

"Surely, Lord".

"Thus, monks, poverty, debt, borrowing, being pressed, beset and bound are all woes for the worldly wanton woeful in the world is poverty and debt".[12]

For the Buddha birth as a human being is a very precious thing. It cannot be sorrow as described in the first Aryan Truth. To the removal of *Dukkha* the Buddha attached great importance. The Buddha's Dhamma certainly is not pessimistic. The philosophy of the Buddha gives hope to man and faith in the present life. Four Aryan Truths are a later accretion by the monks who had strong Hindu influence. The word Aryan itself proves the point. Therefore, Aryan Truths don't form part of the original gospel of the Buddha. Indeed, the Buddha aimed at bringing positive purpose to human life, through his philosophy of *Madhyama Marga*, which is neither the path of pleasure nor the path of self-mortification. It avoids both the extremes. Since Aryan Truths propagate extremes of life i.e., sorrow and cessation of life, they cannot subscribe Middle Path. The scientific study of the middle path denies its relation with (Hindu) Aryan Truths, instead proposes Dalit Truths to fulfil into the scheme of modern Buddhism. Catvari Dalita [13] Satyani (Four original Noble Truths) are as follows:

(1) Life is both happiness and suffering
(2) This is the reality of Life
(3) One has to maximise happiness to minimize suffering
(4) The path that leads to maximise happiness is Majjhima Patipada (Middle Path) i.e., Dalita Patipada.[14]

Four Aryan Truths make false promise of cessation of suffering after following the Middle Path. The concept of cessation of suffering indeed contradicts with the Middle Path that wants no extremes of life. Four Dalita Truths are in accordance with the Middle Path. It is the realisation of the fact that suffering is reality of the life; Middle Path is not for cessation of suffering but to reduce the suffering and to get maximum happiness. This is at individual level. If it is applied at community level it works for the happiness and welfare of the maximum number of people - (Bahujana Hitaya and Bahujana Sukhaya).

Life is neither full of sorrow or misery or suffering (dukkha) nor Middle Path can bring about the end to all suffering. The truth is that Life is both happiness and sorrow. The Middle Path helps man to reduce suffering in his life. Because, even if one follows the Middle Path perfectly, the sorrow is the reality of the life, to balance the experience of the life. A husband requires leaving his wife for working at distance places that bring sorrow to the couples however that is inevitable for future happiness. Killing one evil person for the sake of whole community is also inevitable sorrowful act for larger happiness. This is not to propose that the Middle Path is pessimistic but understanding it in more practical way. In other words, the role of man is to maximise his happiness by his best efforts to follow the Middle Path, which is indeed a difficult task. Therefore, the Middle Path recognise the purpose of life as to balance both the extremes of the life. The sorrow is as real as happiness. The Middle Path is meant to give maximum happiness. This is no way to support Aryan Truths. They are too pessimistic in their approach to the life and worldly things.

Ambedkar finds that the recognition of human suffering as the real basis of religion of the Buddha. The real purpose of his religion is the removal of this misery. According to Ambedkar, the Buddha Dhamma if every person followed, it would bring about the end to all suffering. Even though he is more realistic in approach than the Aryan Truths, he suggests absolute cessation of suffering. This is to instill positive hope in the life. He finds three important paths in the Buddha Dhamma that assures any one who follows them to get the highest happiness. The three paths are: (1) the path of Purity; (2) the path of Righteousness; and (3) the path of Virtue.

Path of Purity

Path of Purity prescribes principles of life. They are: Not to injure or Kill; Not to steal or appropriate to oneself anything which belongs to another; Not to speak untruth; Not to indulge in lust; Not to indulge in intoxicating drinks. These principles constitute the standard of life or social code of conduct for regulating a man's life. In every society there are fallen people. There are two classes of Patit (fallen): the fallen one who has a standard and a fallen who has no standard. The presence of fallen men is the common feature of every society. What matters is not so much the fall of the man but the absence of any standard. The one who has no standard of life does not know that he has fallen. Consequently he always remains fallen. The one who subscribes to standard of life knows that he has fallen, so he tries to rise from his fallen state. That is why Buddha Dhamma prescribes standard through its principles of life. Other religions emphasis on the fall of man, because of ideal nature of their philosophy. Whereas Buddhist practical idealism makes oneself realise what supposed to be the basis of life. The principles of life prescribed in the path of purity from a true standard of life according to the Buddha Dhamma.

Astangika Marga

The Buddha recommended Eight Fold Path (Astangika Marga) - the path of Righteousness. This gives in a nutshell the essentials of Buddha's ethics. This path is open to all, monks as well as laymen.[15] The eight folds of the path are classified under three heads, moral precepts (*Sila*), mental development (*Citta*) and knowledge (*Panna*). The Eight Fold Path is as follows.[16]

SILA

Right speech (*Samma Vacca*)
Right deeds (*Samma Kamanto*)
Right means of livelihood (*Samma Ajeevo*)

CITTA

Right exertion (*Samma Vyayamo*)
Right mindfulness (*Samma Satti*)
Right meditation (*Samma Samadhi*)

PANNA

Right resolution (*Samma Sankappo*)
Right view (*Samma Ditthi*)

According to Pali texts, right speech means refraining from speaking falsehood, malicious words, harsh and frivolous talk; Right deeds mean, refraining from killing, stealing and misconduct; Right Means of livelihood meant for, refraining from earning livelihood by improper means; Right exertion means exertion to remove the existing evil thoughts, to keep the mind free from being polluted by fresh evil thoughts, and to preserve and increase the good thoughts; right mindfulness means mindfulness of all that is happening within the body and mind including feelings, and observant of things of the world and at the same time suppressing covetousness (*abhijjha*) and avoiding mental depression (*domanassa*).

Right meditation means: (a) the meditator's mind does not roam (*avitakka-avicara*) about but is concentrated on the object of meditation (*cetaso ekodibhavam*), becomes internally serene, and derives pleasure on account of full concentration. (b) The Meditator's mind is to rise beyond pleasure caused by acquisition of certain virtues and displeasure caused by the thoughts of impermanence, death and so forth and to attain mental equanimity. He still inwardly feels happy and remains alert, being watchful of what is passing in his body and mind, and his body feels at ease and comfort like that of a person after a deep sleep. (c) The meditator's mind remains undisturbed by any kind of feeling, happy or unhappy and as he has got rid of all mental impurities, his mind attains perfect equanimity, and remains alert to the subtlest movement of his mind and body.[17]

Right resolution meant for renunciation and resolution for refraining from hatred and injury to other beings; Right view means realisation of the truth that worldly existence is misery, root of such misery, end of such misery and the path leading to the end of such misery.

The eight-fold path deals with all the aspects of a spiritual life, viz, ethical, psychological and epistemological.

In the *Magga Samyutta*[18] the eight fold path is described as the spiritual guide (*kalyanamitta*) and is shown as conferring all the spiritual benefits that a Buddhist adept would desire to have. The benefits are cessation or eradication of (1) Suffering due to birth, old age and death; there are three kinds of sufferings, viz., sufferings as they are (dukkha), sufferings transmitted from past life (*samskara-dukkhata*) and sufferings due to change (*viparinama dukkhata*); (2) attachment(*ragadvesa*), hatred (*dosa*) and delusion (*moha*); (3) strong desire (*Chanda*), reflection (*vitakka*) and perception (*Sanna*); (4) thirst for worldly objects (*kama-tanha*), for repeated existence (*bhava-tanha*) and for self-destruction (*vibhava-tanha*); (5) impurities of desire (*kamasava*), of re-existence (*bhavasava*) (i.e. in one of the three spheres as worldly beings (*kamabhava*) as gods (*rupa, bhava*) and as higher gods without material body (*anupabhava*), of ignorance (*ajjasava*) and also of wrong views (*ditthasava*); (6) strong attachment to worldly objects (*kamupadana*), to wrong views (*ditth-Upadana*), to rituals and ceremonies (*silabbatupa dana*), and to belief in a self (*attavadupadana*); (7) Seven inclinations (*anusaya*), such as attachment (*kamaraga*) to worldly objects, enmity (*patigha*), wrong view (*ditthi*), doubt about the *triratna* (*vicikiccha*), Pride (*mana*), desire for existence (*bhavaraga*) and ignorance (*avijja*); (8) five kinds of pleasures derived through the contact of five sense - organs with their respective objects; (9) five hindrances (*nivaranas*) to nirvana, viz., strong desire (*kamacchanda*), hatred (*vyapada*), slothfulness (*thinamiddha*), arrogance and suspicions (*uddhacca-Kukkucca*), and doubt about the *triratna* (*vicikiccha*). *Kamacchanda* arises and grows on account of attractive characteristics of objects (*sudhani mitta*) while hatred (*vyapada*) for inimical feelings (*patighas*), *thinamiddha* for sleep, overeating, weakness of mind, *uddhaccakkukkucca* for lack of quietness (*avupasama*) and *vicikiccha* for objects which cause doubt. (10) five lower fetters (*orambhagiyani sammojanani*), viz., belief in a self (*sakkayaditthi*), doubt about the *Triratna* (*vickiccha*), belief in rituals and ceremonies (*silabasta*); strong desire (*kamacchanda*) and hatred (*vyapada*); (11) five higher fetters (*uddhambhagiyani sammojanani*), viz., attachment for existence in the *rupaloka* (i.e. gods with physical body), Pride (*mana*). Arrogance (*uddhacca*) and ignorance (*avijja*).

The positive benefits, derived through the practice of the eight fold path, when it is accompanied by solitude (*viveka*), detachment (*viraga*), cessation of inclinations (*nirodha*) and sacrifice (*Vosagga*) are: (1) attainment of the four fruits of sanctification (*Samannaphalas* i.e. *Sotapatti*, *Sakadagami*, *Anagami* and *Arhatta*). (2) Attainment of higher powers (*abhinna*)[19] (3) Perfection in the thirty seven *Dhammas* leading to full enlightenment (*Bodhi, Bodhi pakkhiya, Dhammas*): (4) And lastly, to the realisation of *Nibana* the immoral (*amata*).

In 'The Buddha And His *Dhamma*', Ambedkar, writing on the *Ashtangamarga*, maintains the continuity of the spirit of the Buddha *Dhamma* which needed changes as a part of modernisation[20].

Samma Ditti requires free mind and free thought. In other words the abandonment of superstition and supernaturalism and the abandonment of all doctrines, which are mere speculations without any basis in fact or experience. The right view is to have disbelief in the sanctity of the (Hindu) *Shastras*, for this one requires giving up of belief in the efficacy of rites and ceremonies.

Samma Sankappo teaches that everyone should have noble and praiseworthy aims, aspirations and ambitions. *Samma Vacca* teaches that one should speak only truth and not indulge in using abusive, slander language towards fellow beings and speech must be sensible and to the purpose. The most important thing of the Right speech is not to have reference to what any superior being may think of one's own action. The norm of right speech is not the order of the superior or the personal benefit to the individual. *Samma Kamanto* teaches right behaviour that every action should be founded on respect for the feelings and rights of others. In other words course of conduct must be in harmony with the fundamental laws of existence.

Samma Ajivo is earning livelihood through good ways, which don't cause injury or injustice to others. *Samma Vyayamo* is primary endeavour to remove *Avijja*, (Nescience), means to remove misunderstanding about the noble truths and to bring into existence states of mind to follow the *Ashtangamarga*. *Samma Satti* is to have constant wakefulness of the mind to watch and ward over the evil passions. *Samma Samadhi* is positive meditation. It gives the mind the necessary motive power to do good deeds with good thoughts.

Path of Virtue

The last sub path of the Middle path is the Path of Virtue that is meant the observance of the virtues called: (1) *Sila*; (2) *Dana*; (3) *Uppekha*; (4) *Nekkhama*; (5) *Virya*; (6) *Khanti*; (7) *Succa*; (8) *Adhithana*; (9) *Karuna*; and (10) *Maitri*.

(1) *Sila* means fear of doing wrong. It is moral temperament. Its literal meaning is character. (2) *Dana* is giving one's possessions and even one's life for the good of others without expecting anything in return. *Dana* means charity in highest form. It is necessary to remove the suffering of the needy and the poor and to promote general good. (3) *Uppekha* is a state of mind remaining unmoved by the result and yet engaged in the pursuit of it. *Uppekha* is necessary for sustained endeavour even though there is no personal gain. (4) *Nekkhama* is renunciation of the pleasures of the world. It is

necessary for selfless work. (5) *Virya* is right endeavour. (6) *Khanti* is forbearance. Not to meet hatred by hatred is the essence of it. (7) *Succa* is truth. (8) *Adhithana* is resolute determination to reach the goal. (9) *Karuna* is loving kindness to human beings. It is necessary to be drawn to the relief of poverty and suffering wherever it exists. (10) *Maitri* is extending fellow feeling to all beings, including foe. These are called as Ten Paramitas. (States of perfection), because these virtues one must practice to his utmost capacity.

Buddhist Ethics

In Buddhist philosophy knowledge and morality are thought inseparable not simply because morality, or doing of good, depends on the knowledge of what is good, about which all philosophers would agree, but also because perfection of knowledge is regarded as impossible without morality, perfect control of passions and prejudices. Buddha explicitly states in one of his discourses that virtue and wisdom purify each other and two are inseparable.[21] Personal purity is the foundation of good in the world. It is necessary to build up sufficient strength of character. That is not just having love but *maitri* (fellowship) with all living beings. In the Buddha Dhamma salvation has been conceived as the blessing of happiness to be attained by man in this life and on this earth by righteousness born out of his own efforts- inward change of heart to be brought about by the practice of self-culture and self-control.

Even though Ambedkar regarded Aryan interpretation of noble truths that life is sorrow, death is sorrow and re-birth is sorrow as a later accretion. He maintained that the true understanding of noble truths is knowing the existence of suffering and the removal of suffering. Of all religions in the world, the religion of the Buddha is only based on the recognition of human suffering and the purpose of it is the removal of this misery. On the basis of the Buddha's middle path, Dalit interpretation of the noble truths Maintains that the Buddha's real noble truth is to realise the fact of the life that is: life is both happy and sorrow and sorrow cannot be removed totally from the life. What one can do is to minimize sorrow. The middle path helps man to minimize misery in life by maximising happiness. Buddha's middle path is nothing but an ethical pact between man and society and between society and nature.

To discuss the ideas about man and the world in Buddha's ethical teachings, it is essential to mention four views, on which his ethics mainly depends, namely: The theory of "Chain of Dependent Origination" (*Paticca - Samuppada*), i.e., conditional existence of the things. The theory of *Kamma*; the theory of change; and the theory of non-existence of the soul. The doctrine of Middle Path was developed in various rather pedantic forms, most important of which was the theory of dependent origination, as series of twelve terms.

Law of Causation *(Paticca - Samuppada)*

There is a spontaneous and universal law of causation, which conditions the appearance of all events, mental and physical. This law (dhamma) works automatically without the help of any conscious guide. In accordance with it, whenever a particular event (the cause) appears, it is followed by another particular event (the effect). On getting the cause, the effect arises. The existence of everything is conditional, dependent on a cause. Nothing happens fortuitously or by change.[22] This view, as Buddha himself makes clear, avoids two extreme views: On the one hand, eternalism or the theory that some reality eternally exists independently of any condition and, on the other hand, Nihilism or the theory that something existing can be annihilated or can cease to be. Therefore, Buddha claims to hold the Middle view, namely, that everything that we perceive possess an existence but it is dependent on something else, and that thing in turn does not perish without leaving some effect.

The twelve folds or 12 Nidanas (causes) of cause and effect theory or Dependent origination are: *Avidya* (ignorance); Samskaras (impressions); *Vijnana* (clear consciousness); *Namarupa* (name and form[23]); *Sadana* (the six organs of sense); *sparsa* (contact of the senses with exterior objects); *Vedana* (feeling); *Trisna* (desire); *Upadana* (clinging, effort);[24] *Bhava* (becoming, beginning of existence); *Jati* (birth, existence); *Jaramaranam, Sokaparidevana Dukh Dauramanasyopayasah* (old age and death, sorrows, lamentation, pain, grief, despondency).[25]

To believe that all compound things are impermanent is Dhamma. According to Ambedkar the doctrine of impermanence has three aspects.[26] There is the impermanence of composite things; of the individual being and; of the self nature of conditioned things. Asanga, the great Buddhist philosopher explains that all things are produced by the combination of causes and conditions and have no independent noumenon of their own. When the combination is dissolved, their destruction ensures.[27]

In other words, the universe is transient (*anicca*). There is no abiding entity anywhere. Every being or object, however stable and homogenous it may appear, is in reality transient and composite. Man, who thinks himself to be eternal and individualized, is actually a compound of five phsychosomatic elements - Body, Feelings, Perceptions, States of Mind, and Awareness. These five vary from minute to minute and there is no permanent substratum to them. In this sense a being of a past moment has lived, but does not live nor will he live. The being of a future moment will live but has not lived nor does live but has not lived and will not live.

In short, a human being is always changing, always growing. He is not the same at two different moments of his life. The old man is evidently not the same person as the baby in arms seventy years ago, and similarly he is not the same as the man of a moment ago. At every instant the old man vanishes, and a new man, caused by the first, comes into being, though a specious continuity is given by the chain of cause and effect which links one with the other. Buddhism knows no being, but only becoming that means being is becoming.

This later on gave rise to what is called Sunyavad. If all things are equally unreal, they are ultimately one and the same. The one thing which alone had real existence could have no predicate; it was therefore called by Nagarjuna "Emptiness", or "the Void "(*Sunnyata*). Ambedkar says that the Buddhist *Sunnyata* does not mean nihilism out and out. It only means the perpetual changes occurring at every moment in the phenomenal world.[28] Therefore, *Sunnyata* in true Buddhist sense is not void or empty. If things were not subject to continual change but were permanent and unchangeable, the evolution of all of life from one kind to the other and the development of living things would come to a dead stop. *Sunnyata* is like a point which has substance but neither breadth nor length.

The Buddha attaches so much importance to the understanding of the theory of cause and effect that he calls this the Dhamma. He asks us to put aside questions of the beginning and the end. And his Dhamma is that being thus, this comes to be from the coming to be of that, this arises. That being absent, this does not happen. From the cessation of that, this ceases. He says that he who sees the *paticca samuppada* sees the Dhamma, and he who sees the Dhamma, sees the *patticcasamuppada*. It is the failure of grasp this stand point which, Buddha asserts, is the cause of all our troubles.[29] According to Rhys Davids, later Buddhism (Mahayanism) does not pay much heed to this theory. But the Buddha himself says that this theory is very profound.[30]

The moral of this doctrine is simple. In Ambedkar words, "Do not be attached to anything".[31] It is to cultivate detachment, detachment from property, from friends, etc., that Buddha said "All these are impermanent".[32]

The essence of the Buddha's teachings is cessation of suffering. Rhys Davids observes that the theory of dependent origination (in its double aspect of explaining the world and explaining the origin of suffering), together with the formula of the eight fold path, gives us "not only the whole of early Buddhism in a nutshell, but also just those points concerning which we find the most emphatic affirmations of *Dhamma* as *Dhamma* ascribed to Gautama".[33]

Buddha's Metaphysics

The Buddha's attempt to avoid metaphysics gives rise to a new kind of metaphysics. In spite of the Buddha's aversion to theoretical speculation, he never wanted to accept, nor did he encourage his followers to accept any course of action without reasoning and criticism. He was extremely rational and contemplative, and wanted to penetrate into the very roots of human existence, and tried to supply the full justification of the ethical principles he followed and taught. Therefore, it was no wonder that he himself incidentally laid down the foundation of a philosophical system.

His philosophy, partly expressed and partly implicit, may be called positivism in so far as he taught that our thoughts should be confined to this world and to the improvement of our existence here. It may be called phenomenolism in so far as he taught that we were sure only of the phenomena we experienced. Therefore, it is a kind of empiricism in method because experience, according to him, was the source of knowledge.

The different aspects of his philosophy come to be developed by his followers along different lines as they were required to justify that the Buddha's teaching, to defend it from the severe criticism it has to face in India and outside, and to convert other thinkers to their faith.

Ten questions[34] are often mentioned by the Buddha as uncertain, ethically unprofitable and so not discussed (*Vyakata)* by him: (1) Is the world eternal? (2) Is it non-eternal? (3) Is it finite? (4) Is it infinite? (5) Is the soul the same as the body? (6) Is it different from the body? (7) Does one who has known the truth (*Tathagatha)* live again after the death? (8) Does he not live again after death? (9) Does he both live again and not live again after death? (10) Does he neither live nor not live again after death?

The Buddha's reluctance to discuss the ten metaphysical questions concerning things beyond our experience and his silence about them came to be interpreted by his followers in different lights. Some took this attitude as only the sign of a thorough going empiricism which must frankly admit the inability of mind to decide non-empirical questions.

According to this explanation, the Buddha's attitude would be regarded as scepticism. Some other followers, mostly the Mahayanists, interpreted Buddha's view neither as a denial of reality beyond objective of ordinary experience, nor as a denial of any means of knowing the non-empirical reality, but only as signifying the indescribability of that transcendental experience and reality. The justification of this last interpretation can be obtained from some facts of the Buddha's life and teachings. Ordinary empiricists believe that our sense-experience is the only basis of all our knowledge; they do not admit the possibility of any non-sensuous experience.

However, the Buddha taught the possibility of man's attaining in *nirvana* an experience or consciousness which was not generated by the activity of the sense. The Supreme Value and importance that he attached to this non-empirical consciousness justify his followers in supposing that he regarded this as the supreme reality as well. The fact that the nemesis of neglected metaphysics overtakes Buddhism soon after the founder's passing away.

Buddhism as an Ethical Religious Movement

Buddhism is primarily, ethical-religious movement. Buddhism finds its special place among all religions, for its importance to ethics. One way of characterising the Buddhist ethical tradition is to note the close association between the central Buddhist insight into reality as selfless (*anatman*) or empty (*Sunya*) on the one hand, and authentic moral activity (*Kamma*) on the other. Insight into selflessness or emptiness informs moral activity, while moral activity supports the cultivation of insight.

Another characteristic of Buddhist ethics is that the moral character of human action is closely associated with the intention that constitutes it. It is simply presumed that actions constituted by good intentions will, by virtue of the universal order that structures reality, lead to good and pleasant results for the individual and for society; and that actions constituted by bad intentions will, by virtue of that same universal order, lead to an unpleasant results for the individual and for society.

An important characteristic of Buddhist ethics is that it combines an adherence to precepts and responsibilities with an emphasis on the rooting out of vices and the cultivation of virtues. These rule-oriented and vice or virtue oriented modes of ethical activity are occasionally seem be to in tension, but Buddhists have largely assumed that they mesh together in a manner that is mutually supportive.

Buddhist communities have differentiated among levels of ethical responsibility and attainment. These levels are often associated with various stages of steriological achievement. They are also commonly correlated with the institutional and social hierarchies that have traditionally characterised Buddhist societies. Finally, it is the humanity, which matters, not divinity, in the Buddhist social thought. Hence it can be said that, Buddhist ethical religious system is nothing but a pragmatic (i.e. *Madhye-marga or* middle path) approach to the operation of human society.

Ambedkar depended on 'reason and rationale', when he constructed Buddhist theory and ideology. He applied, these two scientific principles (i.e. reason and rationale) to decide the social validity of religion. His main is stress on 'purpose'. For everything there is purpose. In modern society purpose is more important than meaning. In other words, Ambedkar concerns more about the purpose of religion and its philosophy than its meaning.

For some, Buddhism is not at all a religion, since it denies 'God'. For others the Buddha is a God so it is a religion. To Ambedkar the traditional meaning of Religion is not acceptable. He feels that Buddhism is a religion without God. Thus, we find in Ambedlar's approach, that meaning is not important but the purpose.

The important issues, which Ambedkar touched in his writings on Buddhism, are (1) Existence of God (2) Existence of soul (3) Karma and (4) Re-birth. He dealt all these issues, with the application of reason and logic. In other words, Ambedkar does not believe in the existence of God and Soul. His Kamma is to do with this world only. Re-birth to him has differed with traditional meaning.

Theory of Soul, Karma and Rebirth

Ambedkar finds contradictions in the doctrines of soul, of Karma and rebirth. The Buddha denied the existence of the soul. But he is also said to have affirmed the doctrine of Karma and rebirth. The Question is if there is no soul how can there be Karma and rebirth. In what sense did the Buddha use the word Karma and rebirth? Did he use them in a different sense than the sense in which the Hindus used them? If so, there is a terrible contradiction between the denial of the soul and the affirmation of Karma and rebirth.

In the Hindu Religion, Atman (soul) is the name given to an entity which was held to be abiding separate from the body, but living inside the body constantly existing from the moment of his birth. Belief in the soul included other beliefs, connected with it. The soul does not die with the body. It takes birth in another body when it comes into being. The body serves as external clothing for the soul.

Indeed, almost all religions, except Buddha's Dhamma, believe on the immortality of soul. A belief in the existence of soul is as common as the belief in the existence of God, the Supreme Being. Ambedkar feels that, the belief in the existence of the soul is as much a source of superstition as the belief in God is. And the belief in the existence of soul is for more dangerous than the belief in God[35]. "For not only does it create a priesthood, not only is it the origin of all superstition but it gives the priesthood complete control over man from birth to death[36]" Ambedkar writes.

In Buddhism, there is no soul, eternal and unchanging, because the Buddha believed in the impermanence of all composed things.[37] What Buddhism really believes in is not the nonmaterial soul which the theists regard as permanent and unchangeable, even after death, but human consciousness that everyone knows from his own experience.

On the basis of Ambedkar's interpretation of Buddhism, it can be explained that, in Buddhism, a sentient Being is a compound thing consisting of certain physical elements and certain mental elements. They are called *Khandas*. The *Rupa Khanda* primarily consists of the physical elements such as earth, water, fire and air. They constitute the Body or *Rupa*. Besides *Rupa Khanda,* there is such a thing as *Nama Khanda,* which goes to make up a sentient being.[38]

This *Nama Khanda* is called *Vinana,* or consciousness. This *Nama Khanda* includes the three mental elements: *Vedana* (Sensation springing from contact of the six senses with the world), *Sanna* (perception), and *Sankhara* (states of mind). *Chetana* (consciousness) is sometimes spoken of along with the three other mental stages as being one of them. A modern psychologist would say that consciousness is the main - spring from which other psychological phenomena arise. *Vinana* is the centre of a sentient being. Consciousness is the result of the combination of the four elements: *Prithi* (earth), *Apa* (Water), *Tej* (Fire) and *Vayu* (Air).[39]

When the Buddha was asked, "How is consciousness produced?" Ambedkar writes, "his answer was, not that the co-existence or aggregation of the physical elements produces consciousness. What the Buddha said was that wherever there was *Rupa* or *kaya* (body) there was consciousness accompanying it".[40] So it is only the body (*Kaya*) that produces consciousness but not all the matter.

Once consciousness arises man becomes a sentient being.[41] Consciousness, therefore, is the chief thing in man's life. Consciousness is cognitive, emotional and volitional. Consciousness is cognitive when it gives knowledge, information, as appreciating or apprehending, whether it is appreciation of internal facts or external things and events. Consciousness is emotional when it exists in certain subjective states, characterized by either pleasurable or painful tones, when emotional consciousness produces feeling. Consciousness in its volitional state makes a being exerts himself for the attainment of same end. Volitional consciousness gives rise to what we call will or activity.[42]

It is said that, in Buddhism, so long a *Khandas* are united, we have being, when the *Khandas* dissolve, the being disappears. This can be well illustrated. Just as fire, though not lying hidden in the two sticks rubbed against each other, originates through friction, in the same way, says the Buddha, appears consciousness (*vinana*) under certain material conditions, and disappears when these conditions cease to exist.[43]

When the wood is burnt out, the fire disappears; just so, when the conditions of consciousness cease, consciousness disappears. To say it briefly, vital organisation is the indispensable substratum of all consciousness. We know consciousness only as phenomena of life, connected with an organisation.[44]

Prof. Narasu an eminent Buddhist Scholar says that, we only know physical processes as dependent on organic processes. Changes in the brain and the nervous system are essential conditions for all phenomena of consciousness. When the blood supply is cut off from the nerve centres, there is instantaneous loss of consciousness. He says,"normal psychology proves that consciousness can have no existence independent of the organism".[45] In fact, this conclusion is strongly supported by mental pathology.

In Buddhism, the relation between matter and consciousness can be put it that matter is predominating in the formation of the physical universe; but human personality is a combination of both material and mental elements. Consciousness (mind) is predominating in the individual life of man. Matter is the substratum in the formation of the world and human personality; but consciousness in human personality is something very active. As the evolution goes on towards the higher stage, consciousness becomes dominant and controls the material conditions of society and creates moral values for the well being of men living together. Even the human consciousness is always in "restless change".[46]

Both being and consciousness are real and accompanying each other. It is said that, the Buddha recognise mind as creative centre in human personality. And human mind plays a significant part in man's social affairs and relations. Mind (Consciousness), precedes things, dominates them, and creates them. If mind is comprehended, all things are comprehended. The first thing to attend is the culture of the mind.[47]

Buddhism, holds that mind should be used not only to change the material conditions, but also for the cultivation of human personality. So the consciousness or mind, if it is well directed, can transform material conditions and it can create values for a better society than the present one.

The Buddha expresses that there is necessity in nature; there are natural laws, which are knowable by man, and it is the knowledge of the necessity of nature and natural laws that can set man free from misery and interruptions caused by man himself and by natural forces as well. What seem, "Accident or chance" to ignorant persons, the Buddha denied them to be divine and emphasized the need of correct comprehensive understanding of all what exists, what reality is, in order to change the living conditions of mankind for larger happiness.

Generally, people believe that the fact of succession is either accidental or due to supernatural power i.e., God. Which means that in both the cases man could not effectively interfere with the course of things. Buddha's dynamic realism explains that there is every scope for human efforts since a series of causes in nature is understandable. And Buddhism refutes the role of accident or chance or divine power in determining human's life.

The causal factors are determinable in their entirety; and the series they give rise to be, therefore, terminable, according to early Buddhism, at least in respect of the misery of existence. Whose removal is the chief problem of life. It was the knowledge of these factors, with the law of contingent causation implicit in it, that "flashed across Siddhartha's mind at last and made him the 'Buddha".[48]

Its chief significance for man is that since misery caused in accordance with a natural and ascertainable law it can be ended by remaining its cause — a discovery which points at the same time to the positivistic and practical basis of Buddha's teaching. The explanation was then extended to all causal phenomena. In this general form, it states that for everything that is, there is an adequate reason why it is so and not otherwise; and the causes accounting for it are at least in theory completely knowable.

Buddhism has no concern with either determinism or determinateness because it is a religion (*Dhamma*) of "self creation".[49] And it holds the theory of free will (not absolute) within the sphere of human beings. Every being is a stage of dynamic becoming. There is a long continuity of existence of man and nature, birth and death. Birth and death are not the predetermined fate of a living being but a corollary of action (Kamma).[50]

The world is a universe of relations and what appears to be permanent and eternally determined, is a phase of temporary existence, an instant in a causal sequence, one ripple in the long line of Waves, the effect of the two or more causes combined.[51] the fatalist view that man's destiny is influenced by the stars is not accepted in the Buddhist philosophy. In the ongoing of the world new events are continuously happening and that the destiny of each individual is to a very great degree dependent upon what the particular individual is and does.[52]

It can be said that, Buddhism does not believe in any fatalism and determinism, in the sense of being determined by fate and god. It holds the view that man's will is always determined in the moment of willing, not wholly by external forces, but by the tendencies, the impulses and purposes, that belongs to man's character. The act of choice is not uncaused; like any other event it is always an element within a causal situation. It is by knowledge of causal order or about things that man can make many more choices. With the knowledge of things, and in the midst of choices, man enables himself to realise the fruits of his free nature.

The Buddha emphasised that, with true understanding of the nature, man may not be the victim of superstition and demagogue in religion and politics. So the knowledge of human nature, of society and thought is important for a man who want freedom from suffering and exploitation. Unless the sufferers know how they are being exploited, they cannot get rid of exploitation being done through the ill-natured social system.

Thus for the Buddhism the universe is soulless. The word

soul of the *Upanisads* is an illusion. The Buddhism is a religion without souls and without God. According to the Buddha there is no soul but there is re-birth. Hindu theorists posed a question that how can there be re-birth if there is no soul. In support of the Buddhist view of re-birth, Ambedkar says, "there can be re-birth even though there is no soul. There is a mango stone. The stone gives rise to a mango tree. The mango tree produces mangoes. Here is rebirth of a mango. But there is no soul. So there can be rebirth although there is no soul."[53]

What happened after death is a Question often asked. The Eternalists said that the soul knows no death: therefore life is eternal. It is renewed by re-birth. But the Annihilationists argued that death is the end of everything and there is nothing left after death. The Buddha was not an eternalist. For it involved a belief in the existence of a separate, immortal soul to which he was opposed. And also he is not an annihilationist. This may raise Question that how can the Buddha not believe in the existence of the Soul and yet say that he is not annihilationist. To make clear the contradiction, it is needed to examine another Question: Did the Buddha believe in re-birth?

Dealing with the question of re-birth, Ambedkar asks, re-birth of what and re-birth of whom. According to the Buddha there are four elements of Existence, which go to compose the body. They are *Pritivi Apa: Tej* and *Vayu.* Now the Question is when the human body dies what happens to these four elements? Do they also die along with dead body? Some says that they do. But the Buddha said no, according to Ambedkar. And he explains that the elements join the mass of similar elements floating in (Akash) space. When the four elements from this floating mass join together a new birth takes place. The elements need not and are not necessarily from the same body, which is dead. They may be drawn from different dead bodies. It must be noted that the body dies. But the elements are ever living. This is what the Buddha meant by re-birth.

The dialogue between Sariputta and Maha-Kotthita, throws great light upon the subject.[54]

Maha-Kotthita asked: "How many factors has the first ecstasy (*Dhyana*) put from it and how many does it retain?

Sariputta replied: "Five of each. Gone are lusts, malevolence, torpor, worry and doubt. Observation, reflection, zest, satisfaction and a focussed heart persist".

Maha-Kotthita asked: "Take the five senses of sight, sound, smell taste and touch, - each with its own particular province and range of function, separate and mutually distinct. What ultimate base have they? Who enjoys all their five provinces and ranges?"

Sariputta replied: "Mind (Mano)".

Maha-Katthita asked:"On what do these five faculties of sense depend?"

Sariputta replied: "On vitality".

Maha-Kotthita asked: "On what does vitality depend?

Sariputta: "On heat".

Maha-Kotthita asked: "On what does heat depend?"

Sariputta replied: "On vitality".

Maha-Kotthita asked: "You say that vitality depends on heat, you also say that heat depends on vitality! What precisely is the meaning to be attached to this?".

Sariputta replied: "I will give you an illustration. Just as in the case of a lamp, the light reveals the flame and the flame the light, so vitality depends upon heat and heat on vitality.

Maha-Kotthita asked: "How many things must quit the body before it is flung aside and cast away like a senseless log?".

Sariputta answered: "Vitality, heat and consciousness".

Maha-Kotthita asked: "what is the difference between a lifeless corpse and an almsman in trance, in whom perception and feelings are stilled?".

Sariputta replied:" In the corpse not only are the plastic forces of the body and speech and mind stilled and quiescent but also vitality is exhausted, heat is quenched and the faculties of sense broken up; whereas in the almsman in trance vitality persists, heat abides, and the faculties are clear, although respiration, observation and perception are stilled and quiescent".

What happens when the body dies? The body ceases to produce energy. Heat means energy in the above discussion. In other words, death means not only cession of production of energy, and whatever energy had escaped from the body joins the general mass of energy playing about in the universe. It is a new addition to the stock of general floating mass of energy. The Buddha's view is in consonance with science. What science affirms is that energy is never lost. In the sense that after death nothing is left would be contrary to science. For it is would mean that energy is not constant in volume. Annihilationists believe that death is the end doesn't stand with the science. The Buddha is an annihilationist so far as soul is concerned and not an annihilationist so far as matter is concerned. According to his philosophy, there is regeneration of matter and no rebirth of the soul.

'Rebirth of whom is the question raised by Ambedkar in his discussion on the Buddha's philosophy on the concent of 'Re-birth'. In the Buddhist scheme of things, it is most improbable that the same dead person takes a new birth. It is possible depends upon the elements of existence of the dead man meeting together and forming a new body. If a new body is formed after a mixture or the different men who are dead then there is rebirth but not the rebirth of the same sentient being. Sister Khema a widely learned woman disciple of the Buddha in her discussion with King Pasenadi, well explained this point.

Once the Buddha was staying near Savatthi at Jeta Grove in Ananthapindika's Aram. On that occasion the sister Khema took up here quarters at Toranavatthu, between Shravasti and Saketa. The Rajah Pasenadi of Kosala journeying from Saketa to Shravasti and midway he put up for one night at Toranavatthu. There he came to know about the stay of the sister Khema and visited her to learn about the Buddha Dhamma. In their discussion, he said to her: "How say you, lady? Does the *Tathagata* exist after death".

"That also, Maharajah is not revealed by the Exalted one".

"How then lady? When asked 'Does the *Tathagata* exist after death?' you reply, "That is not revealed by the Exalted one,' and, when I ask...the other questions, you make the same reply. Pray, lady, what is the reason, what is the cause, why this thing is not revealed by the Exalted one?".

"Now in this matter, maharajah, I will question you. Do you reply, as you think fit. Now how say you, Maharajah? Have you some accountant, some ready reckoner or calculator, able to count the sand in Ganges, thus" There are so many hundred grains, or so many thousand grains, or so many hundreds of thousands of grains of sand"?

"No, indeed, lady".

"Then have you some accountant, ready reckoner or calculator able to reckon the water in the mighty ocean, thus" There are so many gallons of water, so many hundreds, so many thousands, so many hundreds of thousands gallons of water?".

"No, indeed, lady.

"How is that?"

"Mighty is the ocean, lady, deep, boundless, unfathomable".

"Even so, Maharajah, if one should try to define the *Tathagata* by his bodily form, that bodily form of *Tathagata* is abandoned, cut down at the root, made like a palm-tree stump, made some things that is not, made of a nature not to spring up again in future time. Set free from reckoning as body, Maharajah, is the *Tathagata*. He is deep, boundless, and unfathomable, just like the Mighty Ocean. To say, 'The *Tathagata* exists after death' does not apply. To say, 'The *Tathagata* exists not after death' does not apply. To say,'The *Tathagata* both exist and exist not, neither exist nor not exists after death', does not apply.

"If one should try to define the *Tathagata* by feeling, that feeling of the *Tathagata* is abandoned, cut down at the root... yet free from reckoning as feeling is the *Tathagata*, Maharajaha, deep, boundless, unfathomable like the mighty ocean. To say, 'The Tathagata exists after death.... exists not after death,' does not apply.

"So also if one should try to define the *Tathagata* by perception, by the activities, by consciousness....set free from reckoning by consciousness is the *Tathagata*, deep, boundless, unfathomable as the mighty ocean. To say, 'The *Tathagata* exists after death... exists not after death', does not apply".[55]

With the words of the sister Khema, the Rajah Pasenadi of Kosala was delighted, saluted her and went away. On another occasion the Rajah visited the Buddha and got same answer for his question on the re-birth.

Thus, the Buddha's answer to rebirth of what and whom is entirely different from Hindu belief. The Doctrine of Karma also has created same misunderstanding. The similarity in terminology i.e. Karma, Dharma, gives Hindus an easy handle for their false and malicious propaganda. The historical necessity of the

Buddhism is to locate itself in opposition to Hindu social thought - karma dharma. Hindu theory of Karma Dharma is entirely different from Kamma *Dhamma* of Buddhism.

Even though, etymological similarity exists between Buddhist Pali term Kamma and Hindu Sanskrit word karma. The post-modern approach to Dalit tradition defines Buddhist terminology in absolute meaning and clearly differentiates from deliberately highlighted understandings. The Hindu Law of Karma is based on soul and it is hereditary. It goes on from life to life, because of the transmigration of the soul. When a man does Karma, it affects the doer and produces an impress upon his soul. And after the death, his soul escapes with full such impressions. It is these impressions which determine his birth and status in his future life. In other words, if a man is born in a poor family it is because of his past bad karma. If a man is born in a rich family it is because of his past good Karma. If a man is born with a congenital defect it is because of his past bad Karma. This is a very pernicious doctrine. There is no room left for human effort in this interpretation of Karma. Everything is predetermined by the past Karma. Hindu theory of karma is inconsistent with the Buddhist theory of no soul (*Anatta*). The Buddhist doctrine of Kamma cannot be and is not the same as the Hindu doctrine of Kamma. It is simply foolish to talk about the Buddhist doctrine of Kamma being the same as the Hindu doctrine of Karma.

It was the Buddha first to say:" Reap as you sow".[56] The Buddha's Law of Kamma applied only to human action and its effect on present life. He didn't believe in past life's human action and its effect on future life. The doctrine of past Karma is purely Hindu doctrine. It has been introduced into Buddhism by some one who wanted to make Buddhism akin to Hinduism or who did not know what the Buddhist doctrine was.

The basis of the Hindu doctrine of past Karma as the regulator of future life is an iniquitous doctrine. The purpose of inventing such a doctrine is to enable the state or the society to escape responsibility for the condition of the poor and the lowly. Otherwise such an inhuman and absurd doctrine could never have been invented. This is the main reason to hold the view that the Buddha who was known as *Maha Karunika* could not have preached such a doctrine. What exactly is the Buddha theory of Kamma? In the Buddha's theory, there is no 'transmigration' of anything from past life to present. But there is 'inheritance', that past deed is inherited. For example, child inherits the characteristics of his parents. Human birth is genetic.

In the Hindu doctrine of Karma a child inherits nothing from its parents except the body. The past Karma in the Hindu doctrine is the inheritance of the child by the child and for the child, since it is the soul that matters. The parents contribute nothing. The child's soul brings everything. The soul is implanted into the body that is genetic, from outside but Hindu doctrine is unable to specify the source of soul. Since there is no soul in the Buddhist belief, there is no transmigration of past deeds. The Buddha believed that from the moment of man's birth, his kammas (deeds) are taken into account, and as he sows, so he reaps, in future, up to the last breath of his life. One, who acts must, sooner or later, reap the effect. While experiencing an effect, one is sowing seeds a new, thus causing the next wave of life to be high or low according to the one's proceeding actions, here in this present life. And also the Buddha asserts that the status of a man may be governed not so much by heredity as by his environment.

It is the environment that influences man to experience pleasure and pain. Though child inherits characteristics from parents, it is the environment that makes the personality of child and his actions accordingly. Therefore, the actions of childhood influence the future of man and these actions generally depend on the environment in which he live. J.G. Jennigs holds that the Buddha rejected the doctrine of transmigration and taught merely the almost self-evident truism that one generation is affected by the deeds of the proceeding one.[57] Thus, there is no past deeds effect on the status of the present life of a person in the Buddha's philosophy of Kamma.

Man is, by nature, a social being, because he believes in society, and acts together with his fellow beings. He has developed in society. His whole mode of life is social. Therefore, just as it is in his social activity, that he enlarges his perceptions, he begins to form ideas, to think and to develop his conceptions. The basis of man's social activity is, in the Buddha's philosophical term "*Kamma'* i.e. human action or human effort. *Kamma cultivates* human mind, which leads to the individual and social well being. The importance of human effort is the basic idea in the reconstruction of society and the cultivation of human personality.

For the Buddha, man is responsible for what he is and what he may be in the future. In Buddhism, it is the Kamma of Man which maintains individuality in the social order.[58] What a society is depends largely upon *Kammas* without which the image of man cannot be conserved and conceived. The social order rests on "man and nobody else". *Kamma* means man's action and *Vipaka* is its effect. If the social organisation is oppressive and unjust it is because man's *Kammas* create such things. If the social order is good, full of co-operation, it is because men's *Kammas* create such things. In the principle of *Kamma,* what the Buddha wanted to convey was that the effect of human action was bound to follow the deed, it was like a rule. No society could fail to benefit by the good effects of men's good *Kammas* and no society could escape the evil effects of men's bad *Kammas.*[59] The shape and structure of any society definitely depends on what men do by living in a particular environment.

Emphasising the importance of moral values of human society, Prof. Radha Krishnan writes on Buddha, that the vital problem for the Buddha was not how the world spirit, if any, manifests itself in the superhuman realm, but in the individual man and in the empirical world. "What controls the universe is dharma, the moral law. The world is made, not by gods and angels, but by the voluntary choice of men... By substituting the laws of cause and effect for the caprices of demons and gods the Buddha put the noblest system of morality in the place of tribal custom and taboo".[60] It is said that the Buddha knows that the human will is not omnipotent; it works in a material, animal and social environment which impinges at every point on the life of man, though he, by his will and exertion, can modify and re-shape to some extent his environment.[61] This continual interaction between man and his environment is the texture of which history is woven. Hence it can be said that for the Buddha, human efforts count.

What the Buddha said, is that society is based on what men do and how they manipulate their environmental forces. In the absence of any supernatural help, the re-construction of man's social life is not possible without his own *Kamma* or action.

Man has developed his social activities, his perceptions and thoughts; and through this he has continually revolutionised his own conditions of life, and has increased his capacities and powers. It is through action, *Kamma*, that man has been able to affect the life of his own and the existence of human society. Man has wider activities and interests, and in developing these activities and interests, he has affected the course of social development, consciously and co-operatively.

It is commonly accepted by Buddhist that the development of human action or the cultivation of *Kamma* necessarily helped the people bring the members of society together by multiplying cases of mutual support and joint activity, and by making clear the advantage of this joint activity to each individual. Men, in the process of making, have arrived at the point where they have something to say to one another. This something includes the ends to be achieved and the results to be aimed at by co-operation among human beings.

The Buddha attached a moral significance to man's *Kamma*. In Buddhism, man's *Kamma* is the whole mode of individual and social existence. About the divine and man's relationship to it, the Buddha spoke rather as men who, through their own efforts, discovered truth about the nature of things and especially the nature of human life.

Nibbana (Nirvana)

Everything changes according to the Buddhist understanding of nature. Nothing is stable. Everything depends on the chain of cause and effect leading up to its present existence. A series of separate momentary events which continue indefinitely, influencing earlier events on later events in other words the present actions are the results of the past actions in this life itself. The only stable entity in Buddhism is Nibbana[62], the state of bliss reached by the Buddhas and Arhants, or perfected beings. The Buddha, as mentioned in Majjhima Nikaya, said. " I have not said that the Arhant exists after death, and I have not said that he does not exist...because....this is not edifying, neither does it tend to supreme wisdom."[63] This would suggest that Nibbana is believed to be a state neither of being nor of annihilation. It is the realisation that there is no duality, that *Nibbana* and *Sangsara* (the world of manifestation, of illusion, of becoming), that time and eternity, are indistinguishably one. It is conceivable by the unenlightened.

According to Buddha as mentioned in the traditional texts, *nirvana* stops rebirth, which means the extinction of all misery and of the conditions that cause future existence in this world after death. Buddha maintained his silence about the condition of the liberated after death. Then what is the gain of *Nibbana,* if Buddha is not explicit about the fate of a liberated person after death? *Nibbana* gives double gain: stopping of re-birth and future misery, and attainment of perfect peace in this life. It is a relief from all painful experience from which human kind suffers.[64] We can understand this because all of us have experience at least of temporary feelings of relief from some pain or other, such as freedom from disease, debt, slavery, imprisonment.

Buddhist teacher of the later period Nagarjuna tried to convey to Milinda (Menander, the Greek King) the idea of the blissful character of Nibbana. It is profound like ocean, lofty like a mountain peak, and sweet like honey.[65]

Nibbana is not inactivity as its ordinarily misunderstood. It is full of action. The Buddha clearly said that there are two kinds of action. *One*: Action work with attachment, hatred and infatuation (raga, devesa, moha); *two*: Action without all these. The first one strengthens desire to cling to the world and this result into a kamma which cause for rebirth (of same elements). The second one does not create kamma-causing rebirth.[66] In the story of enlightenment also he teaches same thing.[67]

Aldous Huxley has said that Gautama declined to make any statement in regard to the ultimate divine reality. "All he would talk about was *Nibbana,* which is the name of the experience that comes to the totally selfless and one - pointed."[68]

Nibbana is not outside the universe. It is different from that of the world soul of the Hindu Upanishads. The man who finds it never again loses it and when he dies he passes to this state forever, in his parinirvana, his "Final Blowing Out". A Bhikkhu is free to enter 'Parinibbana', while 'nibbana' is enough for a layman.

In Buddhist society, according to Sangha Rakshita, a modern Buddhist scholar of Ambedkarism, the important function of the state is to uphold the moral and spiritual law. Buddhist society is the means to enlightenment. Buddhism demands that the state should recognise the fact that the true goal of life is not to eat, drink and produce the species, but to attain *Nibbana*.[69] Thus, *Nibbana* is Middle Path, that is following the Eight - fold Path. *Nibbana* means release from Passion. The aim of it is to lead righteous life.[70]

Bhikkhu a Social Servant

The last but very important problem, which Ambedkar discussed on Buddhism, was the problem related to the *Bhikkhu*. What was the object of the Buddha in creating the *Bhikkhu?* Was the object to create a Perfect Man? Or was his object to create a social servant devoting his life in service of the people and being their friend, guide and philosopher? These questions Ambedkar had dealt in his writings on the Buddhism. Ambedkar felt the future of Buddhism depends on in answering these real questions. If the *Bhikkhu* is only a perfect man he is of no use to the propagation of Buddhism because though a perfect man he is a selfish man. If, on the other hand, he is a social servant he may prove to be the hope of Buddhism. This questions must be decided not so much in the interest of doctrinal consistency but as Ambedkar felt in the interest of the future of Buddhism.

The followers of Buddhism are divided into two classes: *BHIKKHU* and *UPASAKAS* (Lay followers). The *Bhikkhus* are organised into a sangha while the *upasakas* are not. The Buddhist *Bhikkhu* is primarily a *Parivarajaka.* This institution of *Parivarjakas* is older than that of the Buddhist *Bhikkhu*. The old *Parivarjakas* are persons who have abandoned family life and are a mere floating body of wanderers. They roamed about with a view to ascertain the truth. They have no sangha, have no rules of discipline and have no ideal to strive for. It is for the first time that the Buddha organised his followers into a *sangha* or fraternity, and has given them rules of discipline and set before them an ideal to pursue and realise. This is evidence to prove that there was Buddhism, before Gautam Buddha started his sangha. That might be Adi-Buddhism. The idea of numerous Buddha proves the point.

The sangha is open to all. There is no bar of caste. Insider the sangha the rank is regulated by worth and not by birth. The only distinction observed inside the sangha is that of sex. The *Bhikkhu sangha* is separate in its organisation from the *Bhikkhuni sangha*. The entrants into the sangha are divided into two classes: SHRAMANERAS and BHIKKHUS. Any one below twenty could become a *shramanera.* By taking the TRISARANAS and by taking the ten precepts a boy becomes a *shramanera.*

The three *Trisaranas* are: 'I follow the Buddha; I follow the *Dhamma*; and I follow the *sangha*; The ten precepts are: "I shall abstain from killing; I shall not commit theft; I shall follow *Brahmacharya;* I shall not tell untruth; I shall abstain from indecent and immoral acts; I shall abstain from ornamenting and decorating myself; I shall abstain from luxuries; I shall abstain from the love of gold and silver'.

A *Shramanera* can leave the sangha at any time and become a layman. A *Shramanera* is attached to a *Bhikkhu* and spends his time in the service of *Bhikkhu.* He is not a person who has taken *Parivraja*. The status of a *Bhikkhu* has to be reached in two stages. The first stage is called *Parivraja* and second stage is called *upasampada*. It is after *upasampada* that he becomes a *Bhikkhu.*

A candidate who wishes to take *parivraja* with a view ultimately to become a *Bhikkhu* has to seek a *Bhikkhu* who has the right to act as an *uppadhya*. A *Bikkhu* can become an *uppadha* only after he has spent atleast ten years as a *Bhikkhu*. Such a candidate if accepted by the *uppadhya* is called a *parivrajaka* and has to remain in the service and tutelage of the *uppadhya*.

After the period of tutelage ends it is his uppadhya who has to propose the name of his student to a meeting of the sangha specially called for the purpose for *upasampada* and the student must request the sangha for *upasampada*. The sangha must be satisfied that he is a fit and a proper person to be made a *Bhikkhu*. For this purpose there is a set of questions which the candidate has to answer. Only when the sangha grants permission that *upasampada* is granted and the person becomes a *Bhikkhu.* The rules regulating entry into the *Bhikkhuni sangha* are more or less the same as the rules regulating the entry into the *Bhikkhu sangha.*

A Bhikkhu besides taking precepts takes them also as vows, which he must not break. If he breaks then he becomes liable to punishment. A Bhikkhu vows to remain celebrate, not commit theft, not to boast, not to kill or take life and not to own anything except what the rules allow. A Bhikkhu should not possess more than the following eight articles: Three pieces of cloth to cover his body. A gridle for the lions, An alms-bowl, A razor, A needle, A water-strainer, a Bhikkhu must beg for his food. He must live on alms. He must sustain himself only on one meal a day. Where there is no *vihar* built for the sangha, he must live under a tree.

A *Bhikkhu* does not take a vow of obedience. Outward respect and courtesy to his superiors is expected from the novice. His own salvation and his usefulness as a teacher depend on his self-culture. He is to obey not his superior but the *Dhamma*. His superior has no supernatural gift as wisdom or of absolution. He must stand or fall by himself. For that he must have freedom of thought.

In this background, one needs to estimate the role of a *Bhikkhu* in the Society. The *Bhikkhu* is not an ascetic and nor even the same as the Brahmin of Hindu Religion. A *Brahmin* is a priest. His main function is to perform certain ceremonies connected with birth, marriage and death. These ceremonies become necessary because of the doctrines of original sin, which requires ceremonies to wash it off, and because of the belief in God and soul. For these ceremonies a priest is necessary. And that priest must be a Brahmin by caste in Hindu religion.

A *Bhikkhu* does not believe in original sin, in God and Soul. Therefore, there are no ceremonies to be performed. He is, therefore, not a priest. Ambedkar writes that a Brahmin is born but a *Bhikkhu* is made. A *Brahman* has a caste. A *Bhikkhu* has no caste. Once a Brahman always a *Brahman*. No sin, no crime can unmake a *Brahmin*. But once a *Bhikkhu* is not always a *Bhikkhu*. A *Bhikkhu* is made. So he can be unmade if by his conduct he makes himself unworthy of remaining a *Bhikkhu*.

No mental or moral training is necessary for being a Brahmin. All that is only expected of him is to know his religious lore. Quite different is the case of the Bhikkhu, mental and moral training is his life blood. A Brahmin is free to acquire unlimited amount of property for himself. A *Bhikkhu* on the other hand cannot. This is no small difference. Property is the severest limitation upon the mental and moral independence of man both in respect of thought and action. It produces a conflict between the two. That is why the

Brahmin is always opposed to change. For, to him a change means loss of power and loss of self.

A *Bhikkhu* having no property is mentally and morally free. In his case there are no personal interests which can stand in the way of honesty and integrity. Each Brahmin is an individual by himself. There is no religious organisation to which he is subordinate. A Brahmin is a law unto himself. They are bound by common interests which are material. A *Bhikkhu* on the other hand is always a member of the sangha. It is inconceivable that there could be a *Bhikkhu* without his being a member of the sangha. A *Bhikkhu* is not a law unto himself. He is subordinate to the sangha. The sangha is spiritual organisation.

The *Bhikkhu* is also not like Hindu ascetic who doesn't bother about wordly things and spends life in speculation. The Bhikkhu is to devote himself to self-culture and to serve the people and guide them, without self-culture he is not fit to guide. Therefore, he must himself be a perfect, best man, righteous man and an enlightened man.

For this he must practice self-culture. A *Bhikkhu* leaves his home. But he does not retire form the world. He leaves home so that he may have the freedom and the opportunity to serve those who are attached to their homes but whose life is full of sorrow, misery and unhappiness and who cannot help themselves.

Compassion, which is the essence of the Dhamma, requires that every one shall love and serve and the *Bhikkhu* is not exempt from it. In the words of Ambedkar a *Bhikkhu* who is indifferent to the woes of mankind, however, perfect in self-culture, is not at all a *Bhikkhu*.

He may be something else but he is not a *Bhikkhu*. For Ambedkar, the *Bhikkhu* is a social servant rather than just a perfect man. The future of Buddhism is based on the social service of the *Bhikkhu* to society, too poor and needy.

The greatness of the *Bhikkhu* lies in his service and guidance to society, but not in his just knowledge of the Buddha *Dhamma*. It is his duty to implement the social equality aspect of the Buddha *Dhamma*. On this point the *Bhikkhu* can be graded as high qualified person than Brahmin of Hindu society. Brahmin or ascetic of Hindu society follows the Dharma of inequality.

Difference between Dharma and Dhamma

Dharma of Hinduism neither represents the welfare of whole mankind nor stands for righteousness. Dharma in reality meant to serve the interests of higher *Varnas* or *Jatis* (castes) among Hindus particularly *Brahmans*. Surprisingly, Hinduism is the only religion in the world that has Dharma, that subscribes discrimination against its own Hindus (read Backward castes). This is the main reason for the opposition to the Dharma referring to Buddhist Dhamma by Dalit Buddhists. Dhamma of Buddhism is entirely different from Dharma of Hindu Sanskrit. Dhamma is for all. It serves total human. It is nothing but humanness. The basic difference between Karma-Dharma and Kamma-Dhamma is, former represents just action or deed and latter for moral action or moral deed. The importance of morality and ethical nature is absent in Hindu terminology where as basis of Buddhist terminology is emphasis on moral activity and ethical culture. In short, Karma dharma is Hinduism and *Kamma* Dhamma is Buddhism.

In this connection, Ambedkar raises three Questions: What is Dhamma? What is not Dhamma (Adhamma)? And what is *Saddhamma*?

What is Dhamma? According to Ambedkar: to maintain Purity of life is Dhamma. To reach perfection in life is Dhamma. To live in Nibbana (following eight-fold Path) is Dhamma. To give-up craving is Dhamma. To believe that all compound things are impermanent is Dhamma. To believe that Karma is the instrument of moral order is Dhamma.[71]

The Buddha did not promise to give salvation. He said he was *Marga Data* (way finder) and not *Moksha Data* (Giver of Salvation). The Buddha did not claim any divinity for himself for his *Dhamma*. Man for man discovered it. It was not a revelation. Ambedkar says, that the Buddha never claimed infallibility for his message, unlike the self-claimed gods of other religions of the world. The only claim the Buddha made was that his message was the only true way to salvation, as he understood it. It was based on universal human experience of life in the world.

Ambedkar makes it more clear, "He (Buddha) said that it was open to anyone to Question it, test it and find what truth it contained. No founder has so fully thrown open his religion to such a challenge.[72] This is what the Buddha Dhamma meant for. In one word the Buddha Dhamma is nothing but a social message, as Ambedkar said.

What is not Dhamma (Adhamma) Ambedkar answers that: Belief in the supernatural is Adhamma; Belief in Ishwara (God) is not essentially part of Dhamma; Dhamma based on union with Brahma is a false Dhamma; Belief in soul is Adhamma; Belief in sacrifice is Adhamma; Belief based on speculation is Not-Dhamma; Reading Books of Dhamma is not-Dhamma (i.e. Brahmins emphasised more on knowledge whereas the Buddha concerned the user of knowledge to society); Belief in the infallibility of Books of Dhamma is not-Dhamma.

What is Saddhamma? Ambedkar puts it that, the Dhamma becomes Saddhamma: only when it makes learning open to all; when it teaches that mere learning is not enough. It may lead to pedantry; when it teaches that what is needed is Pradnya; when it teaches that mere Pradnya is not enough it must be accompanied by Sila; when it teaches that besides Pradnya and Sila what is necessary is *Karuna*; when it teaches that more than Karuna what is necessary is Maitri.

Dhamma to be Saddhamma must pull down all social barriers. It must break down barriers between man and man. It must teach that worth and not birth is the measure of man. And it must promote equality between man and man. Talking on the functions of *Saddhamma,* Ambedkar says that it is to cleanse the mind of its impurities and to make the world a kingdom of righteousness. He Quotes the Buddha words to show the importance of mind for Saddhamma. "The mind is, place of origin of all the things; the mind is the master, the mind is the cause".[73]

He says that, if in the midst of the mind there are evil thoughts, then the words are evil, the deeds are evil, and the sorrow which results from sin follows that man, as the chariot wheel follows him (or it) who draws it. It is the mind that commands and it is the mind that contrives.[74]

He also says that, if in the mind there are good thoughts, then the words are good and the deeds are good, and the happiness which results from such conduct follows that man, shadow accompanies the susbstance, a unique amalgam of *Pradnya* or

Prajna (understanding i.e. against superstition) and *Karuna* (Love).[75] Ambedkar says that Dhamma is fundamentally and essentially social. Dhamma is righteousness, which means right relations between man and man in all spheres of life. In other words, society cannot do without Dhamma. The purpose of Dhamma is to reconstruct the world. For Ambedkar, morality is Dhamma and Dhamma is morality. In other words, in Dhamma morality takes the place of God although there is no God in Dhamma. He says mere morality is not enough. It must be sacred and universal.

Another important concept which Ambedkar has discussed is "Ahimsa'. Ahimsa or non-killing forms a very important part of the Buddha's teachings. It is intimately connected with *Karuna* and *maitri*. The question has, however, been raised whether his Ahimsa was absolute in its obligation or only relative. Was it only a principle? Or was it a rule? Ambedkar says, "People who accept the Buddha's teachings find it difficult to accept Ahimsa as an absolute obligation. They say that such a definition of Ahimsa involves the sacrifice of good for evil, the sacrifice of virtue for vice.[76]

Ambedkar says that the circumstantial evidence on the point is that the Buddha had no objection to eating meat if it was offered to him as part of his alms. The monk can eat meat offered to him provided he was not a party to the killing of it. The Buddha resisted the opposition of *Devadatta* who insisted that the monks should be prohibited from eating meat given to them by way of alms. Ambedkar gives another piece of evidence on the point is that Buddha was only opposed to the killing of animals in *Yajna* (sacrifice).

Ahimsa permo Dharma is an extreme doctrine. It is a Jain doctrine. It is not a Buddhist doctrine. Ambedakr mentions another piece of evidence, which is more direct than circumstantial which almost, amounts to a definition of Ahimsa. The Buddha has said: "Love all so that you may not wish to kill any". Ambedkar explains this as a positive way of stating the principle of Ahimsa. From this it appears that the doctrine of Ahimsa does not say "kill not. It says love all".[77]

In the light of these statements it is quite easy to have a clear understanding of what the Buddha meant by Ahimsa. Ambedkar says that it is quite clear that Buddha meant to make a distinction between will to kill and need to kill. He did not ban killing where there was need to kill/What he banned was killing where there was nothing but the will to kill. So there is no confusion in the Buddhist doctrine of Ahimsa. It is a prefectly sound or moral doctrine. Ambedkar puts it "Brahminism has in it the will to kill. Jainism has in it the will never to kill. The Buddha's *Ahimsa* is quite in keeping with his middle path."[78]

In other words the Buddha made a distinction between Principle and Rule. He did not make Ahimsa a matter of rule. He enunciated it as a matter of principle or way of life. Ambedkar says that a principle leaves you freedom to act. A rule does not. Rule either breaks you or you break the rule.[79]

The importance of Dhamma, in Ambedkar words, "In his (Buddha) doctrine there is love to create a longing to own those who are disowned or unowned: to the degraded there is the ennoblement ever present to raise them: to the disinherited and the downtrodden there is equality blazing forth their path to advancement".[80]

Regarding the Buddha, Ambedakr says that he was a believer in the *Madhyama Marga (Majjhima Patipada)*, the middle path, which is neither the path of pleasure nor the path of self-mortification. However, he quotes the Buddha: "I say unto you that to satisfy the needs of life is not an evil: to keep the body in good health is a duty or otherwise you shall not be able to keep your mind strong and clear and have the lamp of wisdom burning".[81]

Ambedkar says that there was no successor to Buddha. He quotes the Buddha words: "The Dhamma must be (his) successor."[82] What critics says about Ambedkar's view of Buddhism? This is the question, which needs to be examined on the basis of reason and rational, apart from the motivation and social background of the critics.

Ambedkar's The Buddha and His Dhamma

In summing up Ambedkar views in his work 'The Buddha And His Dhamma', it is commented that, "The title should be changed from the misleading one of 'The Buddha and His Dhamma' to that of 'Ambedkar and His Dhamma', for he preaches non-Dharma as Dharma for motives of political ambition and social reform".[83]

The critics mainly based their criticism on the five statements of Ambedkar:

1. The Buddha never claimed infallibility for his message.[84]
2. Dhamma is social.[85]
3. The Buddha's law of *Karma* applied only to *Karma* and its effect on present life.[86]
4. The Buddha meant to make a distinction between the will to kill and need to kill.[87]
5. The Bhikkhus are for the purpose of self-culture and social service, especially social services.[88]

D.C. Ahir, a prominent Buddhist scholar, refuted the criticism on Ambedkar and concluded that Ambedkar interpretation of Dhamms was nothing but the true Dhamma of the Buddha.[89] The traditional critics do not agree with the Ambedkar, that the Buddha never claimed infallibility for his message. Their criticism is simply based on idealising or making Buddha with super human powers.

The Buddha did not claim infallibility for his message because it was based on truth and facts, and did not require the support of any dogmatic and supernatural claims. Neither he claimed divine authority for his teachings nor he claimed that his teachings were not capable of further development. "The fact that without any such claim (the Buddha's) teachings are still as true as they were over 2,500 years ago, is a great credit to the Buddha..."[90]

Ambedkar says, the Dhamma is social, in the sense that it is all embracing and for all humanity. Dhamma teaches righteousness, which means right relations between man and man in all spheres of life. Absence of Dhamma in the society means it has no value for suffering humanity. Ambedkar adds equality to Dhamma. The underlying meaning of the Dhamma is a message of equality. Where there is equality, there is hope for individual initiative, progress and attainment of Nirvana, the supreme state of Bliss, the ultimate aim of every Buddhist.

Regarding *Kamma* Ambedkar does not concern about so called Karma in past life. For him what matters is man's environment, and not hereditary connections. In his interpretation of Kamma, man can change his present life by dint of his labour and true efforts. Critics cannot defend their argument that Ambedkar is wrong.

The criticism on the concept of Ahimsa can also be refuted. Ambedkar's interpretation of Ahimsa, can be said, true saying of the Buddha, because the absolute Ahimsa cannot stand the test of the middle path, which is the basic principle of Buddhism. No doubt, the Buddha denounced *Himsa* (violence) and advocated a ban on the killing of animals for the sake of food, sacrifice, sport or pleasure; but it is wrong to interpret that he banned *Himsa* under all circumstances. "It is note worthy that for a prospective *Bhikkhu*, the Buddha has prescribed *interalia* the condition that he should not have run away from the army. This means that the Buddha attached great importance to the defence of the country and did not like soldiers deserting the army with a view to joining the sangha.[91]

Ambedkar's principles of 'the need to kill' and 'the will to kill', can be said as correct in the context of the purpose of the Buddha Dhamma. To kill is entirely a matter of necessity and personal moral responsibility. Every act has to be guided by man's own *Prajna* (wisdom) and *Karuna* (love or kindness). Thus the Ahimsa of Buddhism is differed with the Ahimsa concept of other religions. The Buddha's Ahimsa teaches non-aggressiveness and it also teaches self-defence, if one needs to fight, he must fight. What the Ambedkar has made is the positive interpretation of Ahimsa.

Ambedkar's interpretation of the role of the *Bhikkhu*, is to be justified in the context of the need of social service. In fact Ambedkar sees the future of the Buddhism, through its social validity. Of course for any religion or Dhamma, the purpose is service to human community. If Ambedkar's interpretation of *Bhikkhu*, serves the social cause, there should be no problem in accepting it as the original doctrine of the Buddha.

Why this misunderstanding of the Buddha Dhamma? The critics of the Ambedkar, neither put forwarded any scientific and rational reason nor adopted humanity as their basis. The criticism is mostly based on Hindu interpretation of Dhamma. Applying the Hindu view of Dharma and the meaning of Hindu concepts like Karma, soul, re-birth, ahimsa etc. to the Buddhism cannot be acceptable to true believers of the Buddha. The critics may claim that they are believers in the Buddha Dhamma, but their traditional view of the Buddha Dhamma cannot be called as original doctrine of the Buddha. All this misunderstanding is because of misunderstanding of the purpose of the Buddha Dhamma.

Ambedkar proved that his interpretation of the Dhamma as the original doctrine of the Buddha by putting on test, which is available. Ambedkar defends his views with argument, "if there is anything, which could be said with confidence, it is: He was nothing if rational, if logical. Anything, therefore, which is rational and logical, other things being equal, may be taken to be the word of the Buddha".[92] The first test proves that Ambedkar's views are rational, logical and so it can be said that those who criticise Ambedkar's interpretation of Buddhism, do not have rational and logical base.

The second test, which Ambedkar puts forth is that "the Buddha never cared to enter into a discussion which was not profitable for man's welfare. Therefore, anything attributed to the Buddha which did not relate to man's welfare cannot be accepted to be the word of the Buddha".[93] The traditional critics of the Ambedkar should answer, that what is the problem in accepting the view of Ambedkar, if they serve the human community. Ambedkar's view very much fulfils the eligibility to qualify the test, and there is no doubt in calling them as the Buddha Dhamma.

There is a third test. Ambedkar explains, "it is that the Buddha divided all matters into two classes. Those about which he was certain and those about which he was not certain. On matters, which fell into class I, he has stated his views definitely and conclusively. On matters, which fell into class II, he has expressed his views. But they are only tentative views".[94]

Ambedkar says that in discussing the questions about which there is doubt and difference it is necessary to bear these tests in mind before deciding what the view of the Buddha was there on.[95] On the basis of these three tests, one can decide the originality and validity of the Ambedkar's view on the Buddha Dhamma.

Ambedkar even evaluated the importance of Buddhism in the context of Marxism. He felt that Buddhism was an ideal alternative to communism. Ambedkar held that communism is inadequate to explain the social evils of untouchability and graded social inequality, based on the caste system. According to Marx, the economic factors are the only determinant factor in shaping human history. But Ambedkar says there are many non-economic factors, which really influenced world history. Ambedkar holds that the social status of an individual by itself often becomes a source of power and authority. This is made clear by the way, which the religious saints have held over the common man.

Infact, today, the priestly class (Brahmans) is not rich compared to business, merchant class (Vaishya or Baniya). But a rich person always tries to depend on priest for direction in his social life. Even in ancient and medieval period, rulers (Kshatriyas) though they are highly powerful economically, they depended on Brahmans for assistance in almost all spheres of life. And Brahmans always projected themselves as socially higher than their rulers, which was commonly accepted by ruling Kshatriya class. So, in Indian society, it is not that one's own economic status decides who is to be high in social ladder but is religion. Why do millionaires in India obey pennyless sadhus and fakirs? That religion is a source of power is attested by the history of India.

India is a country, where religious considerations dominate the human interests. It is the country where everything, even such things like elections, and strikes, easily take a religious turn and can easily be given a religious twist.

For Marx the industrial proletariat is the vanguard of total revolution. Ambedkar felt that this concept has no relevance to Indian society. Industrial workers are divided into various castes and caste - Hindu workers do not like to touch the untouchable industrial workers. The caste system has created great divisions amongst the industrial workers themselves. Under such conditions how can the industrial workers be united?

Ambedkar felt that communism has no faith in any moral values and that communist philosophy recognised no universal moral principles. Ambedkar argued that emancipation of the human mind and social religious revolutions ultimately brought about economic changes in societies. So he opposed the economic interpretation of history. To support this view, Ambedkar explained it with examples in his work, 'Annihilation of Caste'. Generally speaking history bears out the proposition that political revolutions have always been preceded by social and religious revolutions. The religious reformation started by Luther was the precursor of the political emancipation of the European people. In England, puritanism founded the New World. It was puritanism that won the war of American Independence and puritanism was a religious movement. The same is true of the Muslim Empire. Before the Arabs became a political power they had undergone a thorough religious revolution started by the Prophet Mohammad.

Even Indian History supports the same conclusion. The political revolution led by Chandragupta (Maurya) was preceded by the religious and social revolution of the Buddha. The political revolution led by Shivaji was preceded by the religious and social reform brought about by the Saints of Maharashtra. The political revolution of the Sikhs was preceded by the religious and social revolution led by Guru Nanak. It is unnecessary to add more illustrations. These will suffice to show that the emancipation of the mind and the soul is a necessary preliminary for the political expansion of people.[96]

Ambedkar offered to give a very sound alternative to Marxism, a way of life based on Buddhism. Ambedkar's ideas are fundamental and they have a universal value. Ambedkar criticised violent way of revolution in communism. According to Marx violence is the mid wife of the old society, pregnant with a new social order. He gave theoretical justification for violence and bloodshed. Ambedkar questioned the Marxists, how a violent revolution leading to dictatorship will lead us to achieve a better society. He emphasised the purity of means in achieving our noble ends.

In his speech on Buddha and Karl Marx in 1956, at Kathmandu, Ambedkar said, that the means that the communists wish to adopt, in order to bring about communism, is violence and killing of the opponents. There lies the fundamental difference between the Buddha and Karl Marx. The Buddha's means of persuading people to adopt the principles was by moral teaching Buddha's doctrine claims that love, not power can conquer anything. That is where the fundamental difference lies. The Buddha would not allow violence; communists do. Ambedkar felt that the communists get quick results because they adopt the means of annihilating men. He was very confident of the Buddha's way though he felt it is a long way, he had no doubt about it, that it is a surest way.

Ambedkar had tremendous faith in the creativity of man. The human mind according to him is the greatest force. If the creativity of man is unfolded the world can be changed. In explaining this argument, Ambedkar said that, the greatest thing that the Buddha had done was to tell the world that the world could not be reformed except by the reformation of the mind of the man and the mind of the world.

Ambedkar's alternative philosophy to Marxism is based on universal values like equality, liberty and fraternity. He elaborates this principle by saying that, 'we must make our political democracy a social democracy as well'. Political democracy cannot last long, unless there lies at its base social democracy. Social democracy means a way of the principles of life.

These principles of liberty, equality and fraternity are not to be treated as separate items. To diverse one from the other is to defeat the very purpose of democracy. Liberty cannot be divorced from equality, equality cannot be divorced from liberty. Nor can liberty and equality divorced from fraternity. Without equality, liberty would produce the supremacy of the few over the many. Equality without liberty would kill the individual's initiative. Without fraternity, liberty and equality could not become a natural course of things.

Ambedkar summed up that, man must grow materially as well as spiritually. Society has been aiming to lay a new foundation as summarized by the French Revolution in three words, 'Fraternity, Liberty, and Equality'. The French Revolution was welcomed because of this slogan.

"We welcome the Russian Revolution because it aims to produce equality. But it cannot be too much emphasized that in producing equality, society cannot afford to sacrifice fraternity or liberty. Equality will be no value without fraternity or liberty. It seems that the three can co-exist only if one follows the way of the Buddha. Communism can give one but not all".[97] Thus Ambedkar offered to the world a sound philosophy as an alternative to Marxism. His philosophy is based on certain universal and eternal values like the scientific approach and love for humanity. The Buddhism which he advocated is nothing but scientific - humanism.

Adi Buddhism or Dalit Buddhism

Indeed Ambedkar never called his idea of Buddhism as Adi-Buddhism or Dalit Buddhism. These are post-Ambedkar identities to the Buddhist ideas propagated by Ambedkar. It is so called because according to Ambedkar, Dalits are the earliest Buddhists. They were treated as Untouchables because of their Buddhist background in ancient India. Adi-Buddhism means earliest Buddhism. It is the original Dhamma of the Buddha.

Ambedkar's Adi-Buddhism put forwards two important arguments regarding the identity and purpose of the Buddha and the Buddhism respectively. The Gautama Buddha was a Kshatriya, according to some historians. Ambedkar School of Historical Thought emphasises the need to review existing notion about the identity of the Buddha on the lines of Adi-Buddhism. Ambedkarite methodology of historical study gives new interpretations. It makes conclusions that the Gautama Buddha belonged to a noble and royal family but was not a Kshatriya by caste. He could be a member of the indigenous dalit tribe. He was not a Kshatriya. To be Kshatriya one had to be Aryan. Gautam Buddha was not an Aryan.

Aryan community was divided itself into four varnas (Jatis): Brahmins, Kshatriya, Vaishya and Shudra. Only Aryan born could claim status of one of those four *jatis*, based on one's occupation. Indeed, this was the worldview of the Aryan society in ancient India. When Aryans met people of different origin (indigenous people) in India, they tried to identify them on the basis of occupation. In the course of time ancient writers called people of non-Aryan ruling families as Kshatriyas. The Gautam Buddha was Kshatriya of this nature. It is evident even with the Asoka and other Mouryan Kings who originally belonged to Murya, a dalit tribe. Some of the Buddhist scholars also called the Gautama as a Kshatriya, in view of his royal birth. He could be a dalit Kshatriya (i.e., ruling class of indigenous origin), but not Aryan Kshatriya. However, calling him as Kshatriya, hides his real identity. The Shakyas, Lichchhavis, Malavas, Kshudrakas, Mallas, Murias and Nagas were ancient dalit tribes of indigenous India (out side the Aryan cultural dominance). Gautama Buddha could be called as dalit by caste, since he belonged to indigenous race.

Gautama, born in a republic clan of Shakyas and inherited egalitarian sentiments. A careful study of republic culture and values reveals the fact that Brahmans had no place in the republics. They also had no role to play either in guiding society or in the polity unlike in monarchy, where Aryan dharma and Aryan values were followed with utmost respect. For example, respect to the Brahmans and allowing them to guide the king, were the most important elements of Aryan polity since Vedic time (1000 B.C.)

In the republic rajas sat on the assembly, held in the motehall, the brahmanas were not included in this group. The brahmanas exercised great influence in monarchy. The brahmanas did not recognise the presence of republic states in their law books testifies the theory that republican tradition was not a part of the Aryan culture. Indeed, King's post had become hereditary during the Rigvedic period itself (1500 B.C.)

The ruling classes of Magadha region like Lichchhavi, Shakya did not practice Aryan culture. Magadha was placed outside the land of Aryas (Aryavarta), covering modern Uttar Pradesh. Indeed the people on non-vedic areas like Magadha were looked down upon by the brahmanas. The brahmanas and kshatriyas showed that indigenous tribes (read Dalits) were ruling the republics and allowing the Aryans to settle in their states who were otherwise foreigners to them. In Magadha, brahmanas gradually held the society under the grip of Aryan culture, even though they had come from outside.

Some of the indigenous tribes later on ruled over larger monarchies - the dynasties like Koshalan, Shishu Nagas, Nandas and Mauryas. The shift from the republican polity to monarchy was the common feature among the dalit ruling classes since 5th C.B.C., till the dawn of Christian era. However, they did not adopt the Aryan polity and Aryan values, even though there was a considerable influence of the brahmanas and kshatriyas on the society, due to the presence of Aryan tribes in the land of dalit tribes. This was also evident in the state of *shakyas*. The increasing infulence of the brahmanas in the society, disturbed the egalitarian structure of the dalit republican state, that made the Gautama to become 'Buddha' (the enlightened) and produced the philosophy to counter brahminical onslaught on dalit culture, traditions and values.

Different sources of history, establish the fact that Gautama

Buddha belonged to non-Kshatriya community. Gautama's participation in the agricultural festivals support the view that he might have belonged to Katthi clan of Shakya tribe. Katthi (Ploughshare / sickle) played major role in agricultural production. The use of iron ploughshare contributed for the larger agricultural production. The agricultural economy of the society mainly based on the use of iron ploughshare, was a significant feature of the period (600-500 B.C.). The possession of the iron implements at larger level might have made Katthi clan to play a dominant role among the whole Shakya tribe. The word 'Katthi' was born out of Pali word 'Khet' means agricultural field.

The Gautama's father was elected ruler of Kapilvastu and headed the republican Katthi clan of the Shakyas. It seemed to be that Katthi was misspelt as Kshatri and incourse of time brahmanical scholars regarded the Gautama Buddha wrongly as Kshatriya in their writings.

It is interesting to note that Katthi clan can be found even today in a dalit community on coastal Andhra Pradesh. Its primary occupation is also agricultural activity, testifies the extent of dalit tradition prevalent all over India since ancient times.

Shakya dalit community of the modern eastern Uttar Pradesh could also be said that as a surviving link of the ancient Shakya tribe of the Gautama. Pali was the state language of Shakyas as common with other dalit tribes of the period and Sanskrit was the language of Aryans. The linguistic identity also proves the Gautama's non-Aryan and non- Kshatriya origin.

The Buddha was depicted in non-Aryan and non-Kshatriya form both in the literary and in the archaeological sources. Neither in the Pali and Sanskrit literature nor in the Buddhist art nor even in the Mathura images (indigenous sculpture) and in the Ajanta Paintings the Buddha was depicted with sacred thread of Aryans, which was common feature of images of all the Kshatriya deities. Without which one could not be either Aryan or Kshatriya. The racial types portrayed in the sculpture of Barhut and Sanchi (about 200 B.C.), related the Buddha to Indo-Mongoloid clans and not to Aryan Kshatriya.[98]

Aggika Bharadwaj of Kasi called the Buddha an out caste. The Buddha did not get a grain of food in the village of Brahmanas.

Sondanda hesitated to salute the Buddha for his dalit origin.[99] All these sources of ancient Indian history reveal that Gautama Buddha's social identity need to be understood in indigenous context.

The purpose of the Buddhism is human welfare. There is no god according to Buddhism, if a god subscribes inequality and irrationality and stands for the interests of particular social group. There is a god in Buddhism, if god means dhamma and represents human welfare. The rationality of god's presence in the religion to be understood in the context of role assigned to god. The importance of Dalit Buddhism lies in defining the humane role of god in the religion.

Ambedkar's critical approach towards the concept of god need to be understood in the context of negative role assigned to god, particularly in Hinduism. The philosophy of Hindu gods could not stand as Ambedkar put it to the 'test of social utility and test of individual justice'. Dalit context understands Hindu god as social inequality and irrationality. And it is to say that Gautama as a god of Marga data. It emphasises redefinition of god. God should not be a Moksha data (saviour) but Marga data (path-shower).

Dalit Buddhism of modern India has brought innovative interpretation to the concept of God in the Buddhist context and viewed God's existence in a more practical manner by adopting the middle path as base for its interpretation than any other streams of Buddhism that understood the theory of God's existence in an idealistic way.

The social-historical approach adopted by the Dalit Buddhism to understand the concept of God of Buddha's time, revealed that there was something more to understand about the reason for the Buddha's silence on the question of existence of God than interpreting it as the Buddha's atheism.

During 6th century B.C., ancient Indian society was dogmatised by brahmanical theism and the God was popularly identified with Brahma, the counterpart of Brahman. In that circumstances Gautama Buddha avoided himself to counter pose as god against Brahma, however maintained silence on the question of existence of god. If it is the Buddha's rational approach to other issues taken as the basis then his silence on the existence of god could be interpreted as god a man's creation, whether that god is Brahma or anybody. And the Buddha rejected the Brahma as god since Brahma represented inhuman activities and interests of Brahmans.

The Buddha said neither yes nor no to the question of existence of god. In the context of Brahma, the Buddha was for 'No'. Brahma couldn't stand for the righteousness and welfare for all. He represented a thin layer of society that tried to exploit the majority in his name and in his dharma that in true sense was adharma. In subsequent history unfortunately Hinduism produced number of gods but subscribed the same dharma and the same role to all of them.

The Buddha's silence on the existence of god, meant not denial of the very concept of god like the materialist of the time whom the Buddha rejected for their extreme views. On the basis of middle path of the Buddha, it could be said that was a rejection of Brahminical (Hindu) worldview of god (read Brahma) and approval of godship with human element. Dalit Buddhism is trying to see the Buddha's silence on god as an effort by the Buddha to rationalize the concept of god. It was his means of rationalising the very nature of the god. Indeed, the original Dhamma of the Buddha is neither materialism nor atheism. It is very much a religion. For some it is a religion without god but for others the Buddha is very much a god. Buddha as a god may not be performing the same duties as prescribed to the gods of other religions. That is why Buddhism is not a theistic religion. It is non-theist but not atheist. For Tibetans Dalai Lama is an incarnation of the Buddha the god. For Ambedkarites the Buddha the god who has born as a modern Bodhisattva Babasaheb Bhimrao Ambedkar. The role-played by the Buddha as a god both in the Dalit Buddhism and Bon Buddhism of Tibet is not as Mokshadata (saviour) but as Margadata (teacher). The opposition to the concept of god by Ambedkar and the Dalai Lama XIV needs to be understood in this context. In fact, both of them along with their followers worshipped the Buddha as a god of Margadata, and not a Mokshadata.

When the teachings of the Buddha reached Ceylon, there appeared Theravada Buddhism. When it reached China it got happily blended with Taoist thought, already prevalent there. The Chinese called it C'han Buddhism. When it reached Japan it was accepted with great veneration; but it soon underwent reframing, assimilating certain philosophic conjuring. It came to be known as Zen Buddhism. Buddhism spread very rapidly up to North America, thorough Afghanistan, Iran, Italy and France. When it reached Tibet, it was *Vajrayana* with tantric practices but it got blended with Bon religion of Tibet. Some call it Lamaism. It spread to almost all the Asiatic countries and reached Greece and Russia. And Modern Indian Buddhism founded and preached by Ambedkar could be rightly called as Dalit Buddhism or Adi Buddhism. C'han Buddhism of China, Zen Buddhism of Japan, Bon Buddhism of Tibet and Adi or Dalit Buddhism of modern India all belonged to original Buddhism of the Buddha that with new identities emerged to withstand new challenges and new social realities. In the past, it was Theravada and later Mahayana. However the fundamental principles of the Buddha were basis of all of them, so as Ambedkar's Adi or Dalit indigenous modern Buddhism the Buddhism propounded, preached and followed by indigenous (Dalits) people of modern India. Indeed, Dalit Buddhism day by day getting popularized as Adi-Buddhism in India in general and particularly in U.P. and South-India.

References

1. Ambedkar, B.R., "Buddha and the Future of His Religion", *Bhim Patrika*, Jallunder, 1980, p. 13.
2. *Ibid.*
3. *Ibid.*, p. 16.
4. Lederle, M.R., *Philosophical Trends in Modern Maharashtra*, Bombay, 1976, p. 173.
5. Parivraja - the way out; an event that refers the Buddha's decision to leave his family and country in search of an answer for human problems.
6. Basham, A.L., *The Wonder That was India*, Rupa & Co, 1992, p. 258.
7. Ambedkar, B.R., *The Buddha and His Dhamma*, (Dr. Babasaheb Ambedkar writings and speeches, Vol.11), Education Department, Government of Maharashtra, Bombay, 1992 p. 57-58.
8. Bashan, A.L., *op cit*, p. 258; After the enlightenment at Gaya, the Buddha gave his First sermon 'Turning wheel of the law' in the deer park of Isipatana Four Noble truths are first part of the discourse and the other one is the Middle Path. This Sutta opens with the statement that one

should avoid the two extremes, one being the life of a worldly man, performing rituals and ceremonies but at the same immersed in pleasures and the other the life of a recluse dedicated to self-mortification's. One has to choose middle path, which will open up the eyes of knowledge and lead a person to the peaceful state and ultimately to enlightenment and nirvana (final emancipation).

9. "He who has thus - attained" - one of the titles of the Buddha.
10. Full discussion occurs in Digha - nikaya - sutta, 22, Warren, H.C., *Buddhism in Translations*, Harvard University Press, Harvard, first print - 1992, pp. 372-74; The abridged form mentioned in A.L. Bashan's *The Wonder That was India*, p. 271, taken from Samyutta Nikaya, V, pp. 421-43.
11. Ambedkar, B.R., *The Buddha And His Dhamma, op. cit.*, p. 510.
12. *Ibid.*, pp. 510-511
13. Since the word Dalit is ever expanding in its meaning according to its social relevance, here it is used to mean original & noble. Dalit means positively and historically indigenous, pride, self-respect, humble, etc.
14. Dalit although doesn't mean Middle (Madhyama, Majjhima), since it carries the meaning 'noble', the Middle Path is called as Dalita Patipada or Dalita Marga to emphasise its 'noble' character. Dalita Patipada also means original patipada or noble path.
15. T.W. Rhys Davids, tr. *Dialogues of Buddha*, I, London, 1950, pp. 62-63.
16. Samyuktta - Nikaya, I, Warren, H.C., *op. cit.*, p. 165
17. *Ibid.*, III, p. 268; & also IV, p. 265.
18. *Ibid.*, V, pp. 64-65.
19. Five higher powers: Divyacaksu (divine eyes), Divya Strotra (divine ears), Paracitta Jnana (reading other's thoughts), Oyrvabuvasa Jnana (remembering one's past existences) and Rddhividhi Jnana (attainment of miraculous powers), Sila (Character), Samadhi (concentration) and Prajna (knowledge) harmoniously cultivated.
20. Ambedkar, B.R., *The Buddha And His Dhamma, op. cit.*, p. 123.
21. In Sonadanda Sutta, Rhys Davids, *op. cit.*, p. 156.
22. Vasuddhimagga, Chap. XVIII, Warren, H.C., *op. cit., pp. 168 f.*
23. Since every human body consists of an aggregate of physical and mental elements, of the five skandhas such as being can be disigned as Nama rupa.
24. The definition Majjhima - Nikaya, I.p. 266 is: Ya Vedanasu Nandi, Tad Upadanam; as to the four Upadanas, see there p. 66; Samyutta, Nikaya, II, Warren, *op. cit.*, p. 3.
25. Warren, *Ibid.*
26. Ambedkar, B.R., *The Buddha And His Dhamma, op. cit.*, p. 240
27. *Ibid.*
28. *Ibid.*, p. 241
29. Mahanidana - Sutta, Warren, *op. cit.*, p. 203.
30. *Ibid.*
31. Ambedkar, B.R., *The Buddha And His Dhamma, op. cit.*, p. 241.
32. *Ibid.*
33. Rhys Davids, T.W., Dialogues, Part III, *op. cit.*, p. 44.
34. Potthapada Sutta, in Dialogues, Part I, Rhys Davids, *op. cit.*, pp. 254-57.

35. Ambedkar B.R., *The Buddha And His Dhaṃma*, *op. cit.*, p. 261.
36. *Ibid.*
37. *Ibid.*
38. *Ibid.*, p. 262
39. *Ibid.*
40. *Ibid.*, p. 263
41. *Ibid.*
42. *Ibid.*
43. Narasu, p. Lakshmi, *The Essence of Buddhism*, Delhi, 1976, p. 225.
44. *Ibid.*, p. 227.
45. *Ibid.*
46. *Ibid.*, p. 225.
47. Ambedkar, B.R., *The Buddha and His Dhamma*, *op. cit.*, p. 104.
48. Hariyanna, M. *Outline of India Philosophy*, London, 1951, pp. 142, 143-44.
49. Thakakusu, J., *The Essentials of Buddhist Philosophy*, 3rd ed., edited by Wing - tist Chan and Charles A. Moore, Honolulu, 1956, p. 37.
50. *Ibid.*
51. *Ibid.*, p. 38.
52. Alston, W.P., and Brandt, R.S., (ed.), *Problems of Philosophy*, Boston, 1975, p. 376.
53. Ambedkar, B.R., *The Buddha And His Dhamma*, *op. cit.*, p. 513.
54. It is said that once when the Buddha was staying at Shravasti in Jeta's Grove in Ananthapindika's Aram, the Maha-Kotthita rising up at even-tide from his meditations, went to Sariputta and asked him to elucidate some of the questions which troubled him. The dialogue that mentioned is one of them. Dialogue quoted in Ambedkar's *The Buddha And His Dhamma*, *op. cit.*, pp. 331-332.
55. The whole discussion is quoted in the Ambedkar's *The Buddha And His Dhamma*, *op. cit.*, pp. 333-336.
56. Ambedkar, B.R., *The Buddha And His Dhamma*, *Ibid.*, p. 338.
57. Jennings, *The Vedantic Buddhism of the Buddha*, Oxford, first print 1947, p. xxxviff.
58. Ambedkar, B.R., *The Buddha And His Dhamma*, *op. cit.*, p. 344.
59. Ibid.
60. Radha Krishnan, S., (tr.) *Dhamma Pada*, Oxford University Press, Oxford, 1950, pp. 33-34.
61. *Ibid.*
62. *Nibbana in Pali, Nirvana in Sanskrit.*
63. *Majjhima Nikaya*, I, p. 431.
64. *Samanna - Phala - Sutta*, Rhys Davids, Dialogues, I, *op. cit.*,p. 84.
65. *Milinda - Panha*, (ed.), by Vadekar, R.D., Bombay, 1940, p. 61.
66. *Anguttara - Nikaya* III, 33, Warren, pp. 215 f.
67. *Majjhima - Nikaya*, 26, *Ibid.*, pp. 339 f.
68. Aldous Huxley, *Perennial Philosophy*, London, 1954, p. 56.
69. Sangharakshita, B., "Buddhism in the Modern World", *in 2500 years of Buddhism*, (ed.), P.V. Bapat, New Delhi., 1956, p. 449.
70. Ambedkar, B.R., *The Buddha And His Dhamma*, *op. cit.*, pp. 395-396.

71. *Ibid.*, Pp. 229-309.
72. *Ibid.*,p. 222.
73. *Ibid.*,p. 282.
74. *Ibid.*
75. *Ibid.*
76. *Ibid.*,p. 345.
77. *Ibid.*,p. 354.
78. *Ibid.*,p. 347.
79. *Ibid.*
80. *Ibid.*,p. 113.
81. *Ibid.*,p. 120.
82. *Ibid.*,p. 216.
83. Jivaka, "Book Reviews: B.R. Ambedkar's The Buddha and His Dhamma", Published in *The Maha Bodhi*, Calcutta, December 1959, pp. 352-53.
84. *Ibid.*, p. 222
85. *Ibid.*, p. 316
86. *Ibid.*, p. 338
87. *Ibid.*, p. 346
88. *Ibid.*, p. 435
89. Ahir, D.C., "A Reply to Sramamera Jivaka's Review of the Buddha and His Dhamma", *The Maha Bodhi*, Calcutta, October 1990, pp. 315-318.
90. *Ibid.*,p. 315.
91. *Ibid.*,p. 317.
92. Ambedkar, The Buddha And His Dhamma, *op. cit.*, pp. 350-351.
93. *Ibid.*,p. 351.
94. *Ibid.*
95. *Ibid.*
96. Ambedkar, B.R., *Annihilation of Caste*, Vol. 1, Pp. 13-14.
97. Ambedkar, B.R., *Buddha or Karlmarx*, Vol. 3, Bombay, 1987, p. 462.
98. Dobeie, M.R., (tr.), *Ancient India and Indian Civilization*, by Paul Masson-Oursel, Helena Williaman Grawska, Philippe Stem., London, 1967, p. 27.
99. Walters, Thomas (tr.), edited by T.W. Rhys Davids and S.W. Bushell, on Yuan - Chwang's Travel in India, Vol. I, Delhi, 1961, p. 288.

Five

Buddhism and the Modern World: The Dalai Lama's Contribution

Tenzen Gyatso, the Dalai Lama XIV, is a great human being with a deep understanding of human nature. He made every effort to encourage the full development of the positive aspects of the human potential and to reduce the negative. The act of violence reveals one aspect of the human personality, but it must be remembered that human mind has a most remarkable potential, the ability to develop infinite altruism and compassion and a brain capable of unlimited knowledge and understanding. This needs to be used in the right way, for it is also capable of unlimited destruction.

Violence Breeds More Violence

The Dalai Lama believes that human beings are not violent by nature and human beings become violent in large part as a result of their environment and circumstances. He says that acceptance of violence as a means of reacting to violent and other crimes can have the opposite impact to what is intended. Killing offenders, however grave the crime they may have committed may serve the short-term goal of removing a potential threat to others. But it does not serve the long term and much more important goal of reducing crime and violence.

In a number of countries people are killed for political "crimes". That is especially harmful in society. Capital punishment is not the solution to the problems of crimes and in many cases capital punishment contributes to the notion that revenge and killing people is justified. He is very much firm in concluding the nature of violence that, Violence breeds more violence and capital punishment is a form of violence.[1]

The Dalai Lama felt that no matter how powerful or how intelligent we are it is virtually impossible to survive without an other human being.[2] He says that, "we need others for our very existence. The practice of compassion and non-violence is one's own self interest".[3] Dalai Lama considers the cultivation of non-violence and compassion as part of his daily practice. He does not consider this as something that is holy or sacred but of practical benefit to himself. He felt that the practice gives him satisfaction, it gives him a peace that is very helpful to have sincere, genuine relationships with other people. As a human being he loves friends, he loves their smiles. He says that human happiness is interdependent. One's own successful or happy future is related to that of others. Therefore helping others or having consideration of their rights and needs is actually not only one's own responsibility but a matter of one's own happiness. He often tells people that, "if we have to be really selfish then let us be wisely selfish. If we are warm-hearted we automatically receive more smiles and make more genuine friends. We human beings are social animals.[4]

Commenting on the present problems faced by Modern Society, the Dalai Lama says that everyday people face with sad news: violence, crime, wars and disasters. And there cannot be a single day without a report of something terrible happening some where. Even in these modern times it is clear that one's precious life is not safe. He opined that, no former generation had to experience so much bad news as we face today; this constant awareness of fear and tension should make any sensitive and compassionate person question seriously the progress of our modern world.

Science and Religion

The Dalai Lama felt that it is ironic that the more serious problems emanate from the more industrially advanced societies. He says, "Science and Technology have worked wonders in many fields, but the basic human problems remain. There is unprecedented literacy, yet this universal education does not seems to have fostered goodness, but only mental restlessness and discontent instead. There is no doubt about the increase in our material progress and technology, but somehow this is not sufficient as we have not yet succeeded in bringing about peace and happiness or in overcoming suffering".[5]

The Dalai Lama arrives to a conclusion that there must be something seriously wrong with our progress and development, and he cautions that if this wrong would be not checked in time there could be disastrous consequences for the future of humanity. However, this does not mean that he is against science and technology. Indeed, he is of the opinion that, they have contributed immensely to the overall experience of human kind; and to our material comfort and well being and to our greater understanding of the world we live in. But his caution is only not to give too much emphasis to science and technology, because he feels that they put us in danger of losing touch with those aspects of human knowledge and understanding that aspire towards honesty and altruism.

The Dalai Lama's main objection to the modern society is that, neglect of spiritual and humanitarian values. Science and Technology, though capable of creating immeasurable material comfort, he felt that they cannot replace the 'age-old spiritual and humanitarian values' that have largely shaped world civilisation, in all its national forms, as we know it today. In the opinion of the Dalai Lama, "no one can deny the unprecedented material benefit of science and technology, but our basic human problems remain; we are still faced with the same, if not more, suffering, fear and tension".[6]

Thus, he feels that, it is logical to try to strike a balance between material development on the one hand and the development of spiritual, human values on the other. In order to bring about this great adjustment, he wants to revive humanitarian values.

He is sure that many people share his concern about the present world wide moral crisis and would join in his appeal to all humanitarians and religious practitioners who also share this concern to help make our societies more compassionate, just and equitable. He says that he does not speak this, as a Buddhist or even as a Tibetan. Nor as an expert on international politics. Rather, he speaks simply as a human being, as an upholder of the humanitarian values that are the bedrock not only of *Mahayana* Buddhism but also of all the great world religions. From this perspective he shares with us his personal outlook that:

(1) Universal humanitarianism is essential to solve global problems;

(2) Compassion is the "pillar of world peace;

(3) All world religions are already for world peace in this way, as are all humanitarians of whatever ideology;

(4) Each individual has a universal responsibility to shape institutions to serve human needs.[7]

Solution to Human Problems

How to solve human problems? The Dalai Lama suggests that through transforming human attitudes, human problems can be solved. He divides the problems, which we face today into two types. Some are natural calamities and must be accepted and faced with equanimity. Others, however, are of our own making. This second type of problems i.e. man-made-problems are created by misunderstanding, and he felt can be corrected. One such type arises from the conflict of ideologies, political or religious, when people fight each other for petty ends, losing sight of the basic humanity. In his own words, "we must remember that the different religions, ideologies and political systems of the world are meant for human beings to achieve happiness".[8] He says that we must not lose sight of this fundamental goal and at no time should we place means above ends. In other words, he wants to be maintained always the supremacy of humanity over matter and ideology.

The Dalai Lama sees the threat of nuclear destruction as the greatest single danger facing human kind, in fact, all living beings on our planet. He appeals to all the leaders of the nuclear powers who literally hold the future of the world in their hands, to the scientists and technicians who continue to create these awesome weapons of destruction, and to all the people at large who are in a position to influence their leaders. He also appeals to them to exercise their sanity and begin to work at dismantling and destroying all nuclear weapons. He says, "We know that in the event of a nuclear war there will be no victors because there will be no survivors! Is it not frightening just to contemplate such inhuman and heartless destruction? And, is it not logical that we should remove the cause for our own destruction when we know the cause and have both the time and the means to do so? Often we cannot overcome our problems because we either do not know the cause or, if we understand it, do not have the means to remove it. This is not the case with the nuclear threat".[9]

The Dalai Lama says that all beings primarily seek peace, comfort and security. He speaks broadly about two types of happiness and suffering, that are mental and physical. He believes that mental suffering and happiness are the more acute. Hence, he stresses the training of the mind to endure suffering and attain a more lasting state of happiness. However, he also has a more general and concrete idea of happiness: a combination of inner peace, economic development and above all, world peace. To achieve such goals he feels it is necessary to develop a sense of universal responsibility, a deep concern for all irrespective of creed, colour, sex or nationality. He says that the premise behind this idea of universal responsibility is the simple fact that, every being wants happiness and does not want suffering.[10]

The Dalai Lama does not want the people to exploit others. He says, "If we adopt a self-centred approach to life and constantly try to use others for our own self-interest, we may gain temporary benefits, but in the long run we will not succeed in achieving even personal happiness, and world peace will be completely out of the question".[11] He requests people to have proper perspective, which of the universal life process, so that the happiness or glory of one person or group is not sought at the expense of others. He wants a new approach to global problems. "In ancient times problems were mostly family-size, and they were naturally tackled at the family level, but the situation has changed. Today we are so interdependent, so closely interconnected with each other, that without a sense of universal responsibility, a feeling of a universal brotherhood and sisterhood, and an understanding and belief that we really one part of one big human family we cannot hope to overcome the dangers to our very existence – let alone bring about peace and happiness".[12]

Increasing trans-national relations resulted into the world becoming smaller and smaller. Modern societies are more and more interdependent now than earlier times. This need of dependency clearly shows that, one nation's problems can no longer be satisfactorily solved by itself alone. Rather by creating mutual interest, attitude and co-operation of other nations. In the words of the Dalai Lama, "A universal humanitarian approach to world problems seems the only sound basis for world peace".[13] The Dalai Lama explains his concept of 'universal humanitarian approach', that, it is both morally wrong and pragmatically unwise to pursue only one's own happiness oblivious to the feelings and aspirations of all others who surround us as members of the same human family. The wiser course is to think of others also when pursuing our own happiness. This will lead to what the Dalai Lama calls "wise self-interest",[14] which hopefully will transform itself into "compromised self-interest", or better still, "Mutual interest".[15] This is what he meant of universal humanitarian approach.

The Dalai Lama propagates right approach to present problems, not just to help present society only, even to the future-generation. He says that we are facing problems because people are concentrating only on their short-term, selfish interests, not thinking of the entire human family. They are not thinking of the earth and the long-term effects on universal life as a whole. He also warns the people that if we of the present generation do not think about these now, future generations may not be able to cope with them. He does not have any doubt that a spiritual approach may not solve all the problems that have been caused by the existing self-centered approach, but in the long run it will overcome the very basis of the problems that we face today. He feels that if humankind continues to approach its problems considering only temporary expediency, future generations will have to face tremendous difficulties. Because the global population is increasing and our resources are being rapidly depleted. And also it is difficult to achieve a spirit of genuine cooperation as long as people remain indifferent to the feelings and happiness of others.

The Dalai Lama suggests that there is a strong need of transforming human attitudes to solve human problems. He wants human attitudes to be based on concept of non-violence, compassion and world peace, human rights and universal responsibility, value for democracy, above all commitment to 'humanity'.

Commenting on the genuine non-violence the Dalai Lama XIV says that, it is related to one's mental attitude. When anybody talk of peace, he says that must mean genuine peace and not merely the absence of war. In this context the Dalai Lama feels that there is more relevance of non-violence and compassion in today's world. He says that, the nature of non-violence should be something that is not passive but active in helping others. Non-violence means that, he adds, "if you can help and serve others you must do that. If you cannot, you must at least restrain yourself from harming others".[16]

The twentieth century, the Dalai Lama thinks, is the most important century in human history, since it has seen many outstanding scientific achievements and yet more human suffering than ever before. However, he feels that the human being in this century is basically the same as 1,000 or 10,000 years ago. Because, in his opinion human community had the same negative feelings of anger and hatred but this century has seen an enormous increase in its destructive power. Keeping in mind the possibility of nuclear holocaust, he looks at the future so bleak and feels that it forced and helped the human kind to think of alternatives. And "this gives great hope".[17]

The Dalai Lama is of the opinion that today more and more people are realizing that the proper way of resolving differences is through dialogue, compromise, negotiations, through human understanding and humanity. He felt that it is a very great sign. This is true, if we look at the people of fifties and sixties. Many of them felt that ultimate decision in any disagreement or conflict could only come through war or weapons that were believed to deter war. The fact is that the events and developments in this century have encouraged the human being to become wiser and maturer. So the Dalai Lama says that people are developing a greater understanding of the meaning of non-violence and of compassion.

"Compassion and love are not matters of religion, though many religions teach these things. When we are born, we do not have any religion but we are not free from human love and affection. This is not a matter of religion. I believe it is a separate thing. What religions do is try to strengthen these qualities which are already there in human nature from birth",[18] the Dalai Lama says. He felt it is essential to make a distinction between religion and human nature, because of the five billion or so people on our planet, not more than about one billion are "believers" or actively follow any organized religion. So he says that we are all members of the same human family and he wants to find ways of cultivating a deeper awareness of love and compassion, with or without religion. At the same time, there is need to understand the negative expressions of the human mind such as anger, hatred and attachment.

Explaining the nature of negative expressions, the Dalai Lama says that when we face some external problem, it is often possible to escape it and find a solution, but when the anger or the hatred is within, we cannot do so easily. He says that once we have an understanding or realization of the nature of our mind, then gradually it would change. As time goes on, our attitude, even to the external enemy would change. With understanding there would be forgiveness and an increase of our inner strength. As a result there would be less fear, less doubt and more self-confidence, tolerance and patience. That is why he considers compassion to be the key to overcome hatred. This is his belief and his daily practice. He finds that through his own little experience, through training, through analytical meditation, he has changed, and feels that if one makes the attempt one can change.

He feels that, since we are human beings, our basic nature is that of love and compassion and in human nature there is a natural feeling for living things. He thinks that the time has come to think about the basic cause of suffering.

For centuries millions of individual followers have derived personal peace of mind and solace in times of suffering from their own particular religious traditions. It is evident too that society in general has derived much benefit from these traditions in terms of the inspiration to ensure social justice and provide help to the needy. Today, the world over, we can find followers of many faiths sacrificing their own welfare in the service of others. So the Dalai Lama believes that this development of altruism is the most important goal of all religious practice.

The Dalai Lama adopts very pragmatic approach in understanding diverse mental dispositions and interests. It is inevitable that different religious traditions emphasise different philosophies and modes of practice, since human beings naturally possess diverse mental dispositions and interests. This diversity is actual source of enrichment. Because of the astounding variety of human beings intellectual and emotional dispositions, we need a variety of religious traditions and practices to meet our sundry needs and their very existence can be our strength.

History shows that coercion rarely yields positive results and in the present circumstances too no one will really triumph through adopting a belligerent and hostile approach. The Dalai Lama says that, since the essence of our diverse religious traditions is to achieve our individual and collective benefit, it is crucial that we are active in maintaining harmony and mutual respect between them. Concerted efforts to this end will benefit not only the followers of our own faith, but also create an atmosphere of peace in society as a whole. What the Dalai Lama wants is that cultivating harmony, respect and tolerance. It is something that we an each start doing in our own lives and in our own actions. On the other hand, if we take the differences between us as grounds for fighting and argument, there will be no end to it. The Dalai Lama feels that all of us will be weakened and diminished, even if one side manages to impose its point of view by force.

Talking on the growing awareness of the meaning of non-violence today, the Dalai Lama says that, its application is not restricted merely to other human beings; it also has to do with ecology, the environment and our relations with all the other living beings with whom we share the planet. He also says that, non-violence can be applied in our day-to-day lives whatever our position or vocation. Although violence is still rife, the trend of world opinion is to recognize that the future is in non-violence. He sees only one way to obtain real happiness that is through a combination of philosophy of non-violence and promotion of science and technology. Because, non-violence develops mental peace while science and technology are related to material progress. The combination of these two obviously produces real human happiness.

At the same time he warns that, the more we pursue material improvement ignoring the contentment that comes of inner growth, the quicker ethical values will disappear from our communities. We shall all experience unhappiness in the long run, when there is no place for justice and honesty in people's hearts, the weak are the first to suffer, but the resentments resulting from such inequity ultimately affect everyone adversely. To avoid this situation, he suggests balancing external material progress with the sense of responsibility that comes of inner development. "It is natural that we should face obstacles in pursuit of our goals. But if we remain passive, making no effort to solve the problems we meet, conflicts will arise and hindrances will grow. Transforming these obstacles into opportunities for positive growth is a challenge to our human ingenuity. To achieve this requires patience, compassion and the use of our intelligence. But to ignore such opportunities is to waste our human potential ... it is extremely important to realize that the graver the crisis we encounter, the greater is our need for patience. Above all, we must not lose our tranquillity",[19] the Dalai Lama explains the positive mental attitude to achieve positive goals.

World Peace and Human Happiness

As earlier mentioned, the Dalai Lama XIV's whole thought is based on two main purposes. One is universal responsibility and other compassion and world peace. He has been consistently pursuing the twin objects of world peace and human happiness with transparent sincerity and dedication. He feels one with those afflicted by strife and violence, for his concern knows no distinctions of race, religion or political affiliations. Being a Buddhist monk, he pleads for tolerance, wisdom and understanding to establish a just and peaceful world order. He has abiding faith in the values based fundamentally on his religious perceptions, spirituality and a sense of universal responsibility for the well being of all living and sentient beings. His thoughts flow from his philosophy of love and compassion. These and his insistence on peaceful and non-violent methods of solving human problems through dialogue as opposed to conflict and violence – form the under current of his message.

The Dalai Lama believes that there is a need for the development of greater sense of universal responsibility. He says that one must learn to work not just for one's own self or his family or nation, but for the benefit of all mankind. He feels that universal responsibility is the best foundation both for personal happiness and for world peace, the equitable use of natural resources and, through a concern for future generations, the proper care for the environment. He believes that, whether a person is rich or poor, educated or uneducated, belonging to any one nation, religion, ideology or another, basically he is just a human being. He means that, one must treat other person just as a human being but not with any other identity. Here he stresses the importance of the one's identity as a human being.

"Love and compassion are the ultimate source of human contentment. Our need for them lies at our very core. Yet, they are often omitted from many spheres of social interaction. Confined to family and home, their practice in public life is typically thought of as impractical even naïve. This is tragic",[20] the Dalai Lama feels. He believes that, the practice of compassion is not a symptom of unrealistic idealism. It is the most effective and practical means to pursue one's own interest as well as that of others. He says that, adopting an attitude of universal responsibility is, first, a matter of personal initiative.

Love and compassion are the basis for harmony and growth. The Dalai Lama explains the meaning of compassion as: "when you have compassion for a very poor person, you are showing sympathy. Because he or she is poor your compassion is based on altruism. On the other hand, love towards your wife, your husband, your children, or a close friend is usually based on attachment. When your attachment changes, your kindness also changes; it may even disappear. This is not true love. Real love is based not on attachment, but on altruism. In this case your compassion will remain a human response to suffering as long as sentient beings continue to suffer".[21] And also he continues to explain that undiscriminating, spontaneous, and unlimited compassion for all sentient beings is obviously not the usual love that one has for friends or family, which is allowed with desire, attachment and ignorance. He says, "the kind of love we should advocate is this wider love that you can have even for some who has done you harm; your enemy.[22]

Explaining the rationale for compassion, the Dalai Lama says that, everyone wants to avoid suffering and gain happiness. "This in turn, is based on the valid feeling of 'I', which determines the universal desire for happiness. Indeed all beings are born with similar desires and have an equal right to fulfill them. If I compare myself with others, who are countless, I feel that others are more important because I am just one person whereas others are many".[23] He even uses, the belief of re-incarnation to explain the rationale behind his belief of importance of compassion, saying that belief in reincarnation means, we are born and reborn countless number of times, and it is conceivable that each being has been our parent at one time or another. In this way, he feels that, all beings in the universe share a family relationship.

It is true to say that, whether one believes in religion or not, there is no one who does not appreciate love and compassion. The Dalai Lama says that the development of a kind heart (i.e., a feeling of closeness for all human beings) does not necessarily involve conventional religious practice. According to him, it is for anyone, who considers himself or herself, above all, a member of the human family. He says that this is a powerful feeling that one should consciously develop and apply. The Dalai Lama makes it clear that every human being wish to gain happiness and avoid suffering. So what is the need of violence and feeling of hatred! What is needed is a true sense of compassion – a true sense of love and respect for others. In this direction, one needs get trained one's mental attitude. In the words of the Dalai Lama, "a useful result of training ourselves to cultivate altruism is that it diminishes the magnitude of our own problems. When faced with a calm and clear mind, problems can be successfully resolved. On the other hand, when our minds are filled with hatred, selfishness, jealousy, and anger, we lose our sense of judgement. We become blind and can make serious errors of judgement. To be happy oneself, one must help others and to do this, a genuine feeling of compassion must be developed".[24]

The Dalai Lama does not believe in creating movements or organisations to promote an idea. He feels that, doing so implies that only one group of people have responsibility for achieving the goal – the rest are exempt. He says that in the present circumstances no one can afford to assume that someone else will solve our problems. In other words, each of us must really take on his or her own share of universal responsibility. He feels that positive changes cannot come quickly. And he says that we need an ongoing effort for determined application, which can accomplish even the most difficult objectives. "When we transform ourselves it affects those whom we come in contact with in positive ways, they in turn influence others and so on. Each action that each of us take makes a difference even though we cannot always obviously see or understand the conseuqneces".[25]

Today even though great economic and material progress is taking place, there seems to be growing violence and discord between people. There appears to be less tolerance, less-compassion and less concern for others. People are more concerned about asserting their rights and perceived needs. Sadly, much of this is in the name of religion. The Dalai Lama believes that the leaders of different religious traditions and those who give people spiritual guidance have a special responsibility, when they explain their own traditions to the public. They should do so explicitly in a context that acknowledges that all religious traditions have the same essential function of giving advice to human beings that would bring them happiness. He is of the opinion that all the different religious traditions are useful to their followers. It is very important to consider this when sometimes in praising one's own tradition. He sees this as a crucial point all religious leaders must keep in mind, to avoid the danger of misunderstanding and which might lead to intolerance.

The Dalai Lama gives a suggestion to all religious leaders to overcome the problem of misunderstanding in dealing with multi-religious traditions and beliefs. For this, he suggests that religious leaders and practitioners should occasionally meet, sit together and get acquainted on a personal level. Then, as problems crop up, they can discuss them freely and intervene quickly. He views that the establishment of such personal relations based on a close personal acquaintance to be of profound significance. He says that religious leaders need to affirm that although different religious traditions contain fundamental differences, they all have the same noble objective of enabling their followers to be happy and good human beings. Frequently those who wish to exploit religion not for the benefit of their followers but their own political or personal needs and power can corrupt this message. What is of greatest significance for today's religious leaders is that their followers are above to live together harmoniously and amicably, desiring new experiences and insights from people of all faiths even on matters crucial or exclusive to their own faith.[26]

In the present modern society one thing is sure, regarding the practice of religion is that, the force can impose no religious system over a period of time. It is true to say that, it is impossible to make everyone accept the same religion and indeed there would be no point in doing so. It is more beneficial to have a variety of religions to suit the range of human interests and dispositions. In fact, co-existence is no longer merely desirable but imperative. What we need today is that the initiative, which must come from the religious leadership. And the Dalai Lama's Mission is very much ahead in this direction to achieve common minimum programme for religious leadership of various religious streams. The Dalai Lama believes that the protection of religious freedom and the diversity in human faiths is a matter of Fundamental Human Rights. He does not find any other alternative but to live in religious harmony. He requests the proponents of different religious systems at least to observe mutual tolerance, if they are unable to show each other respect.

The Dalai Lama says, "We Buddhists have a concept of 'dependant arising' whereby all events are analysed to have causes and effects which function in a chain reaction. Subsequent causes and conditions derive their power from preceding causes and conditions. In this way, the fruit or the result, whether positive or negative, occurs".[27] On the basis of this Buddhist principle (i.e., the theory of dependent origination or universal law causation) he says that if one is cautious about results of one's own action, one can avoid all the problems, which human community is facing today. In other words, he feels that generally, we start responding to events that take place only after things have come to a head and the causes have fructified.

Universal Faith and Responsibility

Many of our human problems are a result of lack of genuine concern and indifferences when things are still at a casual or formative stage. Therefore, to prevent resentment and outbursts of violence that occur over differences of faith, it is essential to be alert when things are still on a casual level – to contain the causes of religious dissension and encourage the causes of religious harmony. The Dalai Lama have the conviction and the faith that by a close look at the abiding message of all faiths, the highest good could be find out and could work for the cultivation of altruism and a firm active commitment for the welfare and happiness of others. He proposes, "Let us all, those who have the responsibility being regarding as leaders of different religions, and followers, work closely together in a spirit of universal responsibility for the future we share together on this planet".[28]

Universal responsibility, which the Dalai Lama envisages, is also based on the purpose of protecting human rights. The fact is that brute force, no matter how strongly applied, can never subdue the basic human desire for freedom and dignity. The modern society witnessing a tremendous and popular movement for the advancement of human rights and democratic freedoms in the world. Indeed, day by day the world is becoming one community. There is a growing awareness of people's responsibilities. Even though so much suffering continues to be inflicted in the name of nationalism, race, religion, ideology and history, there is a new hope emerging for the downtrodden, since people everywhere displaying their willingness to champion and defend the rights and freedom of their fellow human beings. The Dalai Lama undoubtedly stands first among the people who are putting all their efforts for the cause of suppressed humanity.

Human Rights

The Dalai Lama feels that, "no matter what country or continent we come from we have common human needs and concerns. We all seek happiness and try to avoid suffering regardless of our race, religion, sex or political status. Human beings, indeed all sentient beings, have a right to pursue happiness and live in peace and freedom".[29] In the present society there is need for outrightly protecting human rights, since the problem is not confined to any one single group or community or for that matter nation. It is the problem, whole human community is facing. There is need to early realisation that the political, social, cultural and economic development of a society are obstructed by the violation of human rights. Due to all these losses which human community has to face, the protection of these is of immense value and importance.

The Dalai Lama's belief is that the lack of understanding of the true nature of happiness, is the principal reason why people inflict suffering on others. People either think that the suffering of others can somehow be a source of happiness for themselves or that their own happiness is of such importance that the pain of others is of no significance. He believes that this is clearly short sighted. He says, "when we demand the rights and freedoms we so cherish, we should also be aware of our responsibilities. If we accept that others have an equal right to peace and happiness as ourselves, do we not have a responsibility to help those in the need? All human beings, whatever their cultural or historic background, suffer when they are intimidated, imprisoned or tortured".[30]

The forces of liberty and oppression have been in continuous conflict throughout history. But because of people's innate desire for freedom, the forces that represent tyranny, dictatorship and violence have been at receiving end. The emergence of people's power movements, has shown indisputably that the human race can neither tolerate nor function properly under tyranny. This resulted into emergence of modern democracy, which is based on the principle that all human beings are essentially equal, that everybody has an equal right to life, liberty, and happiness. The political, social and cultural freedom that democracy entails is of immense value and importance. When democracy and human rights are under attack it is often proved that, it is because of, the lack of understanding regarding the universal responsibility. The values of democracy and human rights are interlined with the idea of universal responsibility.

The idea of democracy is closer to essential human nature. "We all want to live a good life, but that does not mean just having good food, clothes and shelter. These are not sufficient we need a good motivation. Compassion without dogmatism, without complicated philosophy. Just understanding that others are our brothers and sisters and respecting their rights and human dignity. That we humans can help each other is one of our unique human characteristics," the Dalai Lama says.[31]

If human society loses the value of justice, compassion and honesty, it will face greater difficulties in future. Some people may think that these ethical attitudes are not much needed in the areas of business or politics. The Dalai Lama strongly disagree with it, because, he feels that the quality of all our actions depends on our motivation. He gives example from the field of politics. He says that, a good and honest politician must have a good motivation and seek a better human society. He opines that, politics itself is not bad and it is mistake to say that politics being dirty. He feels that politics is a necessary instrument to solve human problems. He is of the firm view that politics is not bad in itself. However, he says that if politics is practised by people lacking a good motivation, who only have selfish and short-term ends, then of course it becomes bad.[32]

From the Buddhist viewpoint all things originate in the mind. Actions and events depend heavily on motivation. A real sense of appreciation of humanity, compassion and love, are the key points. The Dalai Lama says that if we develop a good heart, then whether the field is science, agriculture or politics, since the motivation is so very important, the result will be more beneficial. With proper motivation these activities can help humanity; without it they go the other way. This is why the compassionate thought is so very important for human kind. Although it is difficult to bring about the inner change that gives rise to it, it is absolutely worth while to try.[33]

The Dalai Lama on Communism

Commenting on communism, he felt that although communism espoused many noble ideals, it failed utterly because it relied on force to promote its beliefs. It is proved that, brute force, no matter how strongly applied, can never subdue the basic human desire for freedom. What happened in the Eastern Europe was not the people's desire for new ideology or anything else, it is just for freedom. The people who led the movement in these countries simply expressed the human need for freedom and democracy. The Dalai Lama feels that it is not enough, as communist systems have assumed, merely to provide people with food, shelter and clothing. What human society desires constantly is space for freedom, democracy and peaceful living.

The Dalai Lama feels that, the peaceful revolutions in the former Soviet Union and Eastern Europe have taught us many great lessons. One is the value of truth. He says that people do not like to be bullied, cheated or lied to by either an individual or a system. He feels that such acts are contrary to the essential human spirit. Therefore, he says that, those who practice deception and use force may achieve considerable short-term success, but eventually they would be over thrown.

The Dalai Lama does not see any contradiction between the need for economic development and the need for respect of human rights. Similarly, he feels that, the rich diversity of cultures and religions should help strengthen rather than obstruct fundamental human rights in all communities. "Underlying this diversity are fundamental human principles that bind every human being as a member of the same human family. Maintaining old traditions can never justify the violations of human rights. It may be the custom to discriminate against people of different race, against women, and against weaker sections of society, but as this is inconsistent with universally recognized human rights, these forms of behaviour should change. The universal principles of equality of all human beings must take precedence" [34] the Dalai Lama feels.

It is not enough to merely state that all human beings must enjoy equal dignity. This must be translated into action. There is need of serious commitment to the fundamental principles of equality, which the Dalai Lama believes that lie at the heart of the concept of human rights and democracy. His vision of a democratic future is global de-militarization; although it sounds bit idealistic, he believes it is most important to re-evaluate the present concept of military establishment. It is not only during times of war that military establishment is destructive. By their very design, they are the single greatest violations of human rights and most regularly the opponents of democracy. The Dalai Lama envisages de-militarised society. Though it looks an unrealistic idea, at least at idealistic level, if all nations decide this as their goal to achieve, in reality something in this direction can be materialised in future.

The Dalai Lama opines that, once an army has become a powerful force, there is every risk that it would destroy the happiness of its own country. He feels that as long as there are powerful armies there would always be the risk of dictatorship. He says, "if we really believe dictatorship to be a despicable and destructive form of government, the anti-thesis of democracy, we must recognise that the existence of a powerful military establishment is one of its main causes. National forces should be gradually disbanded and replaced by collective regional forces.[35]

Information Revolution

Today, the world has become smaller. The revolution in the field of information has brought far away nations, more closer. This paved the way for the emergence of global village and world's people have become almost one community. Now, local problems also are assuming global character, influencing the people across the continents. We find reaction and support from all the quarters of the world, to the Black community in U.S.A, when they are discriminated racially. We have seen the sympathy of Americans to Tibetan people who are fighting for their rights against Chinese oppression. In India when the caste Hindus massacred more than thirty unarmed Dalits[36] in Tsundur, a small village in the coastal belt of Andhra Pradesh in 1991, we had seen the support and sympathy to them from the people belong to far away nations. This clearly shows that due to the development in the modern communications all over world, people from far away nations started reacting to local issues of far away countries.

The modern technological developments by bringing world communities more closely helped to strengthen the feeling of humanity among people. By reacting to the issues, even though which are not directly related to them, people are reimposing their faith in the humanity. In fact, it can be clearly observed that, no ideology, or regional affiliation (ethnic identity), or any other dominant factors are becoming hurdles, to support any issue related to the suppression of humanity. However, it can be found that still the modern society is not altogether stand by humanity. There are nations, communities or groups, still under the colonial or feudal dominance, where abuse of human rights is common practice. Be it at nation level or community or caste level, this is the common phenomenon, which questions the very foundation of human society. The modern society, even after making so much development at the scientific and technological level, it seems to be that it failed utterly in countering the forces, which are making headway against 'Humanity'. The Dalai Lama believes that, to meet these challenges, human beings would have to develop a greater sense of universal responsibility.

Importance of Compassion

The Dalai Lama truly believes that individuals could make a difference in society. As a Buddhist monk, he tries to develop compassion in himself not just from a religious point of view, but from a humanitarian one as well. For him, the propagation of compassion, and thus peace through it, is part of his daily practice. His humble appeal to human world is that to understand each other through the development of compassion. If a greater sense of universal responsibility joins along with the development of science and technology, he feels that individuals can create more peaceful world.

There is a need to realise the importance of compassion in human life. "Non-violence does not mean the mere absence of violence. It is something more positive, more meaningful than that. True expression of non-violence is compassion. Some people seem to think that compassion is just a passive emotional response instead of a rational stimulus to action. To experience genuine compassion is to develop a feeling of closeness to others combined with a sense of responsibility for their welfare. True compassion develops when we accept that other people are just like ourselves in wanting happiness and not wanting suffering and that they have every right to pursue these",[37] the Dalai Lama gives the meaning of compassion. He further explains that true compassion is universal in scope, and it is accompanied by a feeling of responsibility. He says that, to act altruistically, concerned only for the welfare of others, with no selfish or ulterior motive, is to affirm a sense of universal responsibility.

For the Dalai Lama, the true aim of cultivating compassion is to develop the courage to think of others and to do something for them. One of the most powerful emotions disturbing our mental tranquillity is hatred. The Dalai Lama feels that the antidote for hatred is compassion. He says, "we should not think of compassion as being only the preserve of the sacred and religious. It is one of our basic human qualities. Human nature is essentially loving and gentle".[38] He does not agree with the people who assert that human beings are innately aggressive, despite the apparent prevalence of anger and hatred in the world. He feels that, right from the moment of birth, a human being requires love and affection. He says that without love one could not survive, and human beings are social creatures and concern for each other is the very basis of human's life.

The Dalai Lama believes that a positive outlook could affect an individual. Anger may seem to offer an energetic way of getting things done, but such a perception of the world is misguided. The only certainity about anger and hatred is that they are destructive, no good ever comes of them. The Dalai Lama says, "if we live our lives continually motivated by anger and hatred, even our physical health deteriorates. On the other hand people who remain calm and open-minded, motivated by compassion are mentally free of anxiety and physically healthy".[39] He says that at a time when people are so conscious of maintaining their physical health by controlling their diets, exercising and so forth, it makes sense to try to cultivate the corresponding positive mental attitudes too.[40]

The development of human society is based entirely on people helping each other. Every individual has a responsibility to help guide the community in the right direction. If society loses this essential humanity, which is its foundation, society as a whole will collapse. The Dalai Lama questions that, what point would there then be in pursuing material improvement? He feels that, action motivated by compassion and responsibility would ultimately bring good results, and that anger and jealousy might be effective in the short term, but would ultimately bring only trouble. According to him, fear is another major obstacle to individual's inner development. Suspicion brings fear. It is compassion that creates the sense of trust, without it one cannot communicate with other honestly and openly. Therefore, the Dalai Lama says that developing compassion is one of the most effective ways of reducing fear. Compassion is fundamentally a human quality so its development is not restricted to those who practice religion. Nevertheless, religious traditions have a special role to play in encouraging its development.

It is the Dalai Lama's belief that, for the world in general, that compassion is more important than 'religion'. Because, he believes that the common factor among all religions is that, whatever the philosophical differences between them, they are primarily concerned with helping their followers become better human beings. He says that consequently, all religions – encourage the practice of kindness, generosity and concern for others, in other words compassion. This is why he finds conflicts based on religious differences to be so sad and futile.[41] This can be explained in another way, that the Dalai Lama prefers compassion instead of religion if it is not based on compassion. It is for the people to decide whether religion preaches compassion or is based on violence and social inequality. And it is for the people to decide whether all religions are accepting compassion as a whole or partly as their base.

Probably, the Dalai Lama allows individual's rationale to prevail in selecting the religion wholly based on compassion. Here, doubt may arise to many that, is there any religion not based on compassion. Probable answer is, must be, otherwise how can there be religious conflicts. Either all these religions accept compassion or reject it outrightly. This may be the cause for religious conflicts. If religions are really based on compassion, the believers or followers of all the religions should not accept the means of hatred, anger, violence as their option to resolve their differences.

History showed that with exception to Buddhism, no other religion adopted pragmatic approach towards human society. This acted as major hindrance in the growth of scientism in those religious thoughts. Because they may have adapted compassion but in practice they never insisted. This is so because of the lack of realistic approach in the application of their philosophy. For example, Jainism adopted extreme non-violence and history has proved that it is not feasible in day-to-day life. Hinduism is the best example of 'religious contradiction'. In another words, Hindu scriptures contradict with their own-preachings. Hindu Law books talk of love and compassion but they prefer social system based on inequality and inhuman treatment to their own Hindu followers in the name of caste sacredness.

For Buddhism compassion is its foundation and violence is recognised as part of human nature but not preferred as means to resolve human problems. That is why, the Dalai Lama on the one hand says that all religions are same and on the other hand he believes that compassion is more important than religion.

Among the world population (say over five billion), perhaps one billion actively and sincerely follow a formal religion. The remaining over four billion are not believers in the true sense. If it is regarded that the development of compassion and other good qualities as the business only of religion, the majority people would be excluded. But this could not be in any way criteria to decide relation between compassion and human society. The Dalai Lama says that as members of human family, everyone of these people (who are not attached to any religion) has the potential to be inspired by the need for compassion. He concludes that compassion could be developed and nurtured without practicing a particular religion.

The conflicts arise from a failure to understand one another's humanness. The answer is not the development and use of neither greater military force, nor arms race to solve the problems and to avoid conflicts faced by modern nations. The Dalai Lama feels that, the spiritual growth can only help humankind, in the sense that what is required is a sensitive understanding of common human situation. Hatred and fighting cannot bring happiness to any one, even to the winners of battles. Violence always produces misery and thus is essentially countered productive. Therefore, the Dalai Lama says that, it is time for World leaders to learn to transcend the differences of race, culture, and ideology and to regard one another through the common human situation. This would benefit individuals, communities, nations, and the world at large.

Religion in Politics

The Dalai Lama questions the popular assumption that religion and ethics have no place in politics and religious persons should seclude themselves as hermits. He feels that such view of religion is too one-sided; it lacks a proper perspective on the individual's relation to society and role of religion in individuals' life. He says that, ethics is as crucial to a politician as it is to a religious practitioner. He explains that dangerous consequences would follow when politicians and rulers forget moral principles. Whether the religion is based on the belief in God or Karma, the Dalai Lama feels that, ethics is the foundation of every religion.[42]

Human qualities, such as, morality, compassion, decency, wisdom and so forth have been the foundations of all civilisations. These qualities must be cultivated and sustained through systematic moral education in a conducive social environment so that a more human world may emerge. He says that the qualities required to create such a world must be inculcated right from the beginning, from childhood. He does not want to wait for the next generation to make this change. He wants the present generation to attempt a renewal of basic human values. "If there is any hope, it is in the future generations, but not unless we institute major change on a world wide scale in our present educational system. We need a revolution in our commitment to and practice of universal humanitarian values".[43]

The Dalai Lama wants humanitarian and religious leaders to strengthen the existing civic, social, cultural, educational, and religious organisations to revive human and spiritual values, since present-day governments do not shoulder such religious responsibilities. He feels that, where necessary, the new organisations must be created to achieve these goals. He hopes that, by doing so only, a more suitable base could be created for world peace. He says "Living in society, we should share the sufferings of our fellow citizens and practice compassion and tolerance not only towards our loved ones but also towards our enemies. This is the test of our moral strength".[44] One needs to set an example by one's own practice, for one cannot hope to convince others of the value of religion by mere words. One must live upto the same high standards of integrity and sacrifice that one asks of others. To cultivate this sort of high moral atmosphere, even at the individual level, there is need of some effort towards this direction not just depending on only religious leaders.

Purpose of Religion

It is true to say that the ultimate purpose of religion is to serve and benefit humanity. It is so important that religion should always be used to effect the happiness and peace of all beings and not merely to convert others. There are no national boundaries. A religion can and should be used by any people or person who finds it beneficial. What is important for each seeker is to choose a religion that is most suitable to himself or herself. But, the embracing of a particular religion does not mean the rejection of another religion or one's own community.

In fact, it is important that those who embrace a religion should not cut themselves off from their own society; they should continue to live within their own community and in harmony with its members. The best example is that Christian community in India. They, even call themselves, Indian Christians. They adopted almost all their own Indian customs and formalised them in the Christianity. They use *Mangala Sutra*[45] as well as marriage-ring. This clearly shows that religion really does not have any national boundary. Hence, any body can adopt any religion, irrespective of its place of origin.

If any one doubts the credentials of any religion, just because it born in foreign land, the intention must be based on communal overtones. For example, Indian society have seen recently many communal outbursts, due to the false assumption of Hindu communalists that the presence of religions of foreign origin is dangerous to the growth of Hindu institutions, traditions and customs. But, the history of India stands as witness, to say that Indian society could accommodate any foreign element in its fold. For that matter, not only India, even American society allows Hinduism, Islam to grow. This proves that human society in general is same everywhere, be it in Asian continent or American continent. Hence, the growth of human society depends, on its capability to adopt foreign elements in its indegenous system.

The Dalai Lama explains that conversion to another religion doesn't mean escaping from one's own community, but benefiting his community by being a member of it, with newly adopted religious faith. In this regard there are two things important to keep in mind; self-examination and self-correction. "We should constantly check our attitude towards others, examining ourselves carefully, and we should correct ourselves immediately when we find we are in the wrong".[46]

What today needed is that, a human approach to all the problems; Since just material growth cannot solve the problems of modern society, spiritual sense should be developed. The Dalai Lama sees nothing wrong with material progress per se, provided people are always given precedence. It is his firm belief that in order to solve human problems in all their dimensions, there is a need to combine and harmonize economic development with spiritual growth.[47] Although materialistic knowledge in the form of science and technology has contributed enormously to human welfare, it is not capable of creating lasting happiness. In the views of the Dalai Lama, materialistic knowledge could only provide a type of happiness that is dependent upon physical conditions and it cannot provide happiness that springs from inner development independent of external factors.[48]

What is religion to the Dalai Lama XIV? "Religion is not to be found in temples," he said, "religion is to be found in people's hearts. If people are really practicing religion properly, if they have religion in their hearts, conflicts can be avoided. But when you keep religion in the temple and not in your heart, that is when conflict begins. One day, perhaps we will have to begin destroying temples in order to save religion".[49] He differs with the traditionalists' view of religion, who find religion in the place of worship only. In fact, the Dalai Lama's views echo the words of Gautama Buddha who broke away from traditional religion to a more humanistic philosophy, teaching that man must look not to temples but within himself to find his salvation.[50]

Meaning of Dharma

The Dharma, for Dalai Lama, is Buddhism. He defines it as, "A word with many meanings. From the root '*dhr*' which has the sense of upholding, *Dharma* is, therefore that which uphold's one's efforts when one practices in accordance with it. Dharma is law, that is the law governing the arising, existence and passing away of all physical and psychological phenomena. The Dharma is also the traditional way naming the teaching of Lord Buddha".[51] He says that the teachings of Buddha could be used without any contradiction, whether one practice the way of the *sutra* or that of the *Tantra* or both together. Though he believes that the practices of all the schools of Buddhism are the same,[52] he finds differences and variations in the methods of practices and conducts.

The Dalai Lama says, "Methods employed for the practice of Buddha dharma are diverse, depending upon the capacity and inclination of the individual mind. This is because those to be trained are not endowed with the same, uniform standard of intelligence, while others are of mediocre intelligence. As such, Lord Buddha has delivered his teachings in accordance with the intelligence and capacity of the people".[53] But inspite of all these, the Dalai Lama still finds a possibility to give a description of the general method of practising Buddha Dharma as a whole.

From the doctrine's standpoint, the Buddha dharma according to the Dalai Lama consists of four schools of thought. They are (1) *Vaibhasika*, (2) *Sautrantika*, (3) *Vijnanvada* and (4) *Sunyavad*. From the viewpoint of practice, he classified *Buddha dhrama* into three vehicles. They are (1) *Caravakayana* or Hinayana, (2) *Pratyeka Buddhayana*, and (3) *Bodhisatvayana* or *Mahayana*. He combines both *caravakayana* and *pratyeka Buddhayana*, since both are according to him, basically of the same form. He calls both of them as Hinayana. Finally he finds only two major vehicles. They are Hinayana and Mahayana. He further subdivided Mahayana into the vehicle of *Prajnapara Mithayana* or the cause vehicle of perfection and the *Vajrayana* or the effective vehicle of the Adamantine wheel or the Greet Secret. And he also includes the vehicle of esoteric teachings in Mahayana.

The present day circumstances are entirely different from past. The new scientific developments made man to live in easy way of life. However he could not overcome from the self created troubles and conflicts. Almost all religions and cultures have originated almost two thousand years back but still these spiritual ways have the significance in making human life towards "*Sukhada*" (happiness). The Dalai Lama finds that in ancient times problems were mostly family size and were, therefore, tackled at family level, but now the situation is no longer the same. What he meant is that the people today became so interdependent and so closely inter connected with each other that without a sense of universal responsibility, existence or survival would be difficult. He feels that, natural heart to heart human relationship, transcending all artificial barriers like colour and creed, can solve many of the problems that plague our society. In this context he finds Mahayana Buddhism is very much helpful.

The Dalai Lama believes that compassion for others (as opposite to self) is one of the central teachings of Mahayana Buddhism. In his words, "In Mahayana Buddhism, you sacrifice yourself in order to attain salvation for the sake of other beings".[54] He disassociates humanity from any sort of race, religion or of any political affiliation. For him humanity could be found in any body who considers himself first and foremost a member of the human family and who sees things in terms of humanity.[55]

With this sort of understanding regarding human role in scientific society, the Dalai Lama opines that material progress is certainly necessary and is a good thing, as it is of benefit to mankind. He suggests that the essential and more beneficial is that "we should be able to balance material progress with mental development".[56] For the mental development he feels religion is necessary for human society.

The behaviour of true individual, in his opinion, must be, "Respecting others, having compassion for others, such an attitude will not only give happiness to yourself but it also creates a better atmosphere for others, both on the smallest level of individuals or on a national level".[57] He believes that, having a sympathetic heart, a warm heart, a kind heart, is the essence or the most important thing. Irrespective of whether one believes in a religion or not, or no matter what religion or ideology one follows, if one has such an attitude or motive, then even such a violent act as killing some one, the Dalai Lama feels, "if it is done with a really good motive, could go beyond the usual level of killing".[58] On the other hand, if one has very selfish interests, very egoistic feelings, then even if he is externally preaching religion he would in the Dalai Lama words, "basically have wrong attitude".[59]

The Dalai Lama's philosophy finds human society as a community in which every individual is interdependent. It is almost impossible to live independently of each other. Since the natural circumstances are such, it is extremely unfortunate when we have to live under suspicion or when people try to fool one another. "If we have to live under such conditions, then no matter what facilitates we enjoy",[60] the Dalai Lama explodes the myth of happiness and says "we will not have inner peace".[61] If we have love for others, a sense of brotherhood, if we have compassion and respect for others, the Dalai Lama feels, "then even if we are angry we may have this warm feeling or this feeling of trust and of satisfaction at being in this human society".[62] And he claims, "I myself personally try to practice this philosophy as much as possible".[63]

The core principle in his teaching to his followers today is that, the importance of love, compassion, and altruistic attitude. Whether some one believes something or not, believer or non-believer, he says, "so long as you are a member of the human family you need warm human feeling, warm-hearted feeling".[64] The question of world peace, the question of family peace, the question of peace between wife and husband, or peace between parents and children, in his opinion, everything is dependent on that feeling of love and warm heartedness. He feels that, "we are trying to get peace or happiness from outside, from money or power. But real peace, tranquility, should come from within. A basic factor is warm-hearted feeling. Wherever I go, I stress the importance of this thing. Compassion or love is universal religion".[65]

He emphasises on human qualities, which are love, compassion, tolerance, and will. For him, a true human being is to be warm-hearted. Not to have warm feeling in the heart is almost not to have fully the nature of a human being.

The important thing in the Buddhist philosophy, the Dalai Lama feels is interdependence. The main purpose of the Buddha's teaching is, according to him, for temporary benefit as well as long term benefit. The long-term benefit is Buddhahood or enlightenment and nirvana. The temporary benefit is a happy life.

This is what the Dalai Lama, says about the relevance and significance of the Buddha "*Dharma*", in the present day society. Preserving the *Dharma* means preserving the culture. For this purpose the Dalai Lama and his followers are making efforts with hope, aspirations and faith in future.

The Dalai Lama's whole philosophy of compassion and universal responsibility and Humanitarian path and single human family, could be summed up by quoting his feeling:

"Whenever I meet even a 'foreigner' I have always the same feelings:

> 'I am meeting another member of the human family'. This attitude has deepened my affection and respect for all beings. May this natural wish be my small contribution to world peace. I pray for a more friendly, more caring, and more understanding, Human family on this planet. To all who dislike suffering, who cherish lasting happiness. This is my heart felt appeal".[66]

References

1. Dalai Lama XIV, "Violence Breeds More Violence". An Address to the founding Congress of the International League for the Abolition of the Death Penalty by the year 2000, held at the European Parliament in Brussels, December 9 and 10, 1993. Gyaltsen Gyaltag of the office of Tibet delivered

this text. Zurich, from *His Holiness the Dalai Lama, Speeches Statements, Articles and Interviews 1987 to June 1995*, p. 202.

2. Dalai Lama XIV, "Understanding Human Nature Cultivate the Compassion Within", *The Times of India*, December 3, New Delhi, 1992, p. 10. Others for our very existence. The practice of compassion and non-violence is in one's own self interest."
3. *Ibid.*
4. *Ibid.*
5. Dalai Lama, *A Human Approach to World Peace*, London, Fourth Print, 1988, p. 3.
6. *Ibid.*, p. 4.
7. *Ibid.*, pp. 4-5.
8. *Ibid.*, p. 5.
9. *Ibid.*, p. 7.
10. *Ibid.*, pp. 7-8.
11. *Ibid.*, p. 8.
12. *Ibid.*
13. *Ibid.*, p. 9.
14. *Ibid.*
15. *Ibid.*
16. Dalai Lama XIV, "Understanding Human Nature Cultivation Within", *op.cit.*, p. 10.
17. *Ibid.*
18. *Ibid.*
19. Dalai Lama XIV, "India's Deepening Crisis Imperatives of Harmonious Co-existence", *Times of India*, New Delhi, December 9, 1992, p. 10.
20. Dalai Lama XIV, "Universal Responsibility", *The Times of India*, New Delhi, April 4, 1993, p. 10.
21. *Ibid.*
22. *Ibid.*
23. *Ibid.*
24. *Ibid.*
25. *Ibid.*
26. Dalai Lama XIV, "Universal Responsibility And Religions", *The Times of India*, October 11, 1993, p. 10.
27. *Ibid.*
28. *Ibid.*
29. Dalai Lama XIV, "Human Rights and Universal Responsibility", *The Spirit of Tibet: Universal Heritage, Selected Speeches and Writings of H.H. The Dalai Lama XIV*, edited by A.A.Shiromany, New Delhi, 1995, p. 194.
30. *Ibid.*, pp. 194-95.
31. Dalai Lama XIV, "Fundamental Values of Democracy", *The Spirit of Tibet*, *op.cit.*, pp. 238-239.
32. *Ibid.*, p. 239.
33. *Ibid.*
34. *Ibid.*, pp. 240-241.
35. *Ibid.*, p. 243.

36. Ex-untouchables who acquired the new identity called DALITS in recent times and it symbolises their Self-respect and Militancy.
37. Dalai Lama XIV, "Importance of Compassion in Human Life", *The Spirit of Tibet, op.cit.,* p. 252.
38. *Ibid.,* p. 253.
39. *Ibid.,* p. 254.
40. *Ibid.*
41. *Ibid.,* pp. 254-255.
42. Dalai Lama, *A Human Approach to World Peace, op.cit.,* pp. 20-21.
43. *Ibid.,* p. 21.
44. Dalai Lama, XIV, "Individual Power to Shape Institutions," *The Spirit of Tibet, op.cit.,* p. 272.
45. It is to tie to the neck of bride by bridegroom and it symbolises married women.
46. Dalai Lama, *A Human Approach to World Peace, op.cit.,* p. 22.
47. *Ibid.,* pp. 22-24.
48. *Ibid.,* p. 24.
49. *Tibetan Review,* New Delhi, January 1972, p. 14.
50. Kenadi, L., *Revival of Buddhism in Modern India: The Role of B.R. Ambedkar and the Dalai Lama XIV,* New Delhi, 1995, p. 60.
51. Dalai Lama, the XIV, *The Opening of the Wisdom Eye,* Madras, 1972, p. 142.
52. *Ibid.,* p. 9.
53. Dalai Lama, the XIV, "The Practice of Buddhism in Tibet", *Tibetan Review,* New Delhi, May 1968, p. 8.
54. Dalai Lama the XIV, "Towards Universal Responsibility", *Tibetan Review,* New Delhi, July-August, 1975, p. 10.
55. *Ibid.,* p. 11.
56. *Ibid.,* p. 12.
57. Dalai Lama the XIV, "Universal Responsibility", *Tibetan Review,* New Delhi, April, 1976, p. 21.
58. *Ibid.*
59. *Ibid.*
60. *Ibid.,* p. 21.
61. *Ibid.*
62. *Ibid.*
63. *Ibid.*
64. *The Washington Times,* Washington, September 21, 1984.
65. *Ibid.*
66. Dalai Lama, "Individual Power to Shape Institutions", *The Spirit of Tibet, op.cit.,* p. 273.

Six

Buddhism in Modern India

Ideas control the world. They will triumph over the blind forces. For dynamic conceptions which will remodel society, the basic requirement is the presence of a great thinker at particular juncture of History

Today on all sides a seething mass of turbulent life. It is a situation produced by a combination of varied movements, which the world at large passed through during the last few centuries. The intellectual renaissance, the industrial revolution, the political struggle for freedom and democracy and the religious reformation, which almost all the nations faced at different period of History.

While great changes are taking place in every side of life, post industrial - communication, information technological revolution in other words internet revolution on one side and the other side political, cultural and social, there is a good deal of loose and muddled thinking. The world seems to be marching forth into the unknown. There is a general disposition to despise cultural interests and make of life a rougher and ruder thing than in the spacious past.[1]

The stress of the struggle for the bare physical necessities is more formidable than it ever was. Indeed, this has strengthened politics of caste ideology among dominant social groups in Indian society. Hindu idea of ideal society is Varna based social relations manifested in economic and political relations. It has created modern form of subject social groups. It is like a whole nation suffering from social cancer.[2] In these circumstances a nation can think of nothing else. The nation will listen to all quacks who will profess to beat it. The teaching of the Varna Philosophy of Hinduism is mainly responsible for the social unrest. It has been the explosive energy, the social dynamite.

The social tradition derived from the ancient Buddhist culture has taught Indian society an idea of a juster social order. The social unrest in Indian society is a tribute to the work of casteist Hindus. They are more anxious to Hinduise Buddhist religion. However, the future of Buddhism lies in the Dalit community. The silent struggles in the minds of men are important than the spectacular ones on then politico-religious arena.

The integration of social, cultural and political forces is broken up because of Brahmanic Hindu-Hindutva fundamentalism. The secret of life is in the law of development and that is possible only as history has been witnessed whenever Buddhist ideals dominate Indian society. Hindu society is suffering from want of understanding. Understanding of human relations and motives is not a matter of something which can be taught by somebody. It has to come from within. Unless there is prevalence of culture of ethics, culture of social equality and social justice which are indeed alien to Hindu foundations, Indian society cannot develop into progressive state. Buddha walked out of his palace to suffer and recreate. Christ is the man of sorrows. Unfortunately in Hindu history none can be found in this category. Interestingly, Gods in Hinduism profess violent philosophy and wielding dangerous weapons by themselves is idealising violence. The fact is that none who has not suffered to the utmost gets to the foundations of reality.

There is a need for suffering and strength. Hindu seem to be coddling with comforts of social dominance and is willing to use all his intellectual resources ruthlessly in the service of one end, dominance of Brahmanic communities. It seems to have almost a superstitious reverence for caste hierarchy.

The fact of Indian society is the confrontation of different cultures and different religions. Unfortunately, rather than addressing the false ideals like Varna-dharma / Jati, Casteism etc. Within his society, Hindu is trying to unite his society by posing against other religions namely Islam and Christianity. It has brought negative unity. This trend of time being Hindu unity able to suppress the voices of millions of untouchables in Hindu India. The fact as history shows, Hindu lacks ethical sense always in dealing with untouchable groups. This is so because Hindu gets moral backing of his religion to fight against untouchables.

Hindu context of enemy or the other of Hindu has always been located by caste Hindu in the untouchable not in other religions. His new attack on other religions is indeed expression of frustration of failure in minimizing voices of untouchables. This failure is due to Ambedkar who led untouchable consciousness towards Buddhist belief for justice and equality which have been denied to the so called untouchables in Hindu society for centuries.

Even after dominating over almost all aspects of Indian life, Hinduism failed miserably in its efforts to stop Ambedkarism to lead Dalit masses to the Buddhist India. This is because of negative social philosophy of Hindu society. Gita says, *anityam asukham lokam* (life is never ending misery). The Upanisads tell that, the world is *asat*,(unreal); this world is *Mrtyu* (death); this world is *tamas* (darkness). Whereas the Buddha looked at the present world or life is a combination of both happiness and sorrow like day after night. The Madhyemarga (i.e. no extremes in the meaning of life) made the believers of Buddhism to adopt positive path of life that has shaken the foundations of Hindu society. Success of Ambedkarism lies in the positive understanding of Buddha Dhamma. Understanding does not mean learning or skill, but to understand all is to forgive all. It helps to feel the complexity as well as the mystery of life.

Understanding positively the Buddha path symbolises the spirit of revolution. It is for bringing a change in hegemonic systems - social, economic and political through religious or cultural transformation. There are two sides in the Buddha life: (1) meditation, leading to the development of enlightenment and (2) service of humanity. These two — enlightenment and service, constitute the essentials of religion of the Buddha. Unfortunately the Hindu India has failed to understand the real significance of religion that is 'service to humanity'. Hindu India unable to produce one Mother Theresa or one Ambedkar who lived and worked among the poorest of the poor of Indian society. There are reformers plenty in number but there is none to name who worked for transformation of the society.

The Buddha was dissatisfied with the way in which religion was practised in his days and said 'we want mercy, not sacrifice'. What needs is real help, love of humanity and not what Hinduism subscribes i.e., rituals and ceremonies. The Buddha condemned rituals and made out that these rituals do not take us to the Ultimate Truth.

The Buddha looked at the world, as traditional story goes, met the sights of a sick man, an old man and a dead man. Though it is absurd to believe this story, the positive interpretation of the story gives us true meaning of the Buddha Dhamma. Sickman, old man and dead man represents sickness, oldage and death - these are the perils to which human flesh is exposed.

The Buddha then met an Old monk who was looking bright. He asked him,' How is it, in this world so full of sorrow, that you are able to have an appearance of brightness?' The monk replied: 'O, best of men, afraid of birth and death, I have become a monk, a wanderer, without any settled abode, to escape from the tyranny of Time'. Here Time has for its symbol birth and death. If one wants to overcome time, one has to obtain nirvana, that is not merely escape from time. However, traditional interpretators had made a negative view about this story. They preached that the Buddha professed escapism from life and withdrawal from the present worldly affairs. The Buddha, who professed Madhyama marga, how could subscribe such a extreme view that to withdraw entirely from the present life? Nirvana indeed is not escape form the time in the sense that we avoid temporal things but escape from subjection to time. Nirvana is not only time-transcending, it is also time-transforming. Attaining Nirvana is attainment of enlightenment. After enlightenment one indulges in the affairs of the world by trying to transform, though he trys to redeem and make it eternity. It is to live in time with the proper perspective in our mind. In other words, the gospel of the Buddha is: escape from time and at the same time control over time. That is to think about society to transform it (through service to humanity).

The Buddha's whole life is a succession of these two sides. Trying to balance both that is trying by every possible means to attain enlightenment. After enlightenment, the Buddha spent himself in the service of humanity. Wisdom and love constitute the essence of Buddhism. The Buddha emphasised those two things in his teachings. His life itself is a practical illustration that one has to live in this world to acquire wisdom and to spend one's life in the service of humanity.

Buddha said that life is suffering and suffering has a cause and we can escape from suffering by attaining nirvana or enlightenment, i.e. think about society and transform it by service to humanity. It is possible to attain nirvana in this world itself. It is not essential for us to escape into another world. Deep meditation is deep thinking about society. Questioning the problems faced by society and reasoning out solutions. Nirvana is not to withdraw from the world but we participate in it. This could be achieved by intellectual and spiritual struggle.

Nirvana (enlightenment) is pre-requisite for service to humanity. In other words, the understanding about the importance of service to humanity one could get out of constant thinking about society that is enlightenment (nirvana). Unfortunately, Hindu dominance over Indian cultural psyche to some extent is the main reason for not adopting the Buddha path by Indian society. Another reason is lack of the state support to the propagation of ideals of the Buddha in Modern India.

Modern Indian state under democratic polity outwardly accepts Buddhist ideals as state symbols. However, since polity's main concern is vote banks, and Buddhists are less in number, the agenda of Buddhist interests doesn't form part of agenda of mainstream politics. Thanks to the efforts of Ambedkar to bring back the Buddha to the mainstream consciousness. Being a father of Indian Constitution his contribution to Modern Buddhism is invaluable.[4]

Since the Buddhist heritage represented the glorious past of India, the founders of Modern India had readily adopted the Buddhist symbols as National Symbols, namely: the Lion Capital of the Asokan Pillar at Sarnath as the National Emblem and the Buddhist Wheel of Law (Dhammachakra) in the central part of the National Flag. Undoubtedly the architect of the idea of adopting Buddhist symbols into national symbols is Babasaheb Bhimrao Ambedkar, Chairman of the committee which drafted the Constitution of India, who changed the course of history by leading Millions of Dalit masses to the fold of Buddhism.

On the recommendation of B.R. Ambedkar, Pt. Nehru moved the resolution on 22nd July, 1947 to adopt Buddhist symbols as national symbols in the Constituent Assembly. The resolution as follows: Mr. President, it is my proud privilege to move the following Resolution:

"Resolved that the National Flag of India shall be horizontal tricolour of deep saffron (Kesari), white and dark green in equal proportion. In the centre of the white band, there shall be a wheel in navy blue to represent the Chakra. The design of the wheel shall be that of the Wheel (Chakra) which appears on the abacus of the Sarnath Lion Capital of Asoka. The diameter of the wheel shall be approximate to the width of the white band. The ratio of the width to the length of the Flag shall ordinarily be 2:3.... That the wheel is a symbol of India's ancient culture, it is a symbol of the many things that India had stood for through the ages. So we thought that this Chakra emblem should be there and that wheel appears.... For my part, I am exceedingly happy that in this sense indirectly we have associated with this Flag of ours not only this emblem but in a sense the name of Asoka, one of the most magnificient names not only in India's history but in world history. It is well that at this moment of strife, conflict and intolerance, our minds should go back towards what India stood for in the ancient days".

There was unanimous approval to the resolution which adopted National flag in the constituent Assembly. Asoka Dhamma Cakka symbolised with Buddha Dhamma (Wheel of Law of the Buddha) is representing freedom, social equality and justice in modern India.

Another important achievement of Buddhism in Modern India is the adoption of Lion capital of Asoka as the National Insignia. The four lions facing four directions stand for symbol of *Madhyemarga* of the Buddha. In other words, National Insignia consists of 4 Lions underneath Chakra of Dhamma. The wheel represents peace, love, compassion, justice and equality. Lion represent bravery, self respect, violent method if circumstances warranted for the protection of justice.

The image of Lord Gautama Buddha was placed on the Speaker's table when the Indian Parliament met for the first time after independence. Ambedkar in a mood of celebration felt that the Buddha had come to life once again to bless the Indians.

As Ambedkar felt, the modern India accepted the concept of

a welfare state preached and practiced by Asoka. In other words Asoka Dhamma the modernised Dhamma of the Buddha has become declared ideal of modern Indian State. Asoka profounded for the first time in the political history of India, the concept of secular state even though he was a zealous Buddhist Missionary.

Buddhist Sangha was the first evidence of notion of modern democracy and republic set up of ancient Buddhist republics - all these have been adopted by Modern Indian state. Democratic polity and republic state denouncing Hindu concept of monarchy are fundamental features of Buddhist state have been adopted by Modern Indian state thanks to the efforts of B.R. Ambedkar.

The Viceroy House during British rule now became Rashtrapati Bhavan of Independent India where President of India resides is another example of Buddhist culture. A tall meditative Buddha stands in the Durbar Hall, which is used by the President for investiture ceremonies and giving away of state awards. Next to it is the Ashoka Hall named after the Emperor Asoka. The new ministers take their solemn oaths in this Hall. Foreign Ambassadors also present their credentials to the President of India in this Hall. The famous Bull capital of Asokan pillar at Rampurva in Bihar can be seen just in front of the entrance to the Asoka Hall. The top of the 180 feet high central dome of Rashtrapati Bhavan, on which flies the National Flag, also resembles closely the Sanchi Stupa.

The Government of Independent India, to uphold the tradition of Buddhist era, adopted the Saka Era started by Kanishka the great Buddhist emperor. The Saka Era was introduced as the National Era on 22nd March 1957 corresponding to the 1st Chaitra 1879. The Saka year, like the Gregorian one has 365 days normally and 366 days in a leap year.

On 26 January 1950, India became a sovereign Democratic Republic; Preamble of the Constitution of India states:

> "JUSTICE, Social, economic and political;
> LIBERTY of thought, expression, belief, faith and worship;
> EQUALITY of status and of opportunity;
> and to promote among them all FRATERNITY assuring the dignity of the individual".[5]

Ambedkar's personal philosophy is derived from Buddhism. His philosophy is based on three principles: Liberty, equality and fraternity for justice. His philosophy has social context unlike political context as was in French Revolution. The Preamble of Indian Constitution is a fine example of Ambedkar's contribution to Buddhism in modern India.

The Constitution of India was amended in June 1990 and restored concessions to Dalit Buddhists. Thereby the Scheduled Castes order 1950 was amended and the Rights and Privileges admissible to the Scheduled Castes professing Hinduism and Sikkhism were extended to the Scheduled Castes professing Buddhism also. The act of Parliament as published in the Gazette of Government of India is given below:

Gazette Notification
Extra Ordinary Part II - Section 1
Published by Authority
Ministry of Law and Justice
(Legislative Department)

New Delhi, the 4th June, 1990 / Jyaistha 14, 1912 (Saka)

The following Act of Parliament received the assent of the President on the 3rd June 1990, and is hereby published for general information:

The Constitution (Scheduled Castes) orders (Amendment) Act, 1990 - Nov. 15 of 1990.

An Act further to amend the Constitution (Scheduled Castes) Orders, 1950 and the Constitution (Scheduled Castes) (Union Territories) Order, 1951 and to amend the Constitution (Jammu and Kashmir) Scheduled Castes Order, 1956, the Constitution (Dadra and Nagar Haveli) Scheduled Castes Order, (1962), the Constitution (Pondicherry) Scheduled Castes Order, 1964 and the Constitution (Sikkim) Scheduled Castes Order, 1978.

Be it enacted by Parliament in the Forty-first year of the Republic of India as follows:

1. This Act may be called the Constitution (Scheduled Castes) Order (Amendment) Act, 1990.
2. In paragraph 3 of the Constitution (Scheduled Castes) Order, 1950, for the words "or the Sikh", the words, "the Sikh or the Buddhist" shall be substituted.
3. In paragraph 3 of the Constitution (Scheduled Castes)

(Union Territories) Order, 1951, for the words "Or the Sikh", "the Sikh or the Buddhist" shall be substituted.

4. In the proviso to paragraph 2 of the Constitution (Jammu and Kashmir) Scheduled Castes Order, 1956, for the words "Or the Sikh", the words, "the Sikh or the Buddhist" shall be substituted.
5. In the proviso to paragraph 2 of the Constitution (Dadra and Nagar Haveli) Scheduled Castes Order, 1962, for the words "Or the Sikh", the words, "the Sikh or the Buddhist" shall be substituted.
6. In the proviso to paragraph 2 of the Constitution (Pondicherry) Scheduled Castes Order, 1964, for the words "Or the Sikh", the words, "the Sikh or the Buddhist" shall be substituted.
7. In the proviso to paragraph 2 of the Constitution (Sikkim) Scheduled Castes Order, 1978, for the words "Or the Sikh", the words, "the Sikh or the Buddhist" shall be constituted.

Sd: V.S. Rama Devi
Secy. to the Govt. of India

The following orders were issued in July 1990:
No. 12016/28/90-SCD (R.Cell)
Government of India/Bharat Sarkar
Ministry of Welfare/Kalyan Mantralaya
New Delhi, dated 31st July 1990.

To
The Secretary
Scheduled Castes/Scheduled Castes
Welfare Department of all the
State Governments/U.T. Administrations.

Subject: Removal of bar on the Scheduled Caste to Buddhism from being deemed to be members of the Scheduled Castes.

Sir,

A copy of the Constitution (Scheduled Castes) Orders (Amendment) Act, 1990, which received the assent of the President on 03.06.1990 and published in the Gazette of India on 04.06.90, is enclosed for taking further necessary action at your end.

Yours faithfully
Sd/-
(B.N. Srivastava)
Director

Govt. of India Order to all the concern Departments on the concessions to Dalit Buddhists:

IMMEDIATE
No. 1206/28/90-SCD (R.Cell)
Government of India/Bharat Sarkar
Ministry of Welfare/Kalyan Mantralaya
New Delhi
Dated: 20th November, 1990.

To
The Secretary
Social Welfare Department
Department of Dealing with the Welfare of SC/ST
of all the Sate Government/U.T. Administration
Scheduled Castes.

Subject: Removal of bar on the Scheduled Caste converts to Buddhism from being deemed to be members of the Scheduled Castes.

Sir,

In continuation of this Ministry's letter of even number dated 31.07.1990 on the above subject, I am directed to say that with the amendment of the Constitution (Scheduled Castes) Orders (Amendment) Act, 1990, the Scheduled Caste communities which are included in the Presidential Orders and converted to Buddhist religion shall be deemed to be a member of the Scheduled Caste.

2. While issuing the Scheduled Caste certificates to these persons, the same procedure has to be followed as applicable to the member of other Scheduled Caste communities belonging to Hindu and Sikh religions.
3. The form of Caste certificate will also remain the same as

applicable to other Scheduled Caste communities (Annexure).

4. All the State Governments/U.T. Administrations are, therefore, requested to follow the above procedure for issuing Scheduled Caste certificates to the persons professing Buddhist religion provided:
   (a) The name of the community for which Scheduled Caste certificate is to be issued is included in this Presidential Order specifying the Scheduled Castes in relation to the concerned State/Union Territory;
   (b) That the person and his parents actually belong to the community claimed;
   (c) That the persons belongs to that state and to the area within that in respect of which the community has been scheduled and that
   (d) The person claiming to be a Scheduled Caste professes either the Hindu, the Sikh or the Buddhist religion.
5. The certificate issuing authorities may kindly be instructed to make proper verification before issuing such certificates.

Yours faithfully

(B.N. Srivastava)
Director

No. 12016/28/90-SCD(R.Cell) dated 20th Novemner, 1990.

1. The Minister of Personnel, Public Grievances & Pensions, (Deptt. of Personnel & Training), New Delhi.
2. Secretary, UPSC, New Delhi.
3. All Ministers/Departments of the Govt. of India.
4. Secretary, Staff Selection Commission, CGO Complex, New Delhi.
5. Comptroller & Auditor General of India, New Delhi.
6. Secretary, Commission for SC and ST, Lok Nayak Bhavan, New Delhi.
7. Commissioner for SC and ST, R.K. Puram, New Delhi.
8. Secretary, Election Commission, New Delhi.

Sd/-
(B.N. Srivastava)
Director

Today Modern India with all the concern to Buddhism as discussed so far, committed for the Buddhist values. However, Indian society at large has failed to bring change in social attitude of average Indian (read ad Hindu). The social outlook of Indian society is same as was at the time of Independence (i.e., 1947).

Hindu protagonists have been carrying on malicious propaganda against the Dalit Buddhists. Buddhist scholar in foreign countries, misled by the Hindu religious and political leaders, have also been casting apprehensions on the Dalit Buddhism launched by Babasaheb Bhimrao Ambedkar. Indeed, every country which practice Buddhism has its own interpretation of the religion depending on their life styles and beliefs. Rituals, ceremonies, prayers, mode of worship and customs differ in different countries.

Worship of Hindu deities in Buddhist *Devalas*, employment of *Kapurlas* to perform priestly duties, pathetic faith in idol worship, invocation of evil spirits and worship of *Katargama* ceremonies like Bali, Thovil, Sanni Yakuma, Huniyam Rapima, Rata Yakuma, Mahasoma Samayama have no sanction in Buddhism. Even then these beliefs, rituals have been accepted by Buddhist communities according to their traditions in their own countries.

Dalit Buddhism of vast millions of Ambedkarites is based on rationality. The rational has to grow into the spiritual. A spiritual fellowship is the meaning of human history to find out earth and heaven are intermingled. Ambedkar viewed Buddhism from the point of view of the needs of modern India.

It is an age of science and humanism. Religion which is in sensitive to human ills and social crimes do not appeal to the modern man. Religion which make for division, discord and disintegration and do not foster unity, understanding and coherence, play into the hands of the opponents of religion. Dalit Buddhism is working to weed out unnecessary elements that have cropped up in the Buddhist belief system in all these years. It is trying to occupy the consciousness of an average modern man.

Like any other religion (Christianity or Islam) practised by modern societies of different countries, Buddhism has also been practised differently in different countries. In fact, Buddhism has been divided into many schools and sects since the time of Gautama

Buddha. It is even believed that the Buddhism was prevalent and dominant religion of Mohenjodaro people in Indus valley civilization. There were many Buddhas however with scanty historical evidences, for ex. Kunakamana Buddha. Even the history of Gautama Buddha was recorded hundred years after his death. Later the Buddhism has been divided into Hinayana, Mahayana, and *Vajrayana* or *Tantrayana*. In modern world Zen Buddhism and Lama Buddhism are popular in western world. So what is wrong in calling Dalit belief of Buddhism as Dalit Buddhism?

Dalit Buddhism of Ambedkar is aimed to liberate Dalits from the clutches of Hinduism. Ambedkar did not want his people to follow Hinduism. He did not believe in worshiping Hindu gods. He wanted his people to leave Hinduism and embrace Buddhism. If Dalit samaj wants to save itself, it must change the axis of its thought and life. Belief of Religion and God is intrinsic element of human thought. The question is what kind of religion and what kind of God. What requires is a religion of love and brotherhood and God of justice and equality.

Religious system needs to be capable of responding creatively to every fresh challenge. Buddhism is re-designed in the form of Dalit Buddhism to be capable of responding to the new forms of caste discrimination. It is capable of dethroning the social authority of hegemonic communities in Indian society. Hindutva is a modernised Hinduism to respond to the new challenges faced by Hindu (read Brahmin) society of modern India. Hindutva forces are methodised to work against the Dalit interests. Hindutva the cultural from of Hinduism rather weakened the social fabric of whole Indian society. The answer clearly lies in Buddhism for the liberation of Dalit masses and to re-construct a cultural world of their own with the ideals of justice, equality and fraternity.

Ambedkar has contextualised the Buddhism in the Dalit needs. He located the relevance of Buddhism in the Dalit context. The relevance of Buddhism in modern India lies in the service to Dalit society. Modern Buddhism or Dalit Buddhism needs to be Ambedkarised for safeguarding Dalit - bahujan, interests, because Ambedkar wanted to give a doctrinal basis to his religion.[6]

Dalit Buddhism is basically aimed in the construction of positive Dalit identity. The alternative formulation of Buddhism has, thus, to perceive it as a movement for human freedom and as a process for social transformation. In other words, Buddhism is part of the wider struggle against social hegemony, a struggle against caste ideology, untouchability, economic oppressions. Ambedkarism forms the nucleus of Dalit Buddhist identity.

The challenge is to deal with the marginalisation of so-called lower castes and their inferorised self-images which play an important role in constituting their identities. For instance, the Dalit Buddhist identity with an agenda for transforming the existing social structure, if articulated as a religious identity against Hindu casteist identity, could well provide an important strategy for the Ambedkarisation process. The religious identity has the potentiality to annihilate hierarchical order. Hinduism as a religion has served in many ways to legitimise the oppression of the Dalits. Buddhism as a religion of Dalits can provide alternative positive images of Dalit ideals. Cultural inferiorisation of Dalits can be removed with Buddhist identity of Dalits, which aims to provide self esteem.

Dalits as a cultural beings have sense of identity. Their cultural context needs to be positive to acquire capacity for self-representation. Dalits are to strive to recover their self-worth by organising and identifying themselves as a religious group, with a specific cultural and historical identity, which also functions as a shared religious ideology. Forming such identities would allow the Dalits as a religious group to conceive that each one of its members possessed to share in the total privilege or deprivation and a role in constituting this identity. Thus ultimately it could lead to the struggle against the forces of domination in the society. In other words, the collective positive identity is expressed by Dalits through concrete cultural struggle rooted in Buddhism, as well as in the consciousness of Dalits who see themselves as individuals representing and embodying a particular cultural tradition bounded by a collectivity of similar lives.[7]

Religious identity of Dalits is to problematise inferiorised identity i.e., Untouchable or lower caste by problematising the whole Hinduism and to construct a new social collectivity based on the Dalit Buddhist identity. This counter-hegemonic and counter-Hindutva voices of the Dalit, Buddhists articulated in terms of anti-Brahmanism. This collective Dalit Buddhist identity conditioned by historical necessities might get reformulated into various cultural codes expressed in the form of identities based on language ex: Telugu Dalit Buddhist, religion ex: Tamilnadu Dalit Buddhist, and gender, depending on Dalits' perception of reality.

In cases where Dalit Buddhist collective identity is concretely based on an acute sense of 'relative deprivation' the construction of 'the Other' is not just Hinduism but an entire hegemonic structure and the privileged groups that are perceived as a threat to Dalit individual as well as Dalit as a group identity. It is also informed by Indian history, shaped and developed through changing processes of interaction between the superordinate and the subordinate, articulating discourses of resistance and rebellion. Because Buddhism has always played the role for Dalit liberation.

Dalit-Buddhism as an ideology emerged from the dialectic of modern science and Protestantism. It is to acquire legitimacy of religion and God in Dalit life and society. It is nothing but religion playing politics of recognition and self-respect for the purpose of Dalit liberation. The emerging Dalit Buddhist identity, though not yet fully elaborated as a collective religious identity, is countering the homogenising Hindu identity and hegemonising brahmanic authority particularly in Maharashtra, Uttarpradesh and some extent in Andhra Pradesh.

Dalit Buddhism does not treat Dalits as passive recipients of socio-economic changes administered by dominant groups but are active subjects engaged in constant struggle to define their identities in relation to others. Dalit Buddhism is to retrieve Dalits as subjects of their own history. In this context, the historical moments of change is perceived as confrontations rather than transition.

Periyar Rams Swami Naicker the founder of self-respect movement in Tamil Nadu argued?

> "can rats ever get freedom because of cats?
> can fowl ever get freedom because of foxes?
> can Dalits ever get equality because of Hinduism"?[8]

Ambedkar also asks: can lion be sacrificed by Hindus in their temples? He argued that unless the Dalits become Lions they could not face Hindu cultural onslaught on their identity and privileges. Given this concern it can be argued that unless the victims of the past become active social subjects, they would not succeed in erasing their subordination and become liberated and equal. The construction of the self and its other is thus rooted in the concrete Buddhist ideology and not fixed only in terms of any privileged binary such as upper castes versus lower castes, Brahmin versus Untouchable or Buddhist versus Hindu. But the active social self is Dalit Buddhist and the other is Caste Hindu.

Periyar argued, "....you should realise that if all of you are workers, it is because you were all made into Sudras according to Varnashrama Dharma of Hindu religion. Let that pass. If workers are thought of as lowly people, it is because they (Sudras) were thought of as lowly people in Hindu religious dhamma".[9]

Even if any misguided Dalit feels to liberate himself from the Caste problems within Hindu fold, it is not possible and becomes a futile effort, because invocation of a monolithic / unproblematic Hindu identity is not a viable identity given the reality of social philosophy of Hinduism.

The danger of failure of Ambedkarism (including his rational Buddhism) lies in confining Ambedkar's critique within the post-Enlightenment of binary of rationality versus irrationality and opposing Hinduism merely at the level of 'philosophical' disputes. The opposition to Hinduism has to be carried out by encountering concrete situations of power relations. In other words, struggle based on Dalit Buddhist identity must become a site of contestation against Hindu ideology.

Change of religion is prior condition for the liberation of the Dalits. Dalit Buddhism provides social collectivity on Dalits' own terms. The liberation of Dalits will become an unrealisable dream if they are to remain within the Hindu fold. Given this reasoning, Ambedkar advocated conversion of Dalits to Buddhism. Ambedkar wanted Dalits to enter into relations of power based on religious identity. In displacing the current contradictions within the Dalit communities, the Ambedkarism constructs a distinct Dalit Buddhist past/history.

Ambedkar's rationalism wants to end unreason and blind faith in the Hindu Gods. He is opposed to worship of Hindu Gods. Ambedkar however was pleading for real faith in God. He meant by real faith, prayer to God through service and work which would be related to the generating of faith in society. Ambedkar has always tried to see that his people do not lose faith in God. Who is that God of Dalits? Ambedkar looked at Gautama Buddha as *margadata* a great teacher and not as a God. The whole fight of Dalits is against Hinduism and Gods of Hinduism and not against the very concept of belief in God and identities of other religions like Sikkhism, Islam and Christianity.

The question is not about existence of God but belief in God. Social equality, justice, fraternity are not in opposition to God, but to Hindu Gods. Hinduism as a religion represented by Hindu Gods may not be allowing Dalits to gain social respect and opportunities by forming hegemonic identity, but other religions Sikhism, Islam, Christianity and Buddhism and identity of God in these religions are not opposed to Dalit's interests. Ambedkar had consideration to all these religions before he embraced Buddhism. It shows, Ambedkar understood the importance of faith in God for the Dalits. He afraid that belief in God might land up Dalits again in Hindu fold. His rationalised Buddhism is an outcome of this fear. However, there were many instances that prove that Ambedkar recognised the role of God in the religion provided that God stands for Dalit cause.

Dalit Buddhism is a further developed form of rational Buddhism of Ambedkar. Briefly speaking Dalit Buddhism locates itself in the context of Dalit as indigenous tribe lived prior to Aryan invasion to India. They were inhabitants of Indus civilisation and Mohenjodaro was their capital. Their religion was Dhammam or Adi Buddhism, the earliest form of Buddhism. Dalits were the followers of Buddham means God. Buddhism is Adi Buddha the earliest Buddha. Adi Buddha means beginning of enlightenment. Buddham the Dalit God was formless hence not worshiped in the form of any idol. The idol worshipers were dwellers at Harappa who were Dravidans. Therefore Indus civilisation rightly can be termed as Dalito - dravidian civilisation. This brief understanding of Dalit Buddhism makes us to note that Dalits' belief in their own God identified with Buddhism is a historical necessity to strengthen their social bargain capacity in the form of collective religious identity for better social position in the society.

The formation of identity is a dialectical process of inclusion and exclusion and a process of constituting the self and other. Absence of positive Dalit identity makes Dalits to identify themselves with Hindu identity. This subordination of Dalit identity to Hindu identity is because Dalit is a political identity not religious. To dehinduvise Dalit identity it needs to be religiocised by Buddhism.

De-Hinduvisation of Dalits is possible only through the positive social identity based on Buddhist religion. Dalit Buddhist identity cannot be appropriated by Hindu identity because of two reasons: one - Buddhism has identity of world religion, two - identity of Lord Buddham (Adi Buddha) as a God serves Dalit cause. Hindu identity can never be successful because it is fundamentally opposed to Dalit dignity. Hindu identity is to promote Brahminism through the slogan of Hindu unity and to create enmity among oppressed groups. Dalit Buddhism is the inclusion of two identities: Dalit and Buddhist. Dalits need religion of their own and God of their own for spiritualisation of Dalit Samaj to strengthen alternative cultural forms that aim to demolish Hindu images in the Dalit consciousness and in turn to build strong Dalit politics. Thus the true India or Bharat can be evolved on the strength of SANGAM (the ancient Buddhist name, prior to Gautama Buddha, for the Dalit community or Dalit Samaj).

Now the question arises: Is there God in Buddhism? The answer is Big Yes. Then what is the name of the God in Buddhism? All the schools and sects of Buddhism believe that Gautama Buddha is not a God. He is a great teacher for mankind. He showed the path of wisdom, compassion, and reality as essence of life. His philosophy has not born out of context. It is very much in tune with already prevailing Buddhist beliefs. Gautama Buddha revived Buddhism which was in decline at his time. He injected new oxygen into the already existing Buddhism by new orientation. Buddhism of the Gautama Buddha was born out of already prevailing Adi Buddhism. Gautama Buddha rationalised Adi Buddhism and scientised and called it Buddhism.

If Gautama Buddha is not a God then who is the God in Buddhism. As earlier said that Buddhism was prevalent as a religion even before the birth of the Gautama Buddha. The

Buddhism was even a dominant religion of people of Mohenjodaro in Indus civilisation and their God was Buddham who was Adi Buddha, means the beginning of enlightenment. It seemed that they did not worship Adi Buddha in idols but in symbols and mostly had scared writings in the form of short inscriptions with pictures on the seals. Theravada Buddhism still contains most of the features of Adi Buddhism. That is why Ambedkar had embraced Theravada Buddhism.

Gautama Buddha maintained silence on the question of whether God exists or not. But he never said that there is no need of God for man. The Buddha felt that the debate on the existence of God was waste of time and not useful to mankind. But he never said God is not useful to mankind. Everything which is useful to mankind is part of Buddhist belief. If God is useful to mankind then he must be a true God. If God is not useful and harmful to mankind he must be a false God. This is the true understanding of Gautama Buddha's silence on the question of whether God exists or not.

Did Ambedkar deny God? Ambedkar denied the importance of Hindu Gods for human society. He felt there is no need to worship God in Hindu form. He worshiped the Buddha Dhamma as a God. For Ambedkar God is Dhamma - the path of enlightenment, that is *Madhyema Marga*. Dhamma means Middle Path. Is Ambedkar's denial of God coming under the Middle Path. Some scholars misunderstood the whole philosophy of *Madhyama Marga* which led to wrong interpretation of teachings of Gautama Buddha as well as Ambedkar. Both the prophets of Buddhism indeed never said God is not necessary for mankind. Because denial of God is against the Middle Path of Buddhism. How could they go against middle path, which is the very essence of Buddhism.

Gautama Buddha and Ambedkar did not want people to worship Hindu Gods. In the context of Hinduism, Ambedkar said don't worship God but in general he is not against the worship of God. Dalit fight against Varna / Jati Dharma is to do with Hinduism. Dalit question in opposition to God needs to be located in the Hindu context. Dalits' opposition to very belief of God is neither useful to their cause nor in tune with the Middle Path of Buddhism. Dalit success lies in the adoption of Middle Path that is not to believe in Hindu Gods, Hindu social and religious system and Hindu philosophy but at the same time to have faith in the true God, true religious philosophy and true social and religious system.

Buddham is the true God: *Buddham Sharanam Gachami*; the true God of Dalits.

Dhammam is the true religion: *Dhammam Sharanam Gachami*; the true religion of Dalits

Sangham is the true society: *Sangham Sharanam Gachami*; the true society of Dalits.

To establish Sangham the true Dalit samaj or society, there is a need of Dhammam, the true religious philosophy of Buddham, the true God.

At the time of the Buddha, Buddhists recited the tri Sharana. Even Gautama Buddha recited the tri Sharana. When Gautama Buddha recited 'Buddham Sharanam Gachami' which Buddha he was referring about. It was Buddham - Adi Buddha the God of Gautama Buddha. In other words Gautama Buddha and Ambedkar believed in the worship of true God. Ambedkar did not say not to worship God in his 22 Buddhist's Oaths but said not to worship Hindu Gods.

Middle Path is the essence of Dhamma of Adi Buddhism or Dalit Buddhism. Lord Adi Buddha the true God of mankind was very much the God of ancient Dalits since the days of Indus valley civilisation. Pavithra Dhamma was the sacred belief of ancient Dalits. Sangha was ancient Dalit Samaj. Ancient Dalits realised the true God Lord Adi Buddha by following the path of Pavithra Dhamma. Sangha the ancient Dalit Samaj was religio-political society. We find many Buddhist symbols in the form of pictographic writings of Mohenjodaro people on the seals of Indus civilisation. Pavithra Dhamma was the sacred writing of ancient Dalit Buddhists. Retracing Pavithra Dhamma from the available mesopotamian, Pali, Sinhali sources might help us to re-construct the religious ideas, beliefs and traditions of ancient Dalit Buddhists.

The broad understanding of existing Buddhist ideas, beliefs in the Dalit context, make us some extent to trace the religious beliefs of ancient Dalits in the form of Pavithra Dhamma. As it is discussed earlier that the ancient Dalits were followers of

Adi Buddha and *Pavithra Dhamma* the sacred writings inscribed on the seals of Indus and mentioned in the Contemporary Mesopotamian texts.[10] The major sources are Indus seals and Mesopotamian records to know religion, culture, society, polity and economic life of ancient Dalits. Hindu literature like Rigveda and other Vedas etc are also useful for the purpose.

The Mesopotamian records mention the word Meluha for Indus region. The ancient name of the river Indus was Meluha. Sindhu is Sanskrit name, given by Hindus (Aryans), who invaded India. Therefore Sindhu civilisation is not right to identify Meluha river civilisation. Recently, hindu historians are trying to dig out mythical Sarasvati river to identify Indus Civilisation. Some historians called it Harappa civilisation just because Harappa was the first site found by the archaeologists. Identity of Sarasvati river civilisation to Indus region is unhistorical. It is an effort to communalise identity of Indus region. Harappa is just a name of one sight and not as important as Mohenjodaro. Harappa civilisation is misnomer widely popularised by some historians because of its similarity with the Hindu word 'Hara'. Harappa is a politicised term given by motivated historians.

According to a tradition, Lord Adi Buddha was the God of ancient Dalit tribe whom the Dalits called as Buddham means true God. Ancient Dalit Buddhists believed that God Lord Buddham first created Mother Meluha from whom created first man called Bharat, from their union born the whole humanity of Dalit race, the indigenous people of the land called Bharat. Dalits built great civilisation on the banks of river Meluha (Indus). Intra - tribal conflicts cropped up. Dalits fought themselves for supremacy over each other to rule the land of Bharata. Consequently they divided themselves into two groups namely - 'Dalit and Dravidian'. They made Mohenjodaro and Harappa as their capitals respectively to rule over the land of Bharat. Aryans the barbaric nomadic tribes form central Asian region invaded the land Bharat and destroyed the great Dalit civilisation. The destruction of Meluha culture or Dalito-dravidian culture forced the dalit and dravidian tribes to migrate different places. Aryans followed the policy of divide and rule. They alligned with Dravidians who became part of Aryan culture and were co-opted into the Aryan social system as *Shudra*.

Some of Dalits were captured by Aryans and made them untouchables and some who were untouched by Aryan culture lived in forests and in course of time developed new tribal identities and new religious beliefs.

Dalits were forcibly converted to Hindu religion by Aryan rulers. Thus Dalits were divided into numerous castes and subcastes because of Hindu religion. Dalit was originally a Buddhist tribe, split into several castes after forcible conversion to Hinduism. Therefore Dhammam or Adi Buddhism was religion of ancestors of Dalits. Adi Buddhism is acceptance of the will of God Lord Buddham, the Adi Buddha, that is Dhammam, the Adi Dhamma the path of enlightenment or Madhyama Marga (Middle Path) to attain (Sangham) heaven on this earth and in this world. Dalit Buddhists regard Gautama Buddha, Asoka and Ambedkar as the three great prophets of Buddhism. Gautama Buddha developed Buddhism out of Adi Buddhism. His Dhamma is continuity of already prevalent Adi Dhamma of his times. Gautama Buddha is not a moksha data. He is a *Margadata*. Dalit Buddhists of modern India believe that Gautama Buddha showed Marga (true path) - Adi Dhamma.

Modern Dalit Buddhism is the product of Ambedkarism. Ambedkar liberated Dalits from Hinduism to come back to the religion of their ancestors. He declared in the Yeola conference on 13, October, 1935 that he was born a Hindu, but he would not die a Hindu. In the Bombay conference on 30-31, May 1936, he declared that conversion was the only path to freedom for untouchables. He declared after his conversion to Buddhism, "This conversion has given me enormous satisfaction and pleasure unimaginable. I feel as if I have been liberated from hell".[11] For Ambedkar Hinduism is hell and Buddhism is heaven on earth.

Ambedkarism has contributed for the development of Dalit Buddhism in Modern India.[12] Buddhism has made tremendous progress in independent India. As against less than two lakh Buddhist population in 1947, India now has around one crore Buddhists. A large number of Buddha viharas have come up in various parts of India. Many Bhikkhus and Buddhist scholars have contributed in the post - Ambedkar era for the growth of Buddhism in Modern India.

Post–Ambedkar development of Buddhism

Among Buddhist societies the Maha Bodhi Society of India (Calcutta), The Buddhist society of India (Bhartiya Baudh Maha Sabha, Bombay), Trailokya Baudha Maha Sangha Sahayaka Gana (Pune), Bengal Buddhist Association (Calcutta) are important one. There are other Buddhist societies in India who are also important. They are namely: (1) Lohit Bodhi Society (Arunachal Pradesh), (2) All Assam Buddhist Association (Assam), (3) International Brotherhood Mission (Assam) (4) Ladakh Buddhist Association (Jammu & Kashmir) (5) Indian Buddhist Council (Maharashtra) (6) All Tripura Rajya Buddhist Association (Tripura) (7) Punjab Buddha Mahasabha (Jalandhar) (8) Sikkim Buddhist Association (Sikkim) (9) All Mizoram Buddhist Association (Mizoram) (10) Meghalaya Buddhist Association (Meghalaya).

(I) The contribution of the Buddhist society of India to Modern Buddhism is worth to be discussed. The Buddhist society of India or Bhartiya Baudh Maha Sabha is located at Ambedkar Bhavan, Gokuldas Pasta Road, Dadar, Bombay - 400 014. It was founded by Ambedkar in 1955 to take care of the interests of Dalit Buddhists. Under the auspices of the Buddhist society of India, Ambedkar embraced Buddhism. Yashwant Ambedkar, son of Ambedkar was elected President of this society after the death of Ambedkar. He organised the first All India Buddhist conference in Bombay to coincide with the inauguration of the memorial stupa at Chaitya Bhoomi in November 1968. After the death of Yashwant Ambedkar his wife Mrs. Miratai Ambedkar was elected President of the Buddhist society of India.

The second All India Buddhist conference was held by the society at Nagpur in October 1980. The third All India Buddhist Delegates conference of the Buddhist society of India was held at Ambedkar Bhavan, New Delhi, on 18-19 March 1989. Some of the important branches of the Buddhist society of India are:

(1) Bhartiya Baudh Maha Sabha, Ambedkar Bhavan, Rani Jhansi Road, New Delhi - 110 055.
(2) Bhartiya Baudh Maha Sabha, Lucknow, Uttar Pradesh.
(3) Buddhist society of India, Siddharth Niwas, Hyderabad - 4, Andhra Pradesh.

(4) Buddhist society of India, Buddha Vihara, Siddharth Nagar, Jalandhar - 144003, Punjab.
(5) Bhartiya Baudh Maha Sabha, Babar Bhaika Pitha, Madan Jhampa Road, Baroda, Gujarat.

(II) The people's Education Society founded by Ambedkar on 8 July 1945 is also one of the important Buddhist organisations in Modern India. It's works are mainly in the field of education. It is situated in Anand Bhavan, near fountain, Dr. Dadabhai Naorji Road, Bombay - 1.

Ambedkar had established Siddharth College of Arts, Science and Commerce (1946), Siddharth College of Commerce and Economics (1953) and Siddharth College of Law (1956). The People's Education Society since has established two more colleges at Bombay namely Dr. Ambedkar College of Commerce and Economics at Wadala (1972) and Dr. Ambedkar College of Law at Wadala (1977).

Ambedkar also had established Siddharth Night High School at Buddha Bhavan, Bombay. People's Education Society since then established many institutions at Bombay, which are namely: Dr. Babasaheb Ambedkar memorial Research Centre, Rajgriha, Dadar; Siddarth College of Mass Communications, Anand Bhavan; Siddharth Institute of Industry and Administration, Anand Bhavan; Siddharth English Medium School, Wadala; and Siddharth Vihar Hostel, Wadala. The Institutions established at the New Mumbai campus are: Marathi Medium Secondary School and Junior College; Dr. Babasaheb Ambedkar Public School; Junior College of Education; and Marathi Medium Primary School.

At the Nagasenvana campus at Aurangabad, Ambedkar had established in 1951 the Milind Mahavidyalaya, a multifacultied college. In course of time it developed into three independent Colleges, namely Milind College of Science; Dr. Babasaheb Ambedkar College of Arts and Commerce (1960); and Milind College of Arts (1963). Another College, Dr. Ambedkar College of Law, was established at Aurangabad in 1968. The other institutions at Aurangabad are: Milind Multi - purpose High School (established by Ambedkar in 1955); People's Education Society's College of Physical Education; People's Education Society's English Medium Primary and Pre-primary School; Matoshri Ramabai Ambedkar High School, New Aurangabad; and Buddhist centre.

The People's Education Society had also established the education institutions which are namely: Dr. Ambedkar College of Arts, Science & Commerce, Mahad; Dr. Ambedkar College of Arts and Commerce, Yerwada, Pune; Nagasen High School, Nanded; Nagasen Vidyalaya and Nagasen Junior College of Arts and Commece; Gautam Vidyalaya, Pandherpur, Maharashtra; Nagasen Vidyalaya, Bangalore. The People's Education Society has also established hostels at Bombay, Mahad, Dapoli, Aurangabad, and Nanded for the benefit of Dalit Buddhists.

(III) Trailokya Bauddha Maha Sangha Sahayaka Gana situated in Dapodi, Pune is also working among Dalit Buddhists. It was founded in March 1979 by Sangharakshita an English Buddhist Monk. He was influenced by Ambedkar. He helped the new Buddhist movement in India to survive and grow. He was a Theravada Monk later converted to Mahayana and like Ambedkar believed that Buddhism is one irrespective of the presence of numerous sects and groups and all must work and grow together.

Dhammachari Lokamitra another England born missionary took up the Dhamma work after Sangharakshita left for London. He started the Trailokya Bauddha Mahasangha in Pune in 1979. He attributed the spirit and inspiration behind the foundation of the Mahasangha to the Dhamma Diksha day celebrations at the Deeksha Bhoomi in Nagpur in October 1978 held by Dalit Buddhists. He witnessed the gathering of half a million Dalit Buddhists in one place at the Deeksha Bhoomi. The 'Trailokya Buaddha Mahasangha Sahayaka Gana' is mostely active in Maharashtra. It also spread its activities in Goa, Gujarat, Madhya Pradesh, Uttar Pradesh and Andhra Pradesh.

The Sahayaka Gana is primarily a lay Buddhist organisation. Members of Gana are much more than the ordinary upasakas and they are called Dhammacharis and Dhammacharinis. Trailokya Bauddha Maha Sangha Sahayaka Gana is not a monastic order. Most of its members are house holders while some are not. Those who take the Brahmacharya precept, lead the fully celibate life, even taking the yellow robes; are called as Angarikas. The Gana is not interested in converting others to Buddhism. However it works among Dalit Buddhists to follow the foot steps of Babasaheb

Bhimrao Ambedkar. It teaches Ambedkar and Buddhism. The centres of the Gana after intensive classes on Buddhism and meditation. It also undertakes social programmes under the name of the Bahujan Hitay. Its social work consist of two types namely (1) Wealth and education in urban and (2) hostels for village children. It also involved in publications of Buddhist literature.

There are number of Buddha Viharas contributing for popularising Buddhism in Modern India. Most of the Viharas have come up after Ambedkar conversion to Buddhism. Maharashtra is studded with Buddha Viharas. Nagpur being the place of Ambedkar's Dhamma Deeksha, it has the largest number of Buddha Viharas. Delhi has the second largest concentration of Buddha Viharas. Today in India thanks to growing popularity of Ambedkarism, in almost every state, a number of Viharas have come up. The rapid increase in the number of Viharas are due to cater the religious needs of the growing Buddhist population.

Important Buddhist Centres

(A) Buddha Gaya

Buddha Gaya in Bihar was the place where Siddhartha Gautama Buddha attained Sambodhi, Supreme Enlightenment and became a Buddha, the Enlightened one. Because of the place of Enlightenment, the Buddhist countries of South East Asia built many Buddhist temples and Viharas at Buddha Gaya. The important temples are: the Burmese Temple, the Tibetan Temple, the Chinese Temple, Thai Buddhist Temple (wat Thai), Bhutanese Temple, Japanese Temple (Indosan Nipponi), Daijokyo Buddhist Temple, Karmapa Tibetab Temple, Korean Temple, Twaiwanese Temple, Tai Bodhi kam monastery, Vietnamese Monastry, Bangladesh Buddhist Monastery, Sakyapa Monastery and Internation Meditation Centre near the Great Maha Bodhi Temple.

(B) Rajgir

Rajgir in Bihar (Rajagriha, the capital of Bimbisara during the time of the Buddha) is the place of Vishwa Shanti Stupa (world peace pagoda). It was built by Fuji Guruji, the founder of the Japan Buddha Sangha. It is 160 feet high, gold-topped Pagoda. Rajgir has also a Burmese Buddhist Temple.

(C) Nava Nalanda Mahavihara:-

Bhikku Jagdish Kashyap founded the Nava Nalanda Mahavihara at Nalanda in Bihar. There are also other Buddhist Temples at Nalanda namely: The Japanese Buddhist Temple, Chinese Buddhist Temple, Tibetan Buddhist Temple and Thai monastery.

(D) Sarnath

The ancient name of Sarnath was Isipatana. The holy Isipatana was the place where the Gautama Buddha had delivered His First Sermon. Angarika Dharmapala constructed the Mulagandhakuti Vihara and was inagurated in November 1931. Today, Sarnath consists of Buddhist Temples belonged to Burma, China, Japan, Korea, Thailand and Tibet.

(E) Sravasti

It was famous in ancient period for its Jetavana Monastery built by Anathapindika for the use of the Buddha and where the Buddha had spent about 19 Vassas (Retreats). In modern times it has Srilankan, Burmese, Thai and Chinese temples.

(F) Kushinagar

It is a place of Buddha's Maha Parinirvana. Ven. U. Chandramuni Dhamma - Guru of Babasaheb Bhimrao Ambedkar established Burmese Buddha Vihara. The Buddhists of Korea, Japan, Thailand and Tibet have recently established Buddhist Temples and monasteries at Kushinagar.

There are number of Buddhist centres in modern towns and cities in India: **(1) Deeksha Bhoomi:** Nagpur is the place of Deeksha Bhoomi, where great prophet Ambedkar performed the Great miracle on 14th October 1956 the holiest prophets day or Deeksha Diwas of Dalit Buddhists. It is believed that Pavithra (sacred) prophet Gautama Buddha from heavens came down to the Deeksha Bhoomi to bless Ambedkar and showed him the path of true Dhamma. It is to remind the readers that according to the belief of Dalit Buddhists the path to realise true God is the Path of Pavithra Dhamma (Madhyama Marga or Middle Path as a way of life to reach to the hights of satisfaction or bliss of life). The grand memorial Stupa (Pagoda) has been constructed at Deeksha Bhoomi.

Bhadant Anand Kausalyayan, a Punjabi Buddhist monk had contributed greatly to make Deeksha Bhoomi a living religious centre of Dalit Buddhism. He established Buddha Vihara, Bhikku Niwas and sacred Bodhi Tree at Deeksha Bhoomi. It is a sacred shrine of Dalit Buddhists. Every year in October, on the Vijaya Dashmi Day millions of Dalit Buddhists from all over India gather at Deeksha Bhoomi for Great Prayer and to remember their liberator.

Among more than 40 Buddha Viharas in Nagpur the most important Vihara apart from Deeksha Bhoomi is the Vihara in Indore established by Bhadant Surai Sasai, a Japanese monk settled in India, who almost liberated Great Maha Bodhi Temple, Buddha Gaya from the clutches of the Hindu dominated Management Committee.

Bhadant Anand Kausalyayan founded another famous Buddhist centre and called it 'Buddha Bhoomi', at Khairi near Nagpur. At Chicholi near Nagpur, there is another important Buddhist centre which includes a Buddha Vihara and Ambedkar Museum, established by Bharatiya Bauddha Parishad (Indian Buddhist Council) in 1975.

(2) Chaitya Bhoomi: Chaitya Bhoomi stupa at Shivani Park, Bombay (Mumbai) is another holy place of Dalit Buddhists. It was built on the site where Ambedkar was cremated on 7th December 1956 and it was unveiled on 24 November 1968.

There are also many important Viharas in Mumbai (Bombay). Babasaheb Ambedkar himself built Nalanda Vihara at Khar. The people's Education Society built Siddharth Vihara at Wadala. Bahujana Vihara is another important one was built by Dharmananda Kosambi at Parel and was late taken over by the Maha Bodhi Society in 1950. Japanese Buddha Vihara was built by Fuji Guruji at Worli.

Indeed, Maharashtra is the state with a largest Dalit Buddhist population. In every town in Maharashtra there are number of Buddhist Viharas. Ambedkar had himself installed an image of the Buddha in the Buddha Vihara at Dehu road, Pune, which was consecrated on 25 December the day of Christmas in 1955.

There is a remarkable edifice in Pune called as the 'Dhammachakra Pravartan Maha Vihar' at Dapodi. It was built by

Trailokya Baudha Mahasangha. It is the most impressive Vihara built in Maharashtra in modern times. It has a large shrine room, a library with a good collection of books on Buddhism, Ambedkarism and social work. It also consists of Bahujana Hitay Trust, a residential training centre in Dhamma and social work.

(3) Janma Bhoomi: MHOW in Madhya Pradesh is the birth place of Babasaheb Bhimrao Ambedkar. The Govt. of Madhya Pradesh has constructed a Buddhist stupa in memory of Ambedkar. Madhya Pradesh was the ancient land of Buddhism. The most important modern Buddha Vihara is the Cetiyagiri Vihara at Sanchi in which are preserved the sacred relics of Sariputta and Mahamoggallana, situated on the Chetiya Giri Hills.

(4) Bangalore: Maha Bodhi Society, Bangalore was founded by Ven. Achariya Buddharakkhita in 1956. The society has built Maha Bodhi world peace Buddha Temple and was inaugurated on the Buddha Purnima day May 14, 1995. It is a replica of Maha Bodhi Temple at Bodhgaya. The root has a huge Gopuram on the lines of Bodhgaya Temple with two smaller Gopurams in front. The main Gopuram is a nine storyed structure on top of which rises the great Ashokan style stupa. It is a place of worship, meditation and pilgrimage for devotees from India and abroad and also it is a centre for educational, cultural, social and humanitarian service activities.

(5) Ambedkar Bhavan at Delhi: The place where Ambedkar lived and died and still it is regarded as a place for Dalit Buddhists to gather and remember Ambedkar.

(6) Hyderabad: A giant statue of Lord Buddha was erected by Government of Andhra Pradesh is a major land mark in the Buddhist history of Andhra Pradesh. The 60 feet high statue of the Buddha carved from a single rock has been installed on the Gibraltor Rock in the Hussainsagar Lake situated in the middle of the twin cities of Hyderabad and Secunderabad.

(7) Jyotinagar: It is a famous centre of Buddhist knowledge in Assam. International Brotherhood Mission, Jyotinagar, Dibrugarh was founded by Ven. Achariya Bhikkhu Karma Shastry. The I.B. Mission founded Dr. B.R. Ambedkar Ideal Academy (Ashramic School) in Jyotinagar which works for the development of Buddhism. The sacred 'Bone-Relic' of Lord

Gautama Buddha brought by Thai delegation was installed in the shrine room of the Maha Bodhi Vihara constructed by I.B. Mission.

Bhikkhus who contributed to Buddhism in Modern India.

(1) Ven. U. Chandramani Maha Thera

'Saba U' was born in Burma in 1876 in a devout Buddhist family. In 1888, he was ordained as sramanera and was given the name ' Chanda' in place of his original name 'Saba U'. Ven. U. Chandima sent two sramaneras namely Chanda and Surya to Calcutta in 1891 to assist Angarika Dharmapala, the founder of the Maha Bodhi Society. Chanda late became famous as U Chandramani. Chanda went back to Burma in 1899 and pursued Pali studies. He studied Pali Tripitaka and attained mastery in Pali and Buddhist philosophy. He received higher ordination (Upasampada) at the Ramu grama Vihara on the full-moon day of Magha in 1903. Thereafter, he came back to India for missionary work.

Ven. U Chandramani started his missionary work from Kushinagar. Under the guidance of Ven. Mahavira he tried to develop the sacred Nirvana Temple at Kushinagar. The Nirvana Temple was in the possession of the Archaeological Survey of India and was almost left without proper arrangements for Buddhists to worship in the temple. Ven. U Chandramani took up the matter with the Government and managed to get its possession as well as permission to worship in the temple. In 1904 thus the glory was restored to the ancient Nirvana Temple.

The 1500 year old Nirvana statue represents the Dying Buddha reclining on his right side with face turned towards the west. It is belived that the reclining Buddha image is on the very spot where Lord Gautama Buddha had his last breath (attained Maha Parinirvana).

Ven. U. Chandramani translated Dhammapada and Pali Suttas into Hindi. He constructed a Buddha Vihara at Sravasti, Lumbini and Somnath. In 1924, for the first time he organised the Buddha Jayanti function at Kushinagar. In 1927, he repaired and restored the main stupa. The Matha-Kaur Temple at Kushinagar was also built and consecrated by Ven. Chandramani. It was built in 1928 out of the donations of two Burmese Buddhists namely U Pokyo and Upo Hlaing.

Ven. U. Chandramani had made his contribution to thc field of education also. In 1929, he established a free primary School at Kushinagar. In 1934, he started the Buddha High School. In 1936, he established the Maha parinirvana Sanskrit Paathshala which is now functioning at Kasia. He established the Mahavir Junior School at Kushinagar in 1944. As a whole he contributed for the development of Kushinagar as a centre of Buddhism.

Ven. U. Chandramani had the proud privilege of being the Dhamma- Guru of Babasaheb B.R. Ambedkar who embraced Buddhism at his hands on 14 October 1956 at Nagpur and brought millions of Dalits to the fold of Buddhism. Ven. U. Chandramani Maha Thera passed away at Kushinagar on 8 May 1972.

(2) Ven. K. Sriniwasa Nayaka Thera

He was born in Sri Lanka in 1891. In 1900 he was ordained as Samanera. In 1920 he came to India on the invitation of Angarika Dharmapala and involved in the missionary work of the Maha Bodhi society. He concentrated his missionary activities in the Sravasti - Lumbini region and built Buddha Viharas. He travelled extensively in India, Nepal and Burma. He passed away at Sarnath in 1968.

(3) Ven. D. Sasanasiri Maha Nayaka Thera

He was born in 1899 in Sri Lanka. In 1914 he took Pabajja and in 1920 he received Upasampada (higher ordination). On the invitation of Angarika Dharmapala, founder of the Maha Bodhi Society, he came to India to train the Samaneras for spreading Buddhism in India.

Ven. Sasanasiri Maha Nayaka Thera in 1930 became the head of International Buddhist Institute (Dhammaduta Training School). Later he became incharge of almost all the centres of the Maha Bodhi Society. In 1949 finally he settled at Sarnath. There were many famous disciples followed the foot steps of Ven. Sasanasiri namely Bhikkus Katayayana, Rashtrapal, Vimalsheel, Sugatanand, Dharmakirti, Medhankar, Shobhit, Bodhanand, Vishudhanand.

Ven. Sasanasiri has translated Ashvaghosha's Ṡanskrit treatise 'Bodhichariyavatara' into Sinhalese. 'Buddh-Ki-Den' is his most important publication in Hindi. He had served as Professor of Pali in the Dharmapala Degree College, Sarnath. He died in 1966.

(4) Bhadant Anand Kausalyayan

Harnamdas was born in 1905 in a village near Chandigarh and later became Brahmachari Vishvanath under the influence of Arya Samaj. He became Buddhist and rechristined himself as Bhadant Anand Kausalyayan, when he found no satisfaction in the philosophy of Arya Samaj. He embraced Buddhism on 10 February, 1928 in Sri Lanka. He had known B.R. Ambedkar since 1944 and had met him a number of times. Indeed Ambedkar had even consulted him as to the modalities to be adopted at the historic conversion ceremony.

Bhadant Anand Kausalyayan was very much involved with Ambedkarites to spread Dhamma. On 6 December 1956 when Babasaheb suddenly passed away in sleep at his Delhi residence, Bhadant Anand Kausalyayan immediately rushed to 26 Alipur Road and took charge of the arrangements for the great leader's funeral. He accompanied Babasaheb's body to Bombay, along with a dozen other persons. The plane landed at Bombay Airport at 02 a.m. on 7 December and the body was taken to Rajgriha, Ambedkar's residence in Dadar, where it lay in state for public veneration pending preparations for the funeral procession. More than half a million people from all over Maharashtra participated in the funeral procession, the biggest such procession, ever seen in the city of Bombay and it took nearly four hours to cover a short distance from Rajgraha to the local cremation ground near Shivaji park.[13]

When Babasaheb Ambedkar embraced Buddhism on 14 October 1956, along with half a million of his followers at Nagpur, Bhadant Anand Kausalyayan was away in China leading the official Indian delegation to participate in the 2500th Buddha Jayanti celebrations in that country. However he participated conversion ceremony held at the cremation ground of Ambedkar. Indeed, Babasaheb Ambedkar had planned a mass conversion ceremony in Bombay on 16 December 1956. To fulfil his wish an important conversion ceremony was organised at the cremation ground, more than one lakh people were administered the Tri Sarana and Panch Sila on the spot by Bhadant Anand Kausalyayan after under his guidance Babasaheb's Ambedkar's last rites were performed, according to Buddhist tradition and his mortal remains were consigned to the flames in the midst of the chanting of Pali Suttas by the venerable monks.[14]

Babasaheb Ambedkar had left behind him lakhs of Buddhist followers who were in need of a strong Buddhist (religious) leader particularly in Maharashtra. That is why Anand Kausalyayan decided to make Maharashtra his field of activity. He travelled and guided Maharashtra Dalit Buddhists. He also translated Babasaheb Bhimrao Ambedkar's monumental work 'The Buddha and His Dhamma' into Hindi for the benefit of the masses. While doing so, he also laboriously traced all the original sources from the Pali Tripitaka, which Babasaheb had not done. This Hindi edition of 'The Buddha and His Dhamma' was published by the People's Education Society, Bombay in 1960.[15]

Bhadant Anand Kausalyayan had made Deeksha Bhoomi the sacred site where Babasaheb Ambedkar had converted himself to Buddhism. The Bhikkhu Niwas founded by him there soon became a popular centre of learning. His first book was on Ambedkar entitled as 'Yade Baba Na Hote' a biography of Babasaheb Ambedkar in 1968. He also translated 'The Buddha and His Dhama' of Ambedkar into Punjabi.

Bhadant Anand Kausalyayan continuously engaged himself in nourishing and sustaining Ambedkar's Buddhist movement. He left Deeksha Bhoomi in 1982 and founded another Buddhist centre at Kampte Road, Nagpur and named it Buddha Bhoomi. He was a close friend, guide, philosopher and Guru of Dalit Buddhists. He died at Nagpur in 1988.

(5) Bhikkhu Jagdish Kashyap

Jagdish Narain the earlier name of Jagdish Kashyap was born in Bihar in 1908. Former Arya Samaj activist and disenchanted with the Arya Samaj he embraced Buddhism. He met Rahul Sankrityayan at Patna and with his help he was able to go Sri Lanka in 1933 for studies in Buddhism and Pali literature. Later he joined with Rahul Sankrityayan and Anand Kausalyayan to spread the message of Dhamma. Indeed the trio played a major role in a variety of ways in the revival of Buddhism in India.

Jagdish Kashyap moved to Sarnath in 1937. He became part of Maha Bodhi Society. Thus, the trio Rahul Sankrityayan, Anand Kausalyayan and Jagdish Kashyap translated Pali Tipitaka into Hindi. Jagdish Kashyap apart from literary activities was also involved in social work. He was instrumental to start the teaching of Pali in Banaras Hindu University. Later he got an inner call to spread Buddhism in Bihar. He popularised Pali (Magadhi) in Gaya and Nalanda. Nava Nalanda Mahavihara the brain child of Kashyap was started serving the purpose of Buddhism and Pali studies. He translated Tipitaka in Pali (Devanagari).

Jagdish Kashyap had also involved in the Ambedkar and Dalit Buddhist movement. Apart from Maharashtra, he mainly spread Dhamma among Dalits in Rajasthan and Uttar Pradesh. He passed away in 1976 and was cremated at Nalanda in the vicinity of the Nava Nalanda Mahavihara, the Pali Research Institute created by him.

(6) Ven. Neluwe Jinaratana Nayaka Maha Thera

He was born in 1913 in Sri Lanka. In 1929, Ven. P. Vipulatissa Maha Thera ordained Jinaratana as Samanera at Pannagale Vihara and received Upasampada (the higher ordination) at Malwatta Maha Vihara, Kandy in 1933. He came to India in 1936. He joined the Maha Bodhi Society as a Dhammaduta worker. He became the Bhikkhu-in-charge of Sri Dharmarajika Vihara at Calcutta in the year 1938. In 1942 he became Managing Editor of the Maha Bodhi Journal. Finally in 1968 he became General Secretary of Maha Bodhi Society.

Ven. Neluwe Jinaratana was not only involved in managerial affairs of society but he also involved in preaching Dhamma with missionary zeal and devotion and also in social work. He was a founder of the Asian Buddhist Council for peace and one of the Founder Vice Presidents of the International Buddhist Brotherhood Association of Japan. He became a member of the Buddha Gaya Temple Management Committee. He was conferred the title 'Sangha Nayaka of India' by the Sangha Council of Malwatta

Chapter of the Siamese Sect of Sri Lanka in 1958 for recognition of his services rendered to Buddhism. In 1976, an honorary degree of D. Litt. was conferred on him by the Nava Nalanda Maha Vihara, Nalanda. To his credit, he successfully organised the International Conference and Seminar on the contribution of Buddhism to world culture and civilisation in Vigyan Bhawan, New Delhi in March 1977 in commemoration of the 2600th Birth Anniversary of the Buddha. Ven. Jinaratana indeed a true Buddhist missionary who died in 1983 at Kolkata.

(7) Ven. Lakhera Ariyawansa Nayaka Maha Thera

Apurva was born in 1915 in a Barua Buddhist family of the village Lakhera in Chittagong District of Bengal (now in Bangladesh). He was ordained as a Samanera by Ven. Pragyalankar Maha Thera in 1928 and became Ven. L. Ariyawansa. He joined Bhikkhu Training School at Sarnath in 1931 and had learnt Pali and Sinhalese from Ven. D. Sasanasiri Maha Thera. He also visited Sri Lanka for higher studies in Pali and Buddhism.

Ariyawansa joined the Maha Bodhi Society of India as a Dhammaduta worker in 1949, at Calcutta and Sarnath. He became Bhikkhu in-charge of the New Delhi Buddha vihara in 1950. He maintained contact with Babasaheb Ambedkar also. He was instrumental in having the Buddha Purnima (Thrice Sacred Day) declared as a public Holiday in 1953 by the Government of India. He was associated with the 2500th Buddha Jayanti functions organised by the Government. It was also primarily at his instance that in 1964 Mrs. Sirimavo Bandaranaike, Prime Minister of Sri Lanka brought a Bosapling from the historic Bodhi Tree at Anuradhapura for being planted in the Buddha Jayanti Park in New Delhi to commemorate the Birth centenary of Angarika Dharmapala, the founder of the Maha Bodhi Society.

The Kotte Mangala Uposathagara Kalyani Samagri Dharma Maha Sangha Sabha, Sri Lanka honoured Ven. L. Ariyawansa in 1979 with the title of 'Chief Sangha Nayak of North India for his valuable services to Dhamma. Throughout his life he preached and propagated the Dhamma in whole of North India, particularly in Delhi. He was indeed first Indian to join the Bhikkhu Training Centre established by Angarika Dharmapala at Sarnath in 1913.

He was also the first trained Indian Bhikkhu to join the Maha Bodhi Society of India in 1949. He became elected President of Maha Bodhi Society of India in 1992 and died in 1994.

(8) Ven. Dr. U. Dhammaratana

W.K. Jayasekara was born in Sri Lanka in 1917 and became U. Dhammaratana after ordination into Monk. He completed M.A., Ph.D., D.Litt. He joined the Foster Buddhist Seminary in Kandy in 1928 started by Angarika Dharmapala. He was ordained as Samanera by Ven. M. Devananda Maha Thera and given the new name of Uruwala Dhammaratana.

Dhammaratana came to India on the invitation of Angarika Dharmapala in 1931. After completing his studies from the Calcutta Uniersity and Banaras Hindu University, he made Sarnath the centre of his activities. He edited the Hindi Journal 'Dharmaduta' published by the Maha Bodhi Society from Sarnath. In Hindi he wrote on Visuddhimagga. He translated Theragatha, Suttanipata, Khuddakapatha into Hindi. His English works are: The Buddha and Caste System, A Study of Patisambhidamaga, An Introduction to Visuddhi – magga, The Buddha and His Message. He completed his Ph.D. from the University of Calcutta on 'A Comparative Study of the Anatta Doctrine in Pali Nikayas and that of the Madhyamika System of Nagarjuna'. He also associated with the editorial team of the Maha Bodhi Journal, the English monthly published by the Maha Bodhi Society of India from Calcutta.

Dhammaratana spread the message of the Buddha in India as well as in other countries like U.K., U.S.A., Canada and Japan where he conducted Vipasana meditation camps and delivered Dhamma discourses. He became elected General Secretary of the Maha Bodhi Society of India in 1983 after the death of Ven. N. Jinaratana Nayaka Maha Thera. He died in 1985.

(9) Ven. Motivala Sangharatana Maha Nayaka Thera

He was born in 1912 in Sri Lanka. He came to India in 1927. In 1937 he was appointed as one of the Joint Secretaries of the Maha Bodhi Society and Bhikkhu-in-charge of the Mulagandhakuti Vihara, Sarnath. He was chiefly responsible for making Sarnath a living holy shrine. The Sangha Council of the Malwatta Chapter of Siamese Sect, Kandy, Sri Lanka conferred title Sangha Nayaka of India on Ven. Sangharatana in the year 1961 for his services to Buddhism.

Sravasti, the sacred place where the Buddha had spent 25 rainy seasons, was the place chosen by Ven. Sangharatana after his retirement from Maha Bodhi Society in 1969 to spend his rest of life. He changed the face of Sravasti. Sahet – Mahet was given modern look. Due to the efforts of Ven. Sangharatana the old Jetavana Monastery and its surroundings were fenced by the Government of India. The construction of the Sri Lankaramaya Temple was his major contribution for the development of Sravasti. Under the aegis of the Bhartiya Baudha Shiksha Parishad he started a School in Sravasti.

Ven. Sangharatana died in a Lucknow Hospital on 31 December 1984. His body was cremated in Sravasti.

(10) Venerable Nilwakke Somananda Nayaka Thera:

He was born in 1902 in Sri Lanka. He entered the monastic life in 1919 under the guidance of Ven. Elangipitiye Sri Ratanapala Nayaka Thera of Kumbaldiwela Vihara.

He got higher ordination in 1923 at Asgiriya. Under the influence of Angarika Dharmapala, he came to India in 1929. He became 'dhammaduta' worker and started his activities in Madras. He became incharge of the Maha Bodhi Ashram in Perambur in Madras. He was supported in all his activities by well known educationist and Buddhist leader of Madras Prof. Lakshmi Narasu.

As a part of his missionary work in Madras, Ven. N. Somananda conducted weekly lectures on Buddhism and brought out Buddhist pamphlets in simple Tamil language so that common man could understand the Dhamma. He translated Dhammapada in Tamil. His other Tamil works are 'Buddha' and Buddha Dharma Shurrukkam.

Ven. N. Somananda purchased a piece of land at Egmore and constructed buildings for present Maha Bodhi Society and Vihara close to the famous Egmore Railway Station in Madras. The most remarkable achievement was that he was appointed to the post of Chief Monk of the Buddha Gaya Temple in 1953, when it was brought under Buddhist dominated Management Committee by the Bihar Government. He attended the Sixth Buddhist Council held in Burma in 1954 and displayed there his remarkable knowledge of Pali. He also rendered his services for the benefit of Buddhists of Hyderabad in Andhra Pradesh. He was undoubtly erudite scholar of Buddhalogy. Ven. N. Somananda Nayaka Thera died in 1987 in Sri Lanka.

(11) Ven. Dharmarakshita:

He was an Indian Monk born in the year 1923 near Kushinagar the site of Lord Buddha's Maha Parinirvana. His Ph.D. thesis was on 'Buddha Yoga Sadhana'. He became a Samanera and renounced home in 1942. He received his Upasampada (higher ordination) in 1944 from Ven. Chandramani Maha Thera. He studied Tripitaka and the Pali Literature at the Maha Mahinda Oriental College in Sri Lanka under the guidance of venerable Dhammavasa Sanghanayaka Maha Thera and was awarded the degree of Triptakacharya.

He came back to India and joined the Maha Bodhi Society of India as a Dhammaduta worker. Sarnath (the ancient holy Isipatana) was his place of activity. He was Editor of Dharmadutta, the Hindi monthly organ of the Maha Bodhi Society published from Sarnath. He also worked as Lecturer of Pali at the Maha Bodhi College, Sarnath and later became principal of that college.

The most important contribution of Ven. Dharmarakshita to popularise Buddhism was his whole hearted co-operation to the mass movement launched by Ambedkar for the revival of Buddhism. He met Ambedkar, when Ambedkar visited Sarnath in November 1956. It was Ven. Dharmarakshita who made arrangements for Babasaheb Ambedkar's stay at Sarnath for three days from 22-24 November 1956.

Ven. Dharmarakshita compiled speeches of Ambedkar entitled: 'Baudh Dharm he Manav Dharm', which contains an interesting description of his three meetings with Ambedkar: (1) At Kushinagar in 1943; (2) In Burma in 1954; (3) At Sarnath in 1956.

He wrote books in Pali, Hindi and Marathi. His missionary work came to an end with his death in 1977.

(12) Ven. Bulathasinhala Pannarama Mahathera:

He was born in 1926 in Sri Lanka. He was ordained as a Samanera in his childhood itself. At the age of 20 he was given upasampada in the year 1946 by Ven.D. Saddhatissa in Sri Lanka. Ven. B. Pannarama came to India on 5th January 1961 and joined the Mahabodhi Society of India as a Dhammaduta Monk. Since 1969 he was Bhikkhu-in-charge of the Buddhagaya centre of the Mahabodhi Society of India. He became the Senior Vice-President of the Mahabodhi Society of India. He died in 1995 at Colombo, Sri Lanka.

(13) Ven. Aggmaha Pandita Bhadant Gyaneshwar:

He was born in 1936 in Burma (Myanmar). He became Sramanera at the age of 13. In 1954 at the time of the inauguration of the Sixth Buddhist Council (Sangiti) Ven. Gyaneshwar came in contact win Ven. U Chandramani. On the invitation of Ven. U. Chandramani, Ven. Gyaneshwar came to India in 1963. He studied Pali and Tibetan language.

Ven. Gyaneshwar became active after the death of Ven. U. Chandramani in 1972. He expanded the activites of the Burmese Buddhist Mission at Kushinagar. He had been associated with the All India Bhikkhu Sangha. After the demise of Bhadant Anand Kausalyayan in 1988, Ven. Gyaneshwar was elected as Vice-President of the All India Bhikkhu Sangha. Aggmaha Pandita is a title awarded to Ven. Gyaneshwar for his contribution to the spread of Dhamma and for his social and educational activites. He was also honoured by Miss Mayawati then Chief Minister of U.P. for his contribution to the revival of Buddhism in Modern India.

The most important contribution of Ven. Gyaneshwar to the Buddhism is his active participation in the Buddha Gaya Liberation Movement spearheaded by Ven. Surai Sassai, the great missionary from Japan. Government of Bihar reconstituted the Buddha Gaya Temple Management Committee in 1995, in which Ven. Gyaneshwar has been made as a member.

(14) Ven. Kushak Bakula

He was born in 1917 in Ladakh. He was recognised as the re-incarnation of the previous Head Lama, the 20th reincarnation of

Arhat Bakul. He heads Spituk Gompa (monastery) near Delhi. He is a monk of Tibetan Buddhism. In other words he belonged to the Mahayana School of Thought.

Ven. Kushak Bakula has made a lot of contribution to the propagation of Buddhism in Ladakh. Apart from religious activities he involved in social activities. He worked for the socio-economic development of Ladakh people. Later he became a political activist.

(15) Ven. Lama Lobzang

After Ven. Kushak Bakula, the most popular leader of Ladakh was Ven. Lama Lobzang. He was Bhikkhu-in-charge of the Ladakh Buddha Vihara, in Delhi, which was established by Ven. Kushak Bakula. In 1990, he was appointed by the Government of India a member of the National Commission for Scheduled Castes and Scheduled Tribes. He is also President of Asoka Mission Vihara established by Ven. Dhammavara, a Combodian Monk in 1950. He is working in close association with the Maha Bodhi Society of India.

(16) Ven. Mahaguru Norbu Lama

The most remarkable contribution made by Ven. Mahaguru Norbu Lama for the propagation of Buddha Dhamma was that founding the Vishwa Mahayana Buddha Maha Sangha, Lekhapani, Dibrugarh District in Assam. Indeed his area of activities are not stricted only to North – East, he also propagating the Buddha Dhamma in North India and Maharashtra. He is a Patron of the Maha Bodhi Society of India.

(17) Ven. Acharya Buddharakkhita Maha Thera

He was born in 1922 in Manipur. The most interesting fact of this Bauddha Guru is that he is a scholar of both Mahayana and Theravada Buddhism. He studied Mahayana Buddhism in Nepal and Theravada Buddhism in Ceylon. He was conferred the title 'Acharya' in 1952.

Ven. Acharya Buddharakkhita had learnt Vipassan Meditation and Abhidhamma – Psychology in Myanmar. He was also appointed by Government of Burma as one of the Editors of Chatta Sanghayana Editorial Board of the Union Buddha Sasana Council.

He came to Bangalore in 1956 and established the Maha Bodhi Society, which aimed to propagate Buddha Dhamma in Karnataka, a South Indian state. He also established the Buddha Vachana Trust for publishing the Buddhist literature. His famous work is 'Living Legacy of the Buddha'. He founded monthly magazine called 'Dhamma' in 1972. He was editor of the magazine. He also established: (1) Mahabodhi Institute of Pali studies and Buddhology (2) Mahabodhi Maitri Mandala and (3) Arogya Foundation for the benefit of the people.

(18) Ven. Dr. Ellawala Nandissara Maha Thera

Ven. E. Nandissara served Buddhism in Southern part of India. In fact, on the invitation of Maha Bodhi Society, he came to India and joined the Madras branch of the society. During his tenure the New Vihara was erected at Kannet Lane, Egmore, Chennai (Madras).

After the death of Ven.P.Gunaratana, he became General Secretary of the Maha Bodhi Society of India in 1984. In between he worked as a Buddhist Missionary in U.S.A. and finally he returned to Sri Lanka in 1995.

(19) Ven. Potuwila Gunaratana

Born in Sri Lanka and received Upa Sampada in 1943. He joined the Maha Bodhi Society of India and worked as a Dhammaduta. He was requested to take over the role of the General Secretary of Maha Bodhi Society of India. He passed away in 1984.

There are also many other Buddhist monks, thinks who worked and are working for the propagating of Dhamma namely: Ven. Dr. S. Medhankar, Ven. Dharmapal, Ven. Anandamitra, Ven. Dr. Rashtrapal, Ven. Dhammaviryo, Ven. Saddhananda Thero, Ven. G. Prajnananda, Ven. Dr. D. Rewath, Ven. D. Wimala and Ven. Dr. Mapalagama Wipulasara.

Western Buddhist Missionary Activities

Buddhist ethics provided a stabilising influence in a world of continual conflict. Buddhism is a vital force for Dalit identity. Buddhism became integral part of Dalit identity. Buddhism is becoming recognised in the west as an alternative source of vision and values. *The Friends of the Western Buddhist Order* (FWBO) is one such organisation which aims to use Buddhism for the development of Dalits. It differs from the most other Buddhist organisations in respect of commitment to Buddhist ideals in the conditions of modern westen industrialised society and also conditions of Indian society.

The Friends of the Western Buddhist Order (FWBO) was founded by Ven. Sangharakshita in 1968 as a western sangha. The order of the organisation is very crucial. The order consists of men and women who took refugee to the Trisharana. Sangharakshita is their spiritual teacher. FWBO has established indeed its own tradition, not dependent on, but related to other branches of Buddhism like Dalit Buddhism.

Sangharakshita the founder of the Friends of the Western Buddhist Order committed himself to holding the Ambedkar's Dalit Buddhist Movement together, despite vituperative opposition from sections of the Indian press. After 1977 the FWBO, already established in the west, was a prime motivating force sustaining the missionary activity begun by Ambedkar in India. The movement is known as 'Trailokya Bauddha Mahasangha Sahayak Gana', and its main centres are in Pune and Ahmedabad. Its teachings emphasise spiritual practice and the relevance of Buddhism in the modern world.

Dalit Buddhist movement led by Sahayak Gana is different from other forms of traditional Buddhism. It is a socio-political movement. It emphasises strongly on ethical teachings and social identity.

References

1. In India Hindutva politics of cultural nationalism is indeed not aimed at spiritual atmosphere for peace but involves in activating violent forces to disturb the harmony of the society.
2. Bernard Shaw says that a subject nation is like a man suffering from cancer.
3. Probably a Buddhist monk because before Siddhartha Gautama became 'Buddha', already there was Buddhism. History says that there were number of Buddhas who preached Buddhism – tradition of enlightenment before the birth of Gautama Buddha. In other words there was Buddhism earlier to Gautama Buddha.

4. Ambedkar is being called as Jefferson of India for his authoring constitution of India.
5. The words unity and integrity of the Nation have been added to FRATERNITY by the Constitution (forty-second Amendment) Act, 1976.
6. To abolish caste Ambedkar wanted to destroy the sanctity of Sastras. He sates: "You must give a doctrinal basis to your religion – a basis that will be in consonance with Liberty, Equality and Fraternity, insort with Democracy...." see for mere details: Ambedkar, B.R., *Annihilation of Caste,* Thacker, Bombay, 1937, p. 38.
7. Idea of collective cultural identity has understood from the book: *The Politics of cultural Nationalism* by Margurite Barnett, Princeton University Press, Princeton, 1976, p. 163.
8. Anaimuthu, V., *Periya Ee Ve Ra Sinthanigal.* Vol. II, Trichirapalli, Thinkers Forum, 1974, p. 673 (Quoted with modifications to suit Dalit argument).
9. Viduthalai, 20, January 1948.
10. The Mesopotamian records from about 2300 B.C. onwards refer to trade relations with *Meluha.* Indus civilisation can rightly be called as Meluha civilisation or Dalito-dravidian civilisation.
11. Ahir, D.C., *Buddhism,* B.R. Publishing Corporation, Delhi, 1998. p. 114.
12. Anand Teltumbde in his scholarly work says that the Gautama Buddha gave complete freedom to people to amend the *Dhamma* as per the needs of time. (*Ambedkar in and for the post-Ambedkar Dalit Movement,* Sugawa Prakashan, Pune, 1997, p. 28). Accordingly Ambedkar has brought change in the traditional outlook of Buddhism and modernised it.
13. *Op. cit., Ahir, D.C., p. 84.*
14. *Ibid.*
15. *Ibid.*, p. 85.

Seven

Conclusion: Cultural Change as Prelude to Social Change

In the context of religion 'Modernisation' is a perennial idea. Modernism that causes modernisation is a continuous process. According to Oxford - Encyclopedic Dictionary, Modernism is a mode of theological inquiry in which the tradition and doctrines of a religion are examined in the light of modern thought. Understanding the modern thought of Ambedkar and the Dalai Lama means initiating the inquiry in which Buddhist traditions and doctrines are examined. It is a theological inquiry that means study of the nature of God and of the foundations of religious belief. It is a study on the theological system and its interpretation. Are these studies (on theology and religion) relates only to metaphysical questions? Examination of a religion in the context of social behaviour doesn't require drawing conclusion on metaphysical ideas, What it needs is to understand the impact of metaphysical ideas on societal behaviour. Theological inquiry is not necessarily about metaphysical beliefs but social meanings of nature of God and his religion. Theological inquiry supposed to lead to modernistaion of religion aimed at social profit. That is what exactly Ambedkar and Dalai Lama have done to Buddhism.

The basic tenets of Buddhist modernism can be summarised as follows:

1. There is first of all a dire need to purify Buddhism from accretions and superstitions introduced by Brahmanical Buddhists, as well as from the rigid interpretations inherited from earlier times. The fulfilment of this task requires going back to the original sources of Buddhism, the *Tripithakas (Sutta Pithaka* on sermons of Gautama Buddha; *Vinaya Pithaka* on monastic rules and discipline;

Abhidhamma Pithaka on metaphysics) and ancient works on different schools of Buddhism and reinterpreting them. This position the modernists had adopted with the motivation to strengthen the process of revivalism of Buddhism both in Asian and Western countries. In doing so, their use of the sources is different from traditionalists. Though, the revivalism is basic aim of both modern and traditional religious leaders of Buddhism, the latter have taken a literal and rigid approach to the text, while the modernists objective is to discover its spirit and to distinguish between the universal rules of Buddhism and the specific ones that are valid only for a particular period.

2. The modernist questioned the authority of the early medieval interpretations of Buddhism and advocated the exercise of individual judgement, which Ambedkar once described as the principle movement in Buddhism. Every Buddhist, the modernists argued, has the right and duty to seek to understand the Buddhist scripture and later interpretations. This emphasis on the exercise of individual judgement led the modernists to stress the rational aspects of the religion the role of reason, free thinking and individual will. In the process, modernist thinkers underlined the importance of argument by analogy, the principle of desirability, and general interests of the community.

Ambedkar, for instance, emphasised the role of reason in Buddhism. In his work *'The Buddha and His Dhamma'*, he referred to it as the power that enables people to distinguish truth from falsehood. Thus, Buddhist law must be interpreted by reason. As an authority on Buddhism, he put his ideas into practice and gave a number of important legal opinions.

3. The modernist school focused attention on the social and moral aspects of Buddhism (and the Buddhists) rather than on its metaphysical and philosophical ones. Buddhism must be relevant to the needs and problems of ordinary Buddhists. It must help them in the conduct of their daily life. Believing that the teachings of Buddhism are the best

that humanity knows, modernists concluded that no worthwhile idea could be in conflict with Buddhism. Further, they viewed their emphasis on the "this-worldly" aspect of Buddhism as truly Buddhist.

The outcome of the modernisation of Buddhism is an essentially rational and liberal interpretation of Buddhism covering broad range of issues, including political organisation and sources of legitimacy, legislation, economic life, the status of women and education.

In the realm of politics, these two Buddhist modernist thinkers advocated constitutional government, election, and democratic institutions. They opposed despotic rulers and emphasised the importance of people's participation in decision making. Ambedkar's main opposition to Marxism is the authoritarian or dictatorial oriented governance. Both Ambedkar and the Dalai Lama took the spirit to support democratic polity from the ancient Buddhist *sangha,* which was based on the principle of participation and representation of the members. They agreed that tyranny runs counter to Buddhism and had the effect of corrupting the moral fabric of the society.

The Dalai Lama, for example, stressed the civil function of the Buddhist Gurus in the community life. He himself is a fine example for a religious monk's involvement in secular and civil functions of community in the modern society. He is political as well as religious head of a Tibetan community. Although Buddhist modernism tended to be more of an intellectual trend than a political movement, there are examples of activism. The modernist thinkers reconciled Buddhist principles with the new forces of social liberation and in certain cases, as in Tibet, modernist Buddhism furnished the ideology of national resistance.

On relations between Buddhists, the modernists asked Buddhists to unite and put aside differences among sects and schools. On the issues of social justice and economic equity, the modernist position was not ambivalent. In other words, they opposed any social system which based on discrimination and felt need of distributive justice equal distribution of resources and equal opportunities.

In his writings, Ambedkar argued that a parliamentary

system that did not serve the poor was an empty and meaningless show. In his view the uneven distribution of wealth and authority was the chief enemy of progress.

Another issue that attracted a great deal of attention among the modernists was the status of women. They argued that Buddhism liberated women and virtually assured them equal rights. In particular the modernists advocated the right of women to education and work. On the emancipation of women, Ambedkar suggested that they should have elementary schooling if they were to play a role in society. In his later writings, he restated the case by invoking the great concepts of the nineteenth century: freedom, progress, and civilisation.

From the modernist perspective the primary vehicle for social change was educational reform. They pointed out that the progress of west lay in the quality of its educational system. Criticising the traditional educational system based on religious schools and functionaries, they advocated the introduction of rational and empirical sciences into the curriculum, the popularisation of scientific knowledge, and the teaching of foreign languages, for example, English. Thus, Ambedkar, who closely observed European educational institutions, worked to improve the curriculum and administration at Siddhardha College, Bombay (Mumbai), which he established.

The Dalai Lama also, worked to introduce modern and secular education in all Tibetan schools and even allowed Tibetan works translation into foreign language particularly into English. He discarded the old principle of secrecy, and opened Tibetan religious secrets to the world. Both the modernists, felt teaching modern sciences in the educational institutions, would help to build society on rational lines.

The modernist approach seems to be the most capable of providing synthesis between Buddhism and the modern world. In other words both Ambedkar and the Dalai Lama made an attempt to re-interpret Buddhism to suit purposes and conditions in the modern world, although their targets differ. For example Ambedkar concerns with Dalit community and social transformation of Indian society, whereas the Dalai Lama seems to be concerning with post-industrial societies and general conditions in modern society and in particular future of Tibetan community. In fact, both rationalistic and humanistic elements find corner stone of respective philosophies. This marks great transformation in Buddhist ideology in the history of Buddhism.

Both the modernists had taken Buddhist ways in practice. They are the most significant Buddhist leaders in modern India. Ambedkar's attempt to modernise Buddhism had revived Buddhism in modern India. The Dalai Lama's efforts to modernise Buddhism have resulted in the propagation of Buddhism in the west.

They can be rightly called as the founding fathers of Modern Buddhism and Bodhi Sattvas of twentieth century, who interpreted Buddhism for the epoch.

Modernisation is a continuous process. The combination of traditionalists' thesis, and modernists anti-thesis leads to post-modern synthesis. The post-modern approach to theological inquiry of Buddhism produces synthesis of both traditional and modern ideas.

Modernists' ideas are reflections of colonial, post-colonial and post-industrial experience. Their thought of Modern Buddhism is an explanation about social behaviour of religion in these societies. The idea of native economy against foreign (read western) in newly emerged independent countries like India, in late 1940's able to establish political authority through sovereign control over country's economy. Jawaharlal Nehru's policy of mixed economy based on socialist ideas and NAM as realistic foreign policy all these have roots in the modernist middle path of Buddhism, propounded by Ambedkar. Political independence has brought right to vote for masses, thanks to Ambedkar the father of constitution of India. However, social reality of Indian masses was different. The accessibility to economic resources was a faraway dream of millions of downtrodden. The economic reality was reflected in the social behaviour of religion.

State's monopoly over its economy symbolised political patriotism of the time that minimised the role of religion in the Indian society. Political sovereignty of the country was an expression of its right to control economic life of society. Economic nationalism was the dominant political as well as cultural philosophy of the society. Economic environment was the subject of discussion among the intellectual circles. Marxism gained importance. Materialist interpretation to any phenomena of the society was a valid argument. Indian Universities, academicians, intellectuals, educated class all were under Marx Mania. Anything that argued in contradiction to Marxist understanding was regarded as unintellectual, non-academic and polemics. Economic nationalism allowed the political parties to mobilise masses against the idea of capitalism in other words against U.S.A. Marxists and socialists (i.e., Communist Parties came to rule in states like West Bengal, Kerala, & Congress party with socialist ideology emerged as dominant ruling party at national level) enjoyed the fruits of political power out of economic nationalism.

Ambedkar through his Buddhism refuted Marxian idea of state and gave scientific model based on Buddhist ideals for the economic development of the society. Marxist dogma prevented the main stream intelligentsia to give intellectual acceptability to Ambedkar thought. Marxists failure to identify 'caste' as an Indian social reality took them away from Ambedkar. Economic thought of Ambedkar has its roots in social, cultural and religious philosophy of society. He sees role of religion in moulding social & economic behaviour of society. He believes social philosophy of a religion as an important motivating factor of society. Indeed, the dominance of economic nationalism and Marxism prevented Ambedkarism i.e., Modern Buddhism to play grater role in shaping the newly born independent India. Ambedkar's idea of religion finds answer to Indian social reality of his time. Because the social behaviour of caste system has its roots in the religion, and caste is the primary factor for economic mobility of the society.

Indian society at the beginning of the new millennium is making experience of new social realities. Dalits and backwards have succeeded to some extent in capturing political and bureaucratic structure. Newly emerged educated middle class from these communities started demanding more social and cultural space in the society. Traditional Hindu value system finds difficult to have hold on the religious thought of these groups. Once again Buddhism is making inroads into the downtrodden communities. Ambedkar's modern Buddhism is truly becoming attractive alternative religious belief. The recent Hindu revival, expressed through militant activism against Christian and Muslim groups, is indeed a reaction to Buddhist revivalism that initiated by Ambedkar. It is a Hindu effort not to allow Buddhism to acquire space in the nation's religious agenda.

Till recently, economic sovereignty has been the dominant political agenda. With the privatisation and economic globalisation, foreign (western) products are not regarded as enemy of the nation. Economic barriers have been collapsed. The process of liberalisation of economy resulted into state's gradual withdrawal from the active participation in controlling the society its assets and institutions. In the field of social welfare health and education etc., also state wants to maintain its policy of non-participation. Private business houses, multi-national companies, Non-governmental organisations are steadily occupying the space and adopting the role that earlier reserved for the state only. Economic nationalism has lost its importance. It resulted into an identity crisis in the nation's consciousness. First time after independence, Indian nationalism is in search of an identity. Hinduism is the one to respond immediately. Hindu religious assertion is an attempt to fill the space of national identity left by economic nationalism. Cultural nationalism identified with Hinduism replaced economic nationalism.

Cultural nationalism is not necessarily a negative phenomenon. The culture that has a strong religious history can be manipulated for the positive goals. Human development is certainly linked with social behaviour of the society. Religion is the most visible factor to identify one's own national culture. A religion based on strong ethical values not only positively represent the nation, but also provide the space for multi-religious and cultural identities in the society.

The conflict between nations because of different interests is common phenomena in the human history. Nationalism for just political reasons, geographical expansion, economic dominance produces violent action. If a nation identifies with its culture and religion, there won't be a place for violence. Since religion as such doesn't subscribe to violence, cultural nationalism based on the true religious values spreads the message of 'live and let live', peace and development. Ethical values of a religion are capable of generating cultural nationalism, that strive for the human progress rather than destruction.

Communal element in a cultural identity if any, can be tackled only with the strong intervention of moral culture of a religion. The communalism or fundamentalism under the guise of cultural nationalism, which has been witnessed by Indian society in recent times, does possess no religious value. The culture that propagates communal violence is not based on any religion. Without human values and ethical foundations it cannot be a religion and a culture. It is pseudo in nature, inhuman in means, anti-social in content. If religious ethic is human welfare it never become cause of communal tension. The positive cultural nationalism based in true religious values certainly stands for peaceful co-existence of different religious and cultural identities. It is so because religious behaviour is a social behavior and social behaviour that finds its roots in the culture of humanism causes the total society to behave with the ethical principles. The culture, born out of the ethical principles, does not aim to find doctrinal differences among the different religious communities but produces feeling of oneness that enables a society to acquire a strong positive national identity.

The historical problem of the Indian society is that it has failed if not every time but on many occasions to identify itself with a religion that has strong human values and moral traditions. Presence of Hinduism in Indian society caused this failure. Indian society, whenever identified with the Buddhism as its religion, has seen the pinnacles of its glory. *Mauryan* rule particularly of emperor *Asoka* the Great was the fine example in the history. It is the democratic and republican tradition of the Buddhism that shaped the liberal and progressive outlook of Indian society. Buddhism created Indian face that celebrated the diversities of thought through a philosophy of pluralism and tolerance based on non-violence as the supreme religion. The continuity of Buddhist tradition of *Manavata* (humanity) and *Karuna* in the Indian culture created humane image of Indian society. Indeed, 'Bharatiyata' - the Indian way of life is the by-product of '*Budhatiyata*'. Buddhism has given primacy to the welfare of the world and has religious pluralism as its basis. If India is to ever evolve into a vibrant, democratic and just social order where progress, prosperity and peace become its underlying features - Indian society has to identify with the Buddhism.

Vedic Hinduism has failed to create even a just society due to the limitation of its social philosophy that is aimed to maintain the tyrannical *varna dharma* against *Manava Dharma*. As is well known Vedic India was unaware of the ethics of equality and universal religion. Vedic values are dominant elements in the Hindu social thought. According to Veda, the purpose of man's life is to achieve monitory goals. God is a giver of fortunes to earn money in any means, in return he gets a share from the gains. Morality finds no meaning. Ethics not known. It was Buddhism that introduced positive elements like Ahimsa (non-violence), social justice, social equality and universal brotherhood in Indian culture. With the state's support, although Hinduism able to destroy Buddhism as a religion, it could not succeed in its efforts to drive away the Buddhist elements from Indian thought and culture, customs and manners, beliefs and practices and art and architecture. The present form of Indianism - *Bharatiyata*, has underneath its surface, a thick layer of Buddhism. The aim of modern Buddhism is to re-locate Indian culture and religion in the Buddhist identity.

Traditional knowledge systems told Dalits that they were inferior to caste Hindus. Modern knowledge systems, used in Ambedkar technique through religion, informed the Dalits that there lies idealised equality in the Buddhist India. The practical experience reveals different facts. Indeed, Ambedkar himself departs from this idealised equality and lies the foundations for post-modern utilisations of knowledge systems.

In Ambedkar's ideal scheme of Modern Buddhism the Buddha was not a God and not a Mokshadata and visualised ideal Buddhist society that locates Dalits par with other communities on social scale. However, in his later writings, he applied post-modern technique in understanding social dynamics. He worshipped the Buddha as God and called Bhagawan Buddha as the God of the indigenous communities of India. Secondly, rather than aspiring simply social equality through Buddhism, he asked his people to fight for it. 'Struggle' is the basis of his mission. The study of Dalit history in post-modern methodology draws the conclusion that (1) Dalits are the original inhabitants of the land and they can be rightly called as 'indigenous tribes'; (2) Buddhism is the earliest religion of Indian society. It was present in the Indus culture (Dalito-Dravidian Civlisation) and the Gautama Buddha structurised it, institutionalised its philosophy, and caused to its popularity. With that the Buddha emerged as its historical prophet '*Bhagwan*' (God); (3) Post-modern knowledge indeed understands history more in 'what needs', methodology than in 'what was'. It enquires the past but gives importance to the necessity of the present in constructing its idea, concept and method to examine the fact of history. It believes in aiding historically neglected communities in acquiring dominance over established knowledge systems. Its main emphasis is religion (social culture) as primary motivating factor of the history. Application of post-modern method to understand Buddhism, relieves Ambedkar's religious thought from the typical ideolised '*Samadharma*' (all are equal) to the more assertive Dalita Dhamma. In other words Dalits are the indigenous people. They had highly civlised culture in their Mohenjodaro civilisation than the Aryan Hindus who were foreign invaders. Adi-Buddhism (original Buddhism) is the greatest religion of all. Bhagawan Buddha is a great prophet of the *Sama Dhamma*. God is not visible whose heavenly life can be experienced in this life itself. Dalit world view of religion in post-Modern understanding reveals that in opposition to invisible, undescribed God along with the *Margadata* position of the Gautama Buddha, there is clearly described Mara the Saturn's and his world in which the partheon on Saturn's who are 'thread wearing' and weapon wielding' and cruel in nature in killing indiscriminately the indigenous masses. Post-modern Buddhist philosophy constructs its epistemological superiority on the Dalit greatness. It makes Dalits superior as race with great history, proud culture against Aryan - Brahmin -Caste Hindu communities. Post-modern Buddhism or Adi-Buddhism provides more social bargaining capacity to Dalits to do favourable social business with other groups. It protects the claims of Dalits social superiority rooted in history and culture, over other identities particularly Hindu. It recognises Dalit as indigenous and Hindu as foreign. Bahujan as backward communities of modern India and are past of its social vision along with other non-Hindu religious identities.

The Post-modern idea aims to find the role for Buddhism in building a strong national identity through positive religious philosophy and culture. The religious context of Indian society involves the study on Hindu identity and its philosophy. Hindu symbols, values, traditions and nature of ideal images (i.e., Gods & Goddesses) need to be understood in the context of social utility. Hindu identity severely weakened the strength of the Indian society by propounding *varna-dharma*. Hindu thought rather worked as anti-thesis to the social needs of Indian society.

The most important problem that Hinduism has been facing historically is that its failure to become a religion. Hinduism is not a religion. It is a way of life. A way of life is subjected to a test that finds its quality. Ambedkar finds Hinduism as a negative way of life since it is based on Veda, Gita, Ramayana and Mahabharata, above all Manu Charitra.

Every religion provides a code of life. Social principles of a religion forms nucleus of its culture. The strength of religious culture depends on social value of its philosophy. The philosophy that propagates social inequality, injustice, violence and inhumanity through its cultural symbols, ideal images like Gods and Goddesses, rituals etc., is utmost can be called as a way of life; it can not be a religion. Because a religion provides ethical way of life. Hinduism has failed to become a religion because of its weak social ideals. The cycle of violence and destruction has been swift and severe in Hindu thought, which already poisoned millions of lives of many generations for centuries. The society today trapped between crude nationalism and fundamentalism. Religious identity is a social identity. Ethical values should constitute the basis of philosophy of a religion. Negative social philosophy cannot be a religion. Verification of Hindu social philosophy has brought Ambedkar to draw a conclusion that Hindu value cannot energise Indian society. Hinduism does not profess any religious values. Its adherence to casteism proves the point.

The demand for a change in the state policies towards aborigine population i.e., Backward communities may take a while to be translated politically but religion mean while can provide a platform for a large number of Bahujan Indians to come together and challenge past and present legitimates. This can be realised by making Buddhism as a social weapon against the existing religious values.

Buddhist tradition produces positive traits in Indian culture whereas negative traits constitute Hindu Vedic tradition. Due to various historical reasons Buddhists religious identity has become invisible today. This most unfortunate reality brings one thing to our notice that absence of Buddhist religious identity in Indian society means absence of ethical social national unity. Buddhism with its positive social ideals capable of uniting different social and religious groups. And makes the society to identify itself with broader cultural nationalism that accommodates multi-religious identity, and cultural plurality. It assures equal opportunities to Muslims, Christians, Sikhs, Dalits, Tribals and Bahujans (backwards) in controlling national assets, institutions, centres of knowledge, thus creates ethical essence of the state and nationalism. India with the Buddhism as its national religion and culture could emerge as a strong nation a super power that can aspire to play a dominant role in the world affairs.

Appendix – I

My Personal Philosophy

Every man should have a philosophy of life, for everyone must have a standard by which to measures his conduct. And philosophy is nothing but a standard by which to measure.

Negatively, I reject the Hindu social philosophy propounded in the Bhagvat Gita based as it is, on the Triguna of the Sankhya philosophy which is in my judgement a cruel perversion of the philosophy of Kapila, and which had made the caste system and the system of graded inequality the law of Hindu Social Life.

Positively, my social philosophy may be said to be enshrined in three words: Liberty, Equality and Fraternity. Let no one, however, say that I have borrowed my philosophy from the French Revolution. I have not. My philosophy has roots in religion and not in political science. I have derived them from the teachings of my master, the Buddha. In his philosophy, liberty and equality had a place but he added that unlimited liberty destroyed equality, and absolute equality left no room for liberty. In his philosophy, law had a place only as a safeguard against the breaches of liberty and equality; but he did not believe that law can be a guarantee for breaches of liberty or equality. He gave the highest place to fraternity as the only real safeguard against the denial of liberty or equality or fraternity which was another nature for brotherhood or humanity, which was again another name for religion.

Law is secular, which anybody may break while fraternity or religion is sacred which everybody must respect. My philosophy has a mission. I have to do the work of conversion: for, I have to make the followers of *Triguna* theory to give it up and accept mine. Indians today are governed by two different ideologies. Their political ideal setout in the preamble to the constitution affirms a life of liberty, equality and fraternity. Their social ideal embodied in their religion denies them.

B.R. Ambedkar

(All-India Radio Broadcast of of Speech on October 3, 1954)

Appendix - II

Why I Like Buddhism

(Talk given on the B.B.C. London on 12th May, 1956 by B.R. Ambedkar)

In the short time allotted to me, I am asked to answer two questions; First is "Why I like Buddhism" and the second is "How useful it is to the world in its present circumstances."

I prefer Buddhism because it gives three principles in combination which no other religion does. All other religions are bothering themselves with 'God' and 'soul' and 'life' afer death'. Buddhism teaches 'Prajana' (understanding as against superstition and supernaturalism). It teaches 'Karuna' (love). It teaches 'Samata' (equality). This is what man wants for a good and happy life on earth. These three principles of Buddhism make their appeal to me. These three principles should, also make an appeal to the world. Neither God nor soul can save society.

There is a third consideration, which should make an appeal to the world and particularly the South East Asian part of it. The world has been faced with the onslaught of Karl Marx and the Communism, of which he is made the father. The challenge is a very serious one. That Marxism and Communism relate to secular affairs and they have shaken the foundation of the religious system of all the countries. This is quite natural, for, the religious system although today is unrelated to the secular system yet it is the foundation on which everything secular restes. The secular system cannot last very long unless it has got sanction of the religion, however remote it may be.

I am greatly suruprised at the turn of the Buddhist countries in South East Asia towards Communism. It means that they do not understand what Budhdism is. I claim that Buddhism is a complete answer to Marx and his Communism. Communism of

Russian type aims to bring it about by a bloody revolution. The Buddhist communism brings it about by a bloodless mental revolution. Those who are eager to embrace Communism may note that the 'SANGHA' is a Communist organisation. There is no private property. This has not been brought about by violence. It is the result of the change of mind and yet it has stood for 2500 years. It may have detriorated but ideal is still binding. The Russian Communism must answer this question. They must also answer two other questions. One is that why Communist system is necessary for all times. They have done the work which, it may be admitted, the Russians could never have been able to do. But when the work is done, why the people should not have freedom accompanied by love as the Buddhist preached.

The South East Asian Countries must, therefore be wary of jumping into the Russian net. They will never be able to get out of it. All that is necessary to them is to study the Buddha and what he taught aright and to give political form to his teachings. Poverty there is and there will always be. Even in Russia there is poverty but poverty cannot be an excuse for sacrificing human freedom.

Unfortunately the Buddha's teachings have not been properly interpreted and understood. That his gospel was a collection of doctrines and social reforms have not been completely understood. Once it is realised that Buddhism is a social gospel the revival of it would be everlasting even for the world will realise why Buddhism makes such a great appeal to everyone.

Appendix - III

Buddhist Movement in India

A Blue Print by B.R. Ambedkar

[Ambedkar had discussion with the Buddhist Sasana Council of Burma (Myanmar) on the subject of spreading Buddhism in India. He had prepared an enlarged version of his talk in the form of a Memorandum.]

1. To spread Buddhism outside Myanmar be one of the aims of the Sasana Council, then India is the first country they should make the centre of their effort. No other country will yield so much as India will.
2. The reason is obvious. India is the birth place of Buddhism. It flourished in India from 543 B.C. to 1400 A.D. i.e. for nearly 2,000 years. Although the Buddhist religion has vanished the name of the Buddha is still held in great veneration and the memory of his religion is still green. In India Buddhism may be a withered plant; but no one can say that it is dead at the roots. Buddha is regarded by the Hindus as Avatar of Vishnu. In India we don't have to restore veneration for a new prophet as Nebuchnezar has to do for his gods among the Jews. All that we have to do is to bring back his religion. Such easy conditions for a fruitful effort cannot be found in any other country. In them there are well and long established religions and Buddhism would be regarded as an intruder without a passport. So far as India is concerned the Buddha needs no passport nor does he require any visa.
3. Thirdly there are sections among the Hindus who are eager to leave Hinduism and go over to Buddhism. Such are the Untouchables and the Backward Classes. They are against Hinduism because of its doctrine of Chatruvarnma which is best described as the doctrine of graded inequality. In the present stage of their intellectual awakening these

classes are up in arms against Hinduism. Now is the time to take advantage of their discontent. They prefer Bnuddhism to Christianity on three grounds.

(1) Buddhism is not a religion which is alien to India;

(2) The essential doctrine of Buddhism is social equality which they want;

(3) Buddhism is a rational religion in which there can be no room for superstition.

4. There should be no hesitation in launching the movement on the ground that the majority of the people entering Buddhism in its early stages will be coming from lower classes. The Sasana Council must not make the mistakes which the Christian Missionaries in India made. The Christian Missionaries began by attempting to convert the Brahmins. Their strategy was that if the Brahmins could be converted firs the conversion of the rest of the Hindu could not be difficult. For they argued that "if the Brahmins have accepted Christianity why don't you; they are the heads of your religion." This strategy of the missionaries proved fatal to Christians. Why should they? They had all the advantages under Hinduism. The Christian Missionaries in India realised their mistakes and turned their attention to the Untouchable after wasting hundreds of years in their effort to convert the Brahmins. By the time they turned to the Untouchables the spirit of nationalism had grown up and inimical to the country. The result was that the Christian Missionaries could convert very few Untouchables. The Christian population in India is surprisingly small notwithstanding the missionary effort extending over 300 years. They might have converted the whole of Untouchables and the Backward Classes if they had begun with them first.

5. Attention may be drawn to the entry of Christianity in Rome. For it is very instructive. From the page of Gibbon's "Decline and Fall of the Roman Empire" it is clear that Christianity entered first among the lower classes as Gibbon says among the poor and the despised section of the Roman population. The higher classes came in later on. Gibbon ridiculed Christianity as a religion of the poor and the downtrodden. In holding this view Gibbon was

thoroughly mistaken. He failed to realise that it is the poor who need religion. For religion, if it is right religion-gives hope of betterment to the poor who having nothing else need as a soothing action the rich have everything, they need not live on hope. They live on their possession. Secondly Gibbon failed to realise that religion if it is of the right type ennobles people and elevates them. People do not degrade religion.

6. I will now turn to the preliminary steps which must be taken for the revival of Buddhism in India. I mention below those that occur to me:
   1. The preparation of a Buddhist Gospel which could be a constant companion of the convert. The want of small Gospel containing the teachings of the Buddha is a great handicap in the propagation of Buddhism. The common man cannot be expected to read the 73 voluems of the Pali Cannon. Christianity has a great advantage over Buddhism in having the message of Christ contained in a small booklet 'The Bible'. This handicap in the way of the propagation of Buddhism must be removed. In regard to the preparation of Buddha's Gospel care must be taken to emphasise the social and moral teachings of the Buddha. I have to emphasise this. What is emphasised, is meditation, contemplation and *abhidhamms*. This way of presenting Buddhism to Indians would be fatal to our cause.
   2. The introduction of a ceremony like 'Baptism' in Christianity for the lay people. There it really no ceremony of conversion i.e. for becoming a lay disciple of the Buddha. Whatever ceremony of conversion there is, for becoming a Bhikhu, for entering into the *Sangh*. Among the Christians there are two ceremonies (i) for Baptism showing acceptance of Christianity and (ii) for ordination i.e. becoming a priest. In Buddhism there is no ceremony like Baptism. This is the main reason why people after becoming Buddhist slip out of Buddhism. We must introduce a ceremony like the Christian Baptism which every lay person must undergo before he can be called a 'Buddhist'. Merely uttering the *Pancha Sila* is not enough. Many other

points must be added to make a person feel that he is ceasing to be a Hindu and becoming a new man.

3. The appointment of a number of lay preachers who could go about and preach Buddhism and see how far they are following Buddha's Dhamma. The lay preachers must be paid and secondly they may be married persons. In the beginning they may be part time workers.
4. The establishment of a Buddhist Religious Seminary where persons who wish to become preachers could be taught Buddhism and also comparative study of other Religions.
5. The introduction of congregational worship in the Vihara every Sunday followed by a sermon.

7. In addition to these preliminary steps it is necessary to do some other things which require to be done in a big way as aids to our propagation campaign. In this connection I make the following proposals:
   1. Building big temples and Viharas in the four important towns (i) Chennai (ii) Mumbai (iii) Nagpur and (iv) Delhi.
   2. Establishment of High Schools and Colleges in the following towns (i) Chennai; (ii) Mumbai; (iii) Kolkata and (iv) Delhi.
   3. Inviting Essays on Buddhist topics and giving prizes to the first three sufficient in value so as to attract people to make their best efforts to study Buddhist literature. The essays should be open to all, Hindus, Muslims and Christians; to men as well as to women. This is the best way of making people interested in the study of Buddhism.

8. Temples should be so big as to create the impression that some thing big is really happening. High Schools and Colleges are necessary adjuncts. They are intended to create Buddhist atmosphere among younger men. Besides they will not only pay their way but bring a surplus which could be used for other missionary work. It should be remembered that most of the Christian Missions find funds for financing their activities from the surplus revenue which is yielded by the Schools and Colleges they run.

Appendix - IV

Ceremony for Marriage prescribed by Ambedkar in his Letter to Kardak

Dr. B.R. Ambedkar
Member, Rajya Sabha.

26, Alipore Road
Civil Line, Delhi

Dated the 4th December 1956.

Dear Mr. Kardak,

Please refer to your letter of 12th November 1956.

The Buddhist marriage ceremony is simple. There is no 'homa' and there is no 'Saptpadi'. The essence of the ceremony lies in placing an earthen pot newly made, between the bride and the bride-groom on a stool and to fill it brimful with water. The bride and the bride-groom to stand on two side of the pot. They should place a coton thread in the water and pot and each hold one end of the thread in their hands. Some one should sing the Mangal sutta. Both bride and bride-groom should wear white clothes.

Yours sincerely,
Sd/-
B.R. AMBEDKAR

Mr. V.S. Kardak,
41-2, 3rd Marine Street,
Mumbai - 2.

Appendix - V

The Path to Freedom

B.R.Ambedkar's speech in a conference held at Mumbai on 30-31 May 1936, in which he declared that 'Conversion, was the only path to freedom for the Untouchables'.

"There are two aspects of conversion, social as well as religious; material as well as spiritual. Whatever may be the, aspect, or line of thinking, it is necessary to understand the beginning, the nature of untouchability and how it is practiced. Without this understanding, you will not be able to realise the real meaning underlying my declaration of conversion.

In order to have a clear understanding of untouchability and its practice in real life, I want you to recall the stories of the atrocities perpetrated against you. The instances of beating by caste Hindus for the simple reason that you have claimed the right to enroll your children in government schools, or the right to draw water from a public well, or the right to take a marriage procession with the groom on horseback, are very common. You all know such instances, as they happen before your eyes. But very few of you might have realisd as to why, all this happens. What is at the root of their tyranny. To me, it is very necessary, that you understand it.

The instances cited above have nothing to do with the virtues and vices of an individual. This is not a feud between two rival men. The problem of untouchability is a matter of class struggle. It is a struggle between caste Hindus and the Untouchables. This is a matter of injustice being done by one class against another. This struggle is related to social status. This struggle indicates

---

This is an abridged version of the speech translated into English by Vasant W. Moon. It was published in the Maharashtra Government's special issue of "Loka Rajya" on the occasion of Ambedkar Jayanti, April 14, 1981.

how one class should keep its relationship with another class of people. The struggle starts as soon as you start claiming equal treatment with others. Had it not been so, there would have been no struggle over simple reasons like serving chapatis, wearing good quality clothes, fetching water in a metal pot, sitting the bridegroom on the back of a horse, etc.? In these cases you spend your own money. Why then do the high-caste Hindus get irritated? The reason for their anger is very simple. Your behaving on par with them insults them. Your status in their eyes is low; you are impure; you must remain at the lowest rung. Then alone will they allow you to live happily. The moment you cross your level the struggle starts.

The instances given above also prove one more fact. Untouchability is not a short or temporary feature; it is a permanent one. To put it straight, it can be said that the struggle between the Hindus and the Untouchables is a permanent phenomenon. It is eternal, because the high-caste people believe that the religion which has placed you at the lowest level of the society is itself eternal. No change according to time and circumstances is possible. You are at the lowest rung of the ladder today. You shall remain lowest forever.

This means the struggle between Hindus and Untouchables shall continue forever. How you will survive through this struggle is the main question. And unless you think it over there is no way out. Those who desire to live in obedience to the dictates of the Hindus, those who wish to remain their slaves, they do not need to think over the problem. But those who wish to live a life of self-respect and equality will have to think over this. How should we survive through this struggle? For me, it is not difficult to answer this question. Those who have assembled here will have to agree that in any struggle one who holds strength becomes the victor. One, who has no strength, need not expect success. This has been proved by experience, and I do not need to cite illustration to prove it.

The question that arises, which you must now consider, is whether you have enough strength to survive through this struggle? Three types of strength are known to man: (1) Man-power, (2) Finance, and (3) Mental strength. Which of these, you think that you possess? So far as man-power is concerned, it is clear that you are in a minority. The Untouchables are not even compact. They are scattered through the villages. May be you have a little bit of manpower, but finances, you have none. You have no capacity to get redress from the law courts. You are compelled to tolerate insult, tyranny and oppression at the hands of class Hindus without a sigh of the complaint, because you have no capacity to bear the expenses of the courts. As regards mental strength, the condition is still bad. The tolerance of insults and tyranny without grudge and complaint has killed the sense of retort and revolt. Confidence, vigour and ambition have completely vanished from you. All of you have become helpless, unenergetic and pale. Everywhere there is an atmosphere of defeatism and pessimism. Even the slight idea, that you can do something does not enter your mind.

Uptil now, we have discussed why conversion is necessary for material gains. Now, I propose to put forth my thoughts as to why conversion is much necessary for spiritual well-being. What is religion ? Why is it necessary? Let us first try to understand. Several people have tried to define religion. Amongst all of these definitions, only one is most meaningful and agreeable to all. "That which governs people is religion". Although this definition logically appears to be correct, it does not disclose or clarify the nature of rules which govern a society. The question still remains as to what should be the nature of the rules which govern society. This question is more important than that of definition. Because the question of which religion is necessary for man does not depend on its definition but on the motive and nature of the rules that bind and govern a society. What should be the real nature of religion? While deciding this question, another question follows. What should be the relation between a man and society?

The modern social philosophers have postulated three answers to this question. Some have said that the ultimate goal of society is to achieve happiness for the individual. Some say that society exists for the development of the inherent qualities and energies of man and to help him develop himself. However, some claim that the chief object of social organisation is not the development or happiness of the individual but the creation of an ideal society .There is no place for an individual in Hindu society.

The Hindu religion does not teach how an individual should behave with another individual. A religion which does not recognise the individual is not personally acceptable to me.

Three factors are required for the uplift of an individual. They are: sympathy, equality and liberty. Can you say by experience that any of these factors exist for you in Hinduism?

Such a living example of inequality is not to be found anywhere in the world. Not at anytime in the history of mankind can we find such inequality, which is more intense than Untouchability….I think, you have been thrust into this condition because you have continued to be Hindus. Those of you who have become Muslims, are treated by the Hindus neither as Untouchables nor as unequal. The same can be said of those who have become Christians.

Hindus can be ranked among those cruel people whose utterances and acts are two poles apart. They have this Ram on their tongues and a knife under their armpits. They speak like Saints but act like Butchers…

We are not low in the eyes of the Hindus alone, but we are the lowest in the whole of India, because of the treatment given to us by the Hindus. If you have to get rid of this shameful condition, if you have to cleanse this filth and make use of this precious life, there is only one way and that is to throw off the shackles of Hindu religion and the Hindu society, in which you are bound. The taste of a thing can be changed.

But the poison cannot be made Amrit (nectar). To talk of annihilating castes is like talking of changing the poison into Amrit (nectar). In short, so long as we remain in a religion which teaches a man to treat another man as leper, the sense of discrimination on account of caste which is deeply rooted in our minds cannot go. For annihilating castes and untouchability from among the Untouchables, change of religion is the only antidote.

What is there in conversion, which can be called novel? Really speaking what sort of social relations have you with the, caste Hindus at present? You are separate from the Hindus as Muslims and Christians are. So it is their relation with you. Your society and that of the Hindus are two distinct groups. By conversion, no body can say or feel that one society has been split up. You will remain as separate from the Hindus as you are today. Nothing new will happen on account of this conversion.

Only a congenital idiot will say that one has to adhere to one's religion because it is that of our ancestors. No sane man will accept such a proposition. Those who advocate such an argument, seem not to have read the history at all... Moreover, this Hindu religion is not the religion of our ancestors, but it was a slavery forced upon them.

Our aim is to gain freedom. We have nothing to do with anything else. To reform the Hindu society is neither our aim nor our field of action. None should misunderstand the object of our movement as being Hindu social reform. The object of our movement is to gain social freedom. And this freedom cannot be secured without conversion (to another religion) .

The Hindu religion does not appeal to my conscience. It does not appeal to my self-respect... I tell you very specifically, Religion is for Man and not Man for Religion. To get human treatment, convert yourselves. Convert for getting organised. Convert for becoming strong. Convert for securing equality. Convert for getting liberty. Convert so that your domestic life may be happy.

Why do you remain in that religion which insults you at every step? A religion in which man's human behaviour with man is prohibited is not religion but a display of force. A religion in which the touch of human being is prohibited is not religion but a mockery. A religion which precludes some classes from education, forbids them to accumulate any wealth and to bear arms, is not religion but a mockery. A religion that compels the ignorant to be ignorant and the poor to be poor is not a religion but a mockey.

Finally, let me remind you of the last words of the Buddha. Be your own guide: Take refuge in reason: Do not listen to the advice of others: Do not succumb to others: Be truthful; Take refuge in truth: "If you keep in mind this message of the Buddha at this juncture, I am sure your decision will not be wrong".

Appendix - VI

Three Commandments

On 20 July 1942, Dr. Ambedkar was given a reception by the All India Depressed Classes Conference at Nagpur consequent upon his appointment as a member of the Viceroy's Executive Council. In his short speech on this occasion, Babsasheb exhorted his followers to always keep in view 'Three Commandments' so as to ensure that they achieve their objective. "Educate, Agitate and Organise", he said, in reply to the Welcome Address:

"Ladies and Gentlemen: I thank you for the Address you have presented to me.

I wonder if such an Address was at all necessary. Toasts and Addresses have a peculiar history behind them, at any rate, Toast has. The ceremony of drinking to the health of the King as we see it in the English Society came in after the civil war and during the period of restoration. It was originally a matter of compulsion and was forced on those English Regiments which had rebelled against the King. It was to enforce loyalty to the new King that they were forced to drink to the health of the King. Drinking to the health of the King is now universal and nobody cares to inquire about its origin. Its origin, as I told you, lay in the desire to compel doubtful loyalty to proclaim itself. Your loyalty, I know, is not doubtful and I should have thought it was unnecessary to vouchsafe it by means of this Address. Now that you have insisted on my accepting it, I welcome it as a token of the sentiments of love and affection, which you bear towards me. It is a token of your appreciation of what I have done for the Untouchables. This Address proves that you uphold the stand I have taken in Indian politics in the name of the Untochables of India. Our ideal is to be recognised as

---

Report of the Depressed Classes Conference, Nagpur Session, 18-20 July, 1942, p. 51.

honourable partners with the Hindus and the Muslims in running the Government of this country -partners on honourable and equal terms. I can assure you that I will strive to achieve the ideal we have fixed before us.

You have less need of an assurance from me that I will fight for the ideal. I stand in greater need of an assurance from you. You have assured me of your love and affection. It was quite unnecessary. I want an assurance of another kind. It is an assurance of strength, unity and determination to stand for our rights, fight for our rights and never to return until we win our rights. You promise to do your part. I promise to do mine.

With justice on our side, I don't see how we can loose our battle. The battle to me is a matter full of joy. The battle is in the fullest sense spiritual. There is nothing material or sordid in it. For our's is a battle, not a battle for wealth or for power. It is a battle for freedom, It is a battle for the reclamation of human personality which will continue to be suppressed and mutilated if in the political struggle the Hindus win and we loose. My final words of advice to you are educate, agitate and organise; have faith in yourselves and never loose hope. I shall always be with you as I know you will be with me."

Appendix - VII

The Rise and Fall of Buddhism in India

B.R. Ambedkar's address to an international gathering at Colombo, Sri Lanka on 5 June 1950.

"Most people who have studied rise and fall of Buddhism in India would admit that this subject had not been adequately dealt with as it should have been. I have not been able to find any authentic material explaining why Buddhism rose to the height it achieved and why it disappeared in India.

To know a subject thoroughly, one must know its relevant traditions exactly and precisely. Similarly, the significance of Buddhism would not be understood unless the exact circumstances which gave birth to it are understood. I disagree with the view that Hinduism has all along been the religion of India. Hinduism is the latest development of social thought in India.

The religion of India has undergone three changes. Vedic religion which was practiced first gave way, in course of time, to Brahmanism and this in turn to Hinduism. It was during Brahmanic period that Buddhism was born. This was because Buddhism opposed inequality , authority and division of society into various classes which Brahmanism had introduced in India.

It is easy to practice the Vedic religion. In it, performance of yagya (yajnas) is the main puja. The Vedic Aryans used to worship innumerable gods. They used to please them by performing *yagyas*. The puja to be performed for these gods should necessarily be sacred and superb. In those Agrarian times, cows were the chief wealth of the Aryans. Therefore, they used to sacrifice cows to honour their deities. In this way, Vedic Dharma encouraged

---

D.C. Ahir, edited: Dr. Ambedkar On Buddhism, Bombay, 1982, pp. 111- 114.

violence. Brahmins succeeded in organising the society only by adopting Vedic *yagyas*. The Brahmins also divided the society into four sections (varnas)- Brahmin, Kshatriya, Vaishya and Shudra. The division of the society into four varnas (castes) created great inequalities. They said that the Brahmins were born of the Brahma's mouth and Shudras from his feet. Can any body believe that the basic principle of any religion could be to divide the society? Yet this is what Brahmanism has perpetuated. On the other hand, equality is the main feature of Buddhism. The religion of the Buddha gives freedom of thought and freedom of self-development to all. To abjure violence is another essential teaching of Buddhism. It has never taught to achieve salvation by sacrificing animals or any living being to propitiate gods. I would say that the rise of Buddhism in India was as significant as the French Revolution. Prior to the advent of Buddhism, it was impossible to even think that a Shudra would get throne, History of India reveals that after the emergence of Buddhism, Shudras are seen getting thrones. Verily, Buddhism paved way for establishment of democracy and socialistic pattern of society in India. .

It is a perplexing problem how Buddhism, which had acquired a highest place, disappeared from India. There is very little material to tell us about the condition of Buddhism upto 274 B.C. It is however seen that Buddhism was at its climax of popularity in the reign of Asoka. How such a grêat and popular religion lost ground in India is a painful phenomena.

Buddhism appears to have met strong opposition in 184 B.C. when the last Mauryan King was assassinated by his Chief Commander. This was one of the awful actions of the Brahmins to save their religion. But it is a pity that the historians have not given sufficient importance to this incident. While going through the Buddhist literature, I find that 90% followers of the Buddha were Brahmins. Brahmins used to come to the Buddha for discussion and argumentation, and when defeated, used to become faithful to the Buddha and ultimately accepted Buddhism. The Buddhist literature is full of such incidents. Therefore, how is it that Buddhism that had flourished amongst the majority of Brahmins was later on destroyed by the Brahmins themselves.

In my opinion the main reason for this was the family deity's (kula deva) worship. In India, like the village deity and national deity, there were family deities also who were worshipped through the Brahmins. The priests who used to go for worshipping these deities started influencing the affairs of the State through the queens. Asoka after embracing Buddhism discontinued this practice and removed the idols of such deities. Asoka said, "As I venerate the Buddha, the Enlightened One, there is no need to worship any other deity." This action of Asoka disturbed the Brahmins very much as it ended their unfair means of livelihood and exploitation. They pledged to take revenge for this loss.

The Brahmins were of the view that after death, kings go to hell because of their errors and omissions. Therefore, they did not agree to be rulers but preferred to be the Chief Advisers to the Kings. In order to take revenge for the loss they suffered on account of stoppage of kulapuja (family deity's worship). Brahmins gave up the approved motto of being advisers only and tried to grab power. With the help of their well-wisher Kshatriyas, they also organised an united Brahmin- Kshatriya axis against Buddhism. The ascendancy of Brahmanism again in Indian society is one of the reasons for the downfall of Buddhism.

The foreign invasions are also responsible for the decline of Buddhism in India. The Greeks did no harm to Buddhism. There are positive proofs available that the Greeks gave liberal financial assistance for Buddhist activities. The Huns invaded India, and after being defeated by the Guptas, they settled in India. Prior to this, the Huns tried to destroy Buddhism. The religion of the Buddha got the severest blow from the Muslim invasion. They destroyed the Buddhist idols and killed the Bhikkhus. They mistook the great Nalanda University as the Fort of Buddhists and killed a large number of monks thinking that they were soldiers. The few Bhikkhus who escaped the onslaught fled away to the neighbouring countries like Nepal, Tibet and China.

Some of my Hindu friends often ask why Hinduism, which has also idol-worship, survived in India and Buddhism died. My answer is that whatsoever the religion may be, it requires the priest community to preserve it. Due to the shortage of Buddhist monks, Buddhism declined. Efforts were subsequently made by some Buddhists to raise another priesthood in order to revive

Buddhism but their efforts failed. Such is not the case with Hinduism. A Brahmin's son is priest by birth. Therefore, no separate priest community is required to protect their religion. This is why Hinduism survived Muslim onslaught. Moreover, Buddhism as a religion is difficult to practice while Hinduism is not. Besides, the political climate in India had also been inhospitable to its advancement.

I do not agree with the suggestion made by many people in India that Buddhism was destroyed by the dialectics of Shankaracharya. This is contrary to the facts as Buddhism existed for many centuries after his death. In my opinion, Shankaracharya himself was a Buddhist. His Guru too was a Buddhist. Of course, Buddhism declined in India because of the rise of Vaishnavism and Saivisim, the two cults which adopted and absorbed many good points of Buddhism. Today, Hinduism is in a very much changed form. Hinduism which taught and practiced violence earlier has started teaching non-violence. This has been copied from Buddhism. Buddhism may have disappeared in material form but as a spiritual force it still exists in India."

Appendix - VIII

Buddhism can end India's Ills

On May 20, 1951, a grand Buddha Jayanti function was held at Ambedkar Bhavan in New Delhi. Presided over by H.E.M. Daniel Levi, French Ambassador in India, it was attended by all the Diplomats of Buddhist countries, as well as the Buddhist monks in Delhi. This was an address to that distinguished gathering by Ambedkar:

"Hon'ble Chairman, brothers and sisters.

Last year when we assembled here for celebrating this sacred day, the attendance was not encouraging. But this year, the attendance is good. I was very happy to read in the newspapers that a long procession was taken out yesterday and the same was acclaimed by the people. I am happy with the progress made by you in this direction in the course of one year.

When we celebrate the Buddha Jayanti, we have a special purpose in doing so. To celebrate the birthday of Lord Buddha is not a great thing because all who are great must be honoured. But we celebrate the Buddha Day because by doing so, social evils rampant in India can be eradicated.

The most condemnable thing in Hinduism is that it is based on Chaturvarna which divides people artificially. I want to impress upon the Hindus that the prevalent social evils cannot be eradicated without abolishing the caste system. To get rid of the caste and to end other social evils, India must embrace Buddhism as that religion is based upon the ethics of morality, equality and universal brotherhood.

Lord Buddha never believed in caste system. He was the strongest opponent of caste, and staunchest upholder of equality.

Buddha Vihara, New Delhi, 1951 papers; Indian News Chronicle, 22 May, 1951.

He said, "all human beings are equal." There is no distinction between man and man. He further said that, as the water, whether it is from Ganga, whether it is from Jamuna or whether it is from a drainage, when it enters the sea, it is sea water; likewise there is no distinction between men when they enter His religion. All are equal in His religion. The Buddha took people from all the communities as Bhikkhus.

I am surprised at the attitude of the modem Brahmins towards Buddhism. What has happened to them? Why are they opposing re-adoption of Buddhism by India when ninety percent of Bhikkhus at the time of Buddha were Brahmins. I hope they would change their outlook. If modern Hindus believe in a casteless and classless society then there is no reason why they should not embrace Buddhism which had its very foundations ingrained in such a Philosophy. In my view, Buddhism is a sure cure for India's ills, social and economic. As long as caste barriers exist, India can never attain the grandeur and glory of ancient times. India would rise once again to its glory only when people turn to Buddhism, and follow high ethical principles of liberty, equality fraternity and justice preached by the Buddha.

I am determined to revive the great religion of the Buddha, which was once held in high esteem in India. For the millions of poor people, in particular, the depressed and oppressed classes, the embracing of Buddhism is the only way to social emancipation. If the rest of the Hindu society does not co-operate, then we, the Scheduled Castes, will go ahead on our own and try once again to bring back Buddhism to its former glory and prestige in the land of its birth.

Appendix - IX

Three Gurus and Three Deities

On 28 October 1954, Dr. B. R. Ambedkar was felicitated and presented a purse of rupees one lakh and eighteen thousand by his followers at a public meeting at Purendare Stadium, Bombay. Speaking on this occasion, Babasaheb narrated some events of his early childhood, and declared that his life had been influenced by three Gurus-Buddha, Kabir and Phooley, and three Deities-Knowledge, Self-Respect and Character:

"Friends,

You have presented me a purse of Rupees One lakh and eighteen thousand. It has just now been declared that this purse has been presented to me, to celebrate my diamond jubilee. It is just one reason. This is your money and it has been collected for construction of one hall. To give a practical shape to this plan, it was told to people, to collect this money on the occasion of my 60th Birth Day. This fund has been collected through hard labour of toiling poor men and women of our community. And I am a Barrister. I was a member of Executive Council. Therefore, it is shameful to accept your money on the pretension of sickness. Therefore, this whole fund, as I have told you, will be spent on construction of the building. I declare on the occasion that I do not want a single paisa out of it (thunderous claps).

Friends! Today, while sitting here, all the events of my life are coming before my eyes like some movie film where I was born. All those places where my father took me and what ever he had done for me, all these things are before my eyes. But one thing I want to tell you here is, what evidence is there to show that I completed 60 years of my age (laughs).

Dalit Voice. June 16,30. 1990 : Bahujan Voice, April 1989 I' Translation from Marathi By A. K. Kharpade. New Delhi.

Which year I was born? There is no record. My father was in 6th Pioneer Battalion. Then he moved to 7th Pioneer Battalion. At that time he never felt any importance of me as his son. He did not record my date of birth. How minor is this? But even this could not be possible to him. Therefore, today, whatever date of birth I have nobody can say that it is my real date of birth.

But some two-three events can definitely be told about me. I was born at Mhow in Rajputana. My father belonged to Konkan Region. But due to employment, he was required to go to Rajputana. Therefore, I was born at Mhow, is certain. Another thing is that I was born exactly at 12' 0 clock. At that time my father was on duty and my mother was feeling labour pains. My body was big. It is said that my mother felt terrible pains. But when the matron came out and told my father "Go inside, you got a son", at that time the clock was ringing 12'0 clock. The third thing is that I was born on bad stars and the fortune teller told that this boy is very bad. His mother will die soon. Because of this my other brothers and sisters started disliking me. They were always unhappy with me and used to say " This boy will prove to be bad for our mother". At last my mother died soon. These three incidents about my birth can be told.

If you ask about my childhood, I feel surprised about it. Till I was grown up to the age of 12-13 years, everybody felt that I would not be able to do any thing in life.

But many members in the family treated me with affection. Our aunt was there. She used to love me most. She warned all people that child is without mother. Do not be harsh with him. Only because of this I misused my liberty. All people used to feel that I will not be able to do any thing. Those who brought me up, none of them is surviving today. I would have been happy, had they been living today to see this felicitations. Like this I spent my childhood. You may imagine, what a great change has taken place in my life. At the most I would have been a shepherd, running after animals or an ordinary worker toiling in the field. Then I would not have reached this stage. My father always used to tell me that learn some light work of job. I feel like writing an autobiography. I will definitely write a small book on my childhood. I will mention all these stories in it.

It is not that I had some inborn qualities and therefore I reached this stage. The way my life was going, had I allowed to go like that, I would have at the most become some virtuous man. But I had my own self instinct. Whatever turn my life took why and how it got this turn? I would like to tell this to you now.

I have three Gurus. Everybody has a one or other Guru. Likewise I too have My first and supreme Guru is Buddha. My father was a Kabir panthi. When I was 12-13 years old, since then I remember this. My father's house can be said as a centre of religion. Similarly, it can also be said as centre of education. My father was worshipper of education. Similarly he was also very much religious. In my childhood, he made me read Ramayana, Mahabharata, etc. My father used to say "We are poor, but we should not be afraid. Why you cannot be a learned man?" Once I passed some examination. The residents of our chawl decided to felicitate me with the help of Dada Keluskar, but my father said," We do not want felicitations. By such felicitations, this boy will start feeling that he has become some big leader" (Laughs and claps). At last, the function took place and Dada Keluskar presented a book on the life of Buddha to me. After reading this book, I got different enlightenment. After study of Buddhism through that book, I felt like studying it more and more. The impact of Buddhism is very much firm on my mind. And I firmly believe that it is only Buddhism, which can emancipate the world. If Hindus want their country to survive, they must accept the path of Buddha. This is what I always tell them.

My second Guru is Kabir. My father was a follower of Kabir's sect. Because of this the life and philosophy of Kabir has also influenced my life a great deal. In my opinion Kabir could understand the real significance of philosophy of Buddha.

And my third Guru is Jyotiba. He is the real Guru of all non-Brahmins. Darji, Kumbhar, Nais, Koli, Mahars, Mangs and Chambhars to all these castes, it is only Phooley who taught the lessons of humanity. In earlier political movement, we all were going on the path of Jyotiba. Afterwards, Maratha drifted from us. Some of them have gone to Congress to eat the leftovers. One of them R.B.Bole joined Hindu Maha Sabha. He is present here. Let anybody go anywhere. But we will continue to tread on the path of Jyotiba. These are my three Gurus. My life is influenced by their teachings.

After this, I have three deities. Some people worship goddess Mari Aal or god Khandoba. Similarly, I also worship three deities. My first deity is Vidya (Knowledge). Mankind cannot get peace and human dignity without knowledge. Knowledge must be made available to all. It is like an ocean. Buddha once said that Buddhism is very pure. There is no discrimination in it. Shraman, Monk, Brahman, Scavenger, whosoever they may be, all are one. Before joining my Sangh, all rivers or drains, there names may be anything. Yamuna, Brahmaputra, Ganga or Godavari, all these rivers are flowing from different provinces, (before emerging into ocean) once their water becomes one, one cannot say this is the water of Yamuna, Ganga or Godavari. So my Sangha is also like an ocean. There is no caste or creed in it. All are one. As food is essential for survival of man, similarly knowledge is also essential. Without knowledge what can he do? Today, 90% people are illiterate in India. In Myanmar 90% are literate. The reason is Brahmins did not give knowledge to us. Religious dogmas came in our ways and snatched knowledge from us. Our people used to say that stone is our knowledge. Therefore, our religious concepts have gone to extreme low ends. We are all worshippers of stones. Sant Tukaram had at one place said. "If you are to get sons and daughters by offerings (to Gods), then why you need a husband." (Why this fate of our people?). Because we were not given knowledge. Knowledge is a very big thing. I am extremely crazy for knowledge. Any Brahmin may not be possessing so many books, as I am having at Delhi. Total 20,000 books I am having. Thacker and Company is having bills worth thousands on my credit. I can get books on credit anywhere. Where there is a heavy credit on me, I stop my car there only. Such great craze I possess for knowledge. Everybody must have this madness. If a man loves books so much, then only he will become real worshipper of knowledge. I worship knowledge all the 24 hours.

My second deity is Self-Respect. I never begged to anybody. My aim was that I must feed myself and I must secure my people. Due to request of Dr. Paranjape, I agreed to teach Economics in one college. That time they told me to take 13 lectures. I told them

I will take only four. If you agree, give me appointment. Otherwise I am free to go my own way because I wanted to serve my people. For this purpose I required enough time. At Poibavdi in Room Nos. 48 and 50, I have eaten raw grains. But I have not discarded social service and accepted jobs with big salary. I found out some way out. People accepted money, purse and constructed their houses. One leader known to me had given promissory notes of Rs. 47000/-. And when people presented him a purse of one lakh, repaid his loan. I do not want to do like this. I could do for people whatever could be possible, after maintaining myself on my own. I never wanted to go for job. Let any Governor General come, he was friendly with me. But I never begged to anybody saying that I should be given this post or that. For others I might have done something. But let anybody show, that I have written even a small note for myself. But I had great desire to become Executive Councilor. That desire was fulfilled. Once I accepted Councillorship in British regime and once Congress rule. But here also I had a conflict with Congress. Therefore what I want to tell you is that one should not be so much submissive. He must consider himself that he is also somebody. My self-respect is so burning that I consider even 'God' inferior to me.

And my third deity is Sheel (Character). In my life I have not committed any forgery, cheating or some sin for self-interest. I do not remember to have committed any such kind of act. I feel proud about it. I visited England many times. But never drank wine, never smoked a cigarette. I do not have any habit. Books and clothes, these are the only two things I like. To preserve a sheel (character) is a very big virtue, this I have.

So I have three Gurus and three deities. I am influenced by them. I could reach this stage only because of the strength of them. So follow them. You have felicitated me. It is not a felicitation of one individual. As an ideal of these three deities you feel grateful to them. Therefore, you arranged this function. And hence I am accepting this purse."

Appendix - X

Time for Buddhist Revival in India

In the first week of December 1954, Dr. Ambedkar visited Burma (now Myanmar) to participate in the Third Conference of the World Fellowship of Buddhists held at Rangoon. Addressing the Conference, he said:

Distinguished Delegates, Ladies and Gentlemen.

"I have to say this with anguish that in the land where the great Buddha was born, His religion has declined. How such a thing happened is beyond anyone's comprehension".

After saying this, tears came into his eyes and he could not proceed with his speech for a couple of minutes. Then, composing himself, Dr. Ambedkar said:

"Though Buddhism has declined in India yet it has made a great impact on Hinduism. In ancient days, the Brahmins used to sacrifice cows in the hope of attaining heaven. Influenced by the teachings of love and compassion of the Buddha, the Brahmins have not only stopped bloody sacrifices but are also now propagating against cow-killing. This is the greatest victory of the doctrine of non-violence (ahimsa) preached by the Buddha.

The Brahmins have created thousands of gods and goddesses but they do not know which god or goddess would lead them to heaven. Hence, they keep on running around. Unlike Hinduism, Buddhism lays no emphasis on the attainment of heaven. Nor it is necessary. To be happy in the present life, one should practice the ethics of morality, equality and universal brotherhood. This is an eternal truth taught by the Buddha.

I am keen that India should re-adopt Buddhism. I have already taken some steps in this direction. I am the architect of the

---

B.R. Ambedkar, Baudh Oharam hi Manav Oharam (Hindi), edited by Bhikshu Oh.armarakshita, Sarnath, Varanasi, 1967. Translation: D.C. Ahir.

Constitution of India. In the Constitution which I have framed I have provided for the teaching of the Pali language. I have also got inserted the Buddhist Wheel of Law (Dhamma Chakra) in the National Flag of India. I have also got adopted the Asokan Lion Capital of Sarnath as the National Emblem of India. These proposals, I am happy to say, were not opposed by any Member of the Constituent Assembly.

I have established a College in Aurungabad, near Ajanta-Ellora. Today, 2900 students are studying in the Siddharth Colleges in Bombay, and 500 students are getting education in the Aurangabad College. I have already announced that any student who writes the best essay on the life of the Buddha will be given an award of rupees one thousand. The idea of doing this is to encourage the students to study Buddhism. This will naturally lead to the revival of Buddhism. I would like to add here that for establishing these colleges I had taken a loan of rupees twenty-two lakhs from the Government of India. I doubt if I will be able to repay this loan during my life time. Even so, I am planning to establish Buddha Viharas in Delhi, Bombay, Calcutta and Madras where people from all walks of life could come and pay their homage to the Great Buddha. This is how I am planning to popularise Buddhism in India.

India is now ready to receive the message of the Buddha. In fact, in the world of today, India is the only country where suitable climate exists for the propagation of Buddhism. I strongly feel that the gigantic amounts being spent by Myanmar, Sri Lanka and other countries on the lighting and management of the shrines could be usefully used for the propagation of the Dhamma and its revival in India, the land of its birth. Since this is the most opportune time for Buddhist revival in India, I shall continue to work for its revival whether anybody helps me or not.

Appendix - XI

On Past Performance and Future Prospects

To masses: "For the past 30 years, I am struggling to secure political rights for you people. I have got for you reserved seats in Parliament and in State Assemblies. I have got for you proper provisions for education of your children. Today, we can progress. It is now your duty to continue the struggle unitedly for removal of educational, economic and social inequality. For this purpose, you will have to be prepared for all sorts of sacrifices and even to shed your blood".

To leaders: "If somebody invites you in his palace, you may go willingly. But you must not go there by putting your own hut on fire. If that king quarrels with you some day and drive you out of his palace, where will you go? If you want to sellout yourselves you may do so but not at the cost of destroying your organisation. I do not have any dangers from others, but I feel danger from our own people".

To landless labourers: "I am more worried for the landless labourers of the villages. I could not do much for them. I cannot bear their sufferings and plights. The main reason for their sufferings is that they do not have land.

Therefore, they are victims of humiliations and atrocities. Unless and until they have land, they cannot emancipate

---

On 18 March, 1956, Babasaheb Ambedkar paid his last visit to the historic city Agra. Addressing a huge public meeting there on that day, he reviewed the past performance and reflected on future prospects of the movement launched by him. Lamenting that the educated people had deceived him, he gave some useful hints to his followers as to how to take the movement" forward.

Hindi text with Daya Shanker of Agra. Translated by the Editor, Dalit Voice, Bangalore, 1-5 August, 1990.

themselves. I will struggle for it. If government puts any hurdle in it I will lead these people and will also give a legal battle for them, but I shall try to secure land for the landless".

To his followers: "Very soon, I will embrace the religion of Lord Buddha. It is a progressive religion. It is based on equality, liberty and fraternity .I could search this religion through efforts of many years. Now I will become Buddhist very soon." Then as an untouchable I will not be able to live with you. But as a real Buddhist I will continue to struggle for your welfare. I will not tell you to become Buddhist with me. I do not want BLIND FOLLOWERS. Only those who desire to take refuge in this great religion, may embrace Buddhism, so that they remain in this religion with firm convictions and observe its code of conduct".

To Buddhist monks: "Buddhism is a great religion. The founder of this religion Tathagaṭa Buddha has propagated this religion and due to its good aspects it could reach every nook and corner of India. After its great fame, this religion became extinct in 1213 AD. There are many reasons for this. One of the reasons is also that the Buddhist Monks became addicted to living luxurious and restful life. Instead of moving from place to place for propagation of the religion, they started taking rest in Viharas and indulging in writing books in praise (of Kings). Now for re-establishing this religion, they will have to work hard. They will have to move from door to door. We have very few monks in the society. Therefore, the common good people should also propagate the religion and perform its rites".

To Govt. employees: " There is some progress in education in our society. By acquiring education some people have reached the higher positions. But these educated people have deceived me. I was hoping that after acquiring high education they will serve the society. But what I am seeing is that a crowd of small and big clerks have gathered around, who are busy in filling their bellies. Those who are employed in government services, it is their duty that they should contribute willingly 20th part of their salary to the cause. Then only the society will progress. Otherwise only one family will improve. The boy who is educating in a village, the entire society has expectation from him. One educated social worker can prove a boon for them".

To students & youths: My appeal to the students is that after acquiring education, instead of doing some clerical job, he should serve his village or locality people, by which, exploitation and injustice arising out of ignorance can be stopped. Your emancipation lies in the emancipation of the society.

Today my position is like a big pole. Supporting a hunge tent. I am worried about when this pole will not be there. I am not keeping good health. I do not know, when I will go away from you. I am not finding any young man, who will protect the interest of these crores of helpless and hopeless people. If any young man comes forward (to take up this responsibility) then I will go away peacefully".

Appendix - XII

Embrace Buddhism for Emancipation

On 14 October 1956, Babasaheb Ambedkar embraced Buddhism, along with half a million of his followers, at a historic conversion ceremony at Nagpur. Next day, on 15 October 1956, in a three-hour long speech in Marathi, he traced the history of the suffering of the downtrodden through the ages; his life-long struggle to mitigate their sufferings and as to why he had chosen Buddhism:

"Members of Buddhist Brotherhood, Brothers and Sisters, I want to express my thoughts on this important question as to why I have taken the stupendous responsibility of the great task of reviving and propagating the gospel of Lord Buddha. The 'Initiation' (Deeksha) ceremony as you all know, took place yesterday. It has been a difficult task for the thoughtful to evaluate the significance of the 'Initiation' ceremony carried on a gigantic scale yesterday at this place. Some of our friends have suggested that this speech should have preceded the conversion rather than followed it. In grappling with certain knotty and important things, the logical order cannot always be maintained. The forces of history as much as the rules of logic are responsible for this sequence which some find reversed.

Now, the first question that occupies the mind of many is, why should the choice of venue fall on Nagpur? Some people believe that I have purposely chosen this place because this city is the centre of R.S.S. activities and that I wanted to do something spectacular right in front of their eyes, well, that is not true. I have no such motive. I have no desire to irritate or to provoke anybody by scratching his nose nor do I have any time for these kind of childish pranks.

D. C. Ahir, Dr. Ambedkar on Buddhism, People's Education Society, Bombay, 1982, pp. 31-43, 47-50.

Some people are under the impression that another reason why I chose this place and this time for the initiation ceremony was because on the same day and at the same time Rashtriya Swayam Sangh was holding a rally in Nagpur. This ceremony, was intended to juxtapose a striking contrast. That, of course, is not true. Why should we go out of our way to quarrel with RSS? We have no time to do so, nor does it deserve that honour.

The great task that I have taken on my shoulders is so important that every minute that passes has become valuable for me. While selecting this, place for this historical ceremony, I had not the remotest idea of the RSS in my mind. This city of Nagpur was chosen for very different reason.

Those who have studied the Buddhist history of India know that the people who worked in the beginning for the propagation of the religion of Buddha were the 'Nagas'. Nagas were non-Aryans and there existed fierce enmity between the Aryans and the Nagas.

Many a battle was fought between the Aryans and the non-Aryans. Aryans wanted to completely annihilate the Nagas. There are many legends to be found in the Puranas in this connection. Aryans had burnt Nagas. The Sage 'Agastya' saved one Naga and we are supposed to be the descendants of that Naga.

The Nagas were suppressed and oppressed by the Aryans. They needed a great man to liberate them and they found that great man in the person of Lord Buddha. Bhagwan Buddha saved them from decay and extinction. It were the Nagas who spread the religion of the Buddha throughout the world. These people were predominantly the inhabitants of Nagpur. Through the soil of this city; there flowed a river named the 'Nag'. It appears that the Nagas lived on the banks of this river. This is mainly the reason for selecting Nagpur for this great occasion. There is no other reason. The choice of this city for conducting the 'deeksha' initiation ceremony need not cause any misunderstanding.

In choosing this path I have been a target of a number of unkind comments. Some very pungent, some crude. Some people have accused me of misleading my down-trodden, poverty-stricken followers since according to them the path that I have chosen will deprive them of the concessions and privileges which they enjoy now. Some assert that the Untouchables will remain Untouchables no matter what I do in order to emancipate them. Many have suggested that it would not be wise on our part to leave the path that we have been following hitherto for ameliorating our condition. This kind of mischievous talk is likely to cause doubts and fears in the minds of the young as well as the older people belonging to the Scheduled Castes. Therefore, I must answer this question. Removal of the doubts and fears will surely strengthen our movement. I would like to say many things on this question. Those who say we shall be left economically weak and backward are worried about the despicable occupations like scavenging and flaying and tanning.

Their objection pertains to the removal of the dead bodies of animals. Mahars and Chamars stop removing the dead bodies of buffaloes and cows. Mahars and Chamars don't eat carrion was a slogan which was raised by me. Some thirty years ago I launched this movement. This somehow immensely offended our Hindu friends. I asked them, 'You take the milk from the cows and buffaloes and when they are dead you expect us to remove the dead bodies. Why? If you carry the dead bodies of your mothers to cremate, why you do not carry the dead bodies of your 'mother-cows' yourself?

When I put this question to the Hindus they felt irritated. I told them, if you let us remove the dead bodies of your mothers we shall very gladly remove the dead bodies of your cows and buffaloes as well. Many letters written by the Brahmins and other Hindu correspondents appeared in the 'Kesari'. A 'Chitpavan Brahmin' through one of such letters tried to prove that if the untouchables stopped removing the dead bodies of animals they would be put to a great financial loss. He augmented his point by furnishing statistical data in support of his argument. According to him every chamar who removed the dead bodies of the animal earned between Rs. 500 and Rs. 600 per annum from the sale proceeds of the skin, horns, teeth, hoofs and bones of the dead cows. He accused me that I was trying to deprive them of their livelihood by preaching against this practice. My people were in a dilemma; not knowing where I was leading them to. Once I happened to visit Sangmaner a Tehsil in the District of Belgaum.

The author of those letters which had appeared in Kesari met me and repeated the same question. I told him that I would answer this question some time later. Then I answered this question in a public meeting in this manner:

"My people do not have sufficient food to eat. Women have no clothes to cover their bodies. No roof over their heads to give them shelter. No land to grow food-grains. So they are down-trodden and poverty striken. They are oppressed and exploited. Do you know the reason why"?

None replied from among the congregation. Not even the man who had written those letters to the "Kesari". Then I told them 'you had better leave us alone. Good men, we are quite capable of thinking for ourselves. If you are so much anxious about our losses, why not send your friends and relatives to live in the villages and do this dirty job of dragging the dead bodies of animals so that they may earn Rs. 500/- per annum. In addition to that amount I will pay Rs.500/- from my pocket. They will gain doubly. Why miss this opportunity. True, we will suffer a loss but you stand to gain.

Unfortunately nobody has come forward to claim the prize so far. Why on earth do they feel perturbed on seeing us making progress. I can take care of my people for the food, clothing, houses and other things they need. You (Hindus) need not worry about these things. If we do this dirty work, it is said to be profitable and if you do it, it becomes non-profitable. Strange logic it is, isn't it?

Similarly some people say that now that some seats have been reserved for us in the legislature, why should we lose them. I say to them we are glad to vacate them for you. Let the Brahmins, Rajputs and other caste Hindus come forward and fill these up by becoming Chamars, Sweepers and Mahars and take advantage of opportunity .Why should they moan over our loss?

Self-respect is more important than the material gains. Our struggle is for honour, for self-respect, not only for the economic progress alone.

There is a locality in Bombay where prostitutes and whores live. These women who trade in flesh, wake up at about 8 O'clock in the morning and call for the Moslem boys who work in the cheap restaurants, located in the Mohallah, 'O Suleman' they shout out, ' Get some 'Kheema' (minced meat curry) and 'Roti'(Bread)'.

They take 'Kheema Roti' and tea every day. Well, our women do not get 'Kheema' Roti' to eat. Many of the women present here do not get even a square meal every day. They have to content themselves with ordinary 'Roti'and 'Chatni'. They too can get rich and lead the life of infamy and sin if they so desire but they care more for their honour, for dignity and self-respect. This is what we are struggling for, honour and self-respect.

For a man it is his birthright to lead an honourable life. To achieve this aim we must do our utmost. We are prepared to make the greatest sacrifice for achieving this. We are struggling for human dignity which the Hindus had hitherto denied to us. We want to make our life as full and wholesome as possible.

There are many things we may have to sacrifice on our embracing Buddhism, So far as the concessions, such as reservations etcetra are concerned; let me assure you they shall not be lost. After the ceremony, the first problem that I shall devote my attention to would be the problem of the concessions.

Continuance of these concession would require a line of action which may take us to court. I am prepared for such eventuality though I need not reveal at this stage, what line of action I may have to adopt. Those who are capable of achieving the rights, have the strength and capacity to retain them too. We shall have to do a great deal for the progress of this movement. Many problems will crop up after the acceptance of Buddhism. How shall we face the situation? How shall we brave the many difficulties that may arise? I have sufficient strength and material in hand to grapple with problems. I fought for these rights and secured them for you. I assure you, I will get them again for you. Of course, what may happen after my death, I cannot say.

Have confidence in me and the words, I am uttering. There is absolutely no truth in the words of our opponents. I say unto you, pay no heed to their words.

The question of our conversion is being discussed everywhere but I am surprised to see that nobody has asked me the reason why of all the religion I have chosen the religion of Buddha. In any movement of conversion this is a significant question to be asked. At the time of embracing a religion one should ask oneself these question, namely:

1. Which religion should be adopted? And
2. How it should be adopted?

I started the movement of renouncing the Hindu religion in 1935 at Nasik and since then I have been continuing the struggle. A mammoth meeting was held at Yeola in 1935 in which through a resolution a decision was taken to the effect that we should renounce the Hindu religion. In the meeting I had said that though born as a Hindu because I could not help it, I would not die as a Hindu. This conversion has given me enormous satisfaction and pleasure unimaginable. I feel as if I have been liberated from hell. I want each one of you all who got initiated yesterday, to realise this by his own experience. But I do not want any blind followers. I do not like sheep mentality. Those who wish to come under the refuge of Buddha, should do so after counting the cost, for it is a religion very difficult to practise.

For the progress of mankind religion-or to be more precise 'Dhamma' is absolutely necessary. Some followers of Karl Marx believe that Religion is an opium. But this statement of Karl Marx must be taken with a pinch of salt. Those who say so for them religion has no significance-no meaning. Even among us there are many who follow the maxim 'eat, drink and be merry'. All that they want is — bread and butter for breakfast, delicious meals in the afternoon, nice comfortable bed to sleep on and cinema to while away their time. In their life there is no place for religion. I do not somehow agree with them. Owing to the poverty of my father I did not have the opportunity to enjoy any of these luxuries. Till very late in life I suffered excessively and laboured very hard. But this has not made me irreligious.

I know myself what sort of hardships the poor have to bear. We must launch our struggle keeping in view the economic aspects and I am not against this idea. We should progress economically too and endeavour to become independent. I have been struggling myself throughout my life to that end. Not only this, I very much desires mankind to become economically strong. But I have my independent views in this regard.

There is a difference between man and animal. Whilst the beast needs nothing save its daily food for existence, the human being who is endowed with the physique and the sentient mind has to develop both. Mind must be developed side by side with the body. Mind should also be filled with pure thoughts. Personally, I believe that it would not be in the least advantageous to have anything to do with the countries where people believe that 'eat, drink and be merry' should be the motto of life. Keeping in view the masses one should bear in mind that just as we must have a healthy body in order to be free from disease, so in order to keep the body healthy we must also develop the sentient mind, or else it would be futile to say that man is developing and making progress.

Why does the human mind become diseased? The reason is that so long as the human body is not free from suffering, mind cannot be happy. There is a saying by Ramdas, Maharashtrian Saint, that if a man lacks enthusiasm, either his mind or body is in a diseased condition. Now what saps the enthusiasm in man? If there is no enthusiasm, life becomes a drudgery-a mere burden to be dragged. Nothing can be achieved if there is no enthusiasm. Why does one lose enthusiasm? Main reason for this lack of enthusiasm on the part of a man is that an individual loses hope to get an opportunity to elevate oneself. Hopelessness leads to lack of enthusiasm. The mind in such cases becomes diseased.

One who sees no ray of hope of escaping from the present misery lacks the enthusiasm and is always cheerless. When is enthusiasm created? When one breathes in an atmosphere where one is sure .of getting the legitimate reward for one's labours, only then one feels enriched by enthusiasm and inspiration.

If the teachers in school start commenting, 'Oh' This-here, is a Mahar boy. How did he secure the first position in his class? What business has he to stand first in the class?". Only the Brahmins are entitled to secure the first position. Now what enthusiasm, what inspiration, what hope can the Mahar boy have in these circumstances? How will he advance in life and make progress?

For inspiration and enthusiasm one must have a healthy and sound mind. Such a man is capable of surmounting all kinds of difficulties. He has confidence, courage and will to rise and that gives him the inspiration and enthusiasm.

Unfortunately, Hinduism which is founded on the ideologies of inequality and injustice leaves no room for the development of enthusiasm. So long as the Untouchables continue to slave under the yoke of Hinduism, a diabolical creed-they can have no hope, no inspiration, no enthusiasm for better life. They might produce no more than a few hundred clerks-poor clerks who will do nothing except filling their belies. What else can they do. Then we shall need superclerks to protect them from injustices and various kinds of atrocities. Common masses of the untouchables will not gain anything. The Scheduled Castes can never feel enthusiastic about and derive inspiration from Hinduism.

Man derives inspiration if his mind is free to develop. You know the proprietors of mills. They appoint managers in the mills who extract work from the labour. The proprietors remain so much engrossed in their work that they have little time to develop their minds. While they accumulate wealth and become economic giants they remain mental dwarfs. We have started this movement to develop and educate our minds.

If you excuse me for citing my own experience, I may tell you how I got my education. Owing to the poverty I used to attend school with nothing more than a loin cloth on my body. I could not get water to drink in the school. I had to go without water for many days. My mother instructed me to address the strangers with respect. There was a lady peon, Maratha by caste, in our school. Even my satchel was untouchable for her. When thirsty, I was not allowed to touch the tap myself. Untouchability was observed even in Elphinstone College, Bomaby. What can be expected in this kind of circumstances?

Untouchability cannot be removed by education alone. During the British regime I was a member of the Viceroy's Executive Council. Lord Linlithgow was the Viceroy. A certain amount of money was allocated for expenditure on general education. Out of this a sum of three lacs of rupees was sanctioned for Aligarh Moslem University and an equal amount for the Benares Hindu University .While talking to the Viceroy one day I raised this issue. I told the Viceroy that a sum of Rs. 3,00,000 had been given to Aligarh Moslem University and an equal amount had been made available to Benares Hindu University. The Untouchables are neither Hindus nor Moslems. But they are really more backward than either of these communities. An amount proportionate to their population should also be allotted to the Scheduled Castes people for their education. Lord Linlithgow asked me to give in writing whatever I wanted to say in this regard. I submitted a memorandum. Europeans were generally sympathetic in their outlook. He agreed to my proposal and granted a sum of Rs. 3,00,000 for the Scheduled Castes. Now the question arose as to how to spend that money. Viceroy wanted this amount to be spent on the education of the girls belonging to the Scheduled Castes, and suggested Boarding Houses be built for them.

If this money is spent in this manner to build Boarding Houses in order to make the illiterate girls belonging to the Scheduled Castes educated, I thought, soon we shall require money for providing them with good, food too. Poor as our people are, how shall they get these things for their daughters.

From where will our people get money to bear the expenses on food in the Boarding Houses? Our girls do not need any training in the art of cooking. What will be the result of this education and then the question of their marriages?

Meanwhile government spent on other items but withheld the amount earmarked for the education of the Scheduled Castes. I went to Lord Linligthgow once again and had a straightforward talk on this topic. I put this question to the Viceroy, Lord Linlithgow. 'Am I not better than 500 graduates? Yes, of course, you are replied, Lord, Linlithgow. Then I asked him, 'Do you know the reason why I say so? He did not know. I had to convince the Viceroy that a person who received education in a foreign University was as good as 50 graduates of the Indian Universities put together. I am personally equivalent to 50 graduates. My education is so thorough that I am capable of holding any office of the Govt. with confidence. I need such learned men who should be capable of holding the key position whence they should work in the most effective manner for the betterment of the community. If you really want to do something for the uplift of the 'untouchables' you will have to produce such people as would be able to ameliorate their condition. Merely producing clerks will not do.

Lord Linlithgow agreed to my suggestion and the result was that 16 boys belonging to the Scheduled Castes were sent abroad for higher education. Out of these sixteen, some took fun advantage of this opportunity and others did not. They got only half-baked and returned home. The reason is that there exists no enthusiasm for the Scheduled Castes in Hinduism, though such an atmosphere exists for the Brahmins and other castes.

I once went to see Gandhiji. Gandhiji told me that he believed in CHATURVARNA, What kind of Chathurvarna I enquired pointing towards my hand with the little finger in the bottom and thumb on top or this way-with the palm lying flat on the surface of the table and fingers lying side by side what do you mean by the Chaturvarna ? Where does it begin and where does it end? I asked Gandhiji. Gandhiji could not reply in a satisfactory manner.

Besides the lack of cheerful atmosphere, congenial for human development there is no equality in Hindu religion. Brahmin is considered to be superior to the Kshatriya and Kashtriya superior to Vaishya and Vaishya superior to Shudra. It is not based on equality of human beings.

This religion and this social order has ruined us. But this is not going to stop here. This would ruin the Hindus themselves and ultimately India.

I do not accuse the Hindu religion in vain. This religion cannot save anybody. It has no life left in it.

Why has our country lost her freedom time and again? Why we have been subjected to foreign domination so often? It is because this country as a whole never stood the enemy. It was always a small section of the society and whoever overpowered it became the victor. This is mainly due to the pernicious caste system of the Hindus.

Second World War was fought in Europe during the period from 1939-45. The soldiers who were killed in the battles, were immediately replaced by the fresh recruits. Nobody ever paused to say that the credit for winning the war should go to a particular community or section of the society. Whereas in our country in the past if all the Kshatriyas were done away with in the battle, there could be no mobilisation or recruitment according to the Chaturvama since according to this abominable law, Kahatriyas and Kahatriyas alone were entitled to fight. This is what has been happening in the past. This is why country has been enslaved many time, had the right to bear arms not been denied to us, this country would never have lost her freedom or nor could any invader have succeeded in conquering her.

Hinduism cannot save anybody. There is no salvation for anybody in Hinduism. According to the tenets of Hinduism only the so-called higher castes have been benefited. There is no exaggeration in my statement. What have the Shudras or the untouchables gained?

As soon as the wife of a Brahmin woman conceives, she thinks of the High Court whether any post of a Judge has fallen vacant but when our woman becomes pregnant, she cannot think of anything better than a sweeper's post under the Municipal Committee.

This deplorable situation exists only because Hinduism has inculcated this kind of ambitions to the latter. No change in our status can be expected if we continue to be slaves of Hinduism. If we have any hope it is by renouncing the Hinduism and following the path of the Buddha. Let us now consider the principles of Buddhism.

The fundamental principle of Buddhism is equality. Of all the Bhikkhus who joined the order in the time of Lord Buddha about 75% of the Bhikkhus belonged to the Brahimin caste and the remaining 25% were the Shudras. Even then Buddhism was called the religion of the Shudras.

"O Bhikkhus, you belong to different castes and have come from various lands, Just as the great rivers when they have fallen into the great ocean lose their identity just so 'O Brethern, do these four castes Kshatriyas, Brahmins, Vaishyas, Shudras when they begin to follow the doctrine and discipline as propounded by the Tathagatha, they renounce different names, caste and rank and become members of one and the same society".

These are the words of Buddha. There was only one man who raised his voice against the separatism and untouchability and that was Lord Buddha.

In the beginning Lord Buddha got only ten or twelve Bhikkhus. Out of these nine or ten were Shudras. This is evident from the autobiographical 'gathas' of the Bhikkhus entitled as 'Thera Gatha and Therigatha'. Their writings bear testimony to the fact that Buddhism is the only religion, which does not recognise caste and affords full scope for progress.

My political opponents who observe my political activities very keenly say that I am a cunning fox. They say that I want to extract as many concessions for the Scheduled Castes as it is possible to get. On the other hand there are some who wonder as to why I have taken so long to take a decision. In regard to the change of religion. What have you been doing all these years?" They ask. The only reply I can give is this that question of religion is the most difficult and a very serious question. It is a matter of enormous responsibility, really, to educate the people in regard to the merits of this religion and to inculcate in the people the habit of behaving according to the principles of the Dhamma. There is no other person who had to shoulder so grave a responsibility, nor do I think will anybody be called upon to shoulder such a heavy responsibility in future. If I am allowed some more years to live, I shall bring the task I have undertaken today to successful end.

Some people will naturally ask this question, what will the Untouchables gain by embracing Buddhism?" Suffice this to say that it is a worthless question.

Is religion necessary for the well-to-do? No, perhaps not. Those who are holding high positions in life have nice bungalows to live in, money to buy all comforts of life and servants to attend on them, perhaps, have little use for religion.

This reminds me of my German Professor Winterniltz. The Watergang Rabelan Depth' was the book which he recommended and by which I was much inspired. "It is only the poor" he said, "who need religion." Hope is the spring of action in life. Religion affords this hope. Therefore mankind find solace, in religion and that is why the poor cling to religion.

When Christianity made its way into Europe, the situation in and around Rome was appalling. People did not get enough food to fill their bellies. They lived in abject poverty. But do you know who were the people who extended a sympathetic response to the call of Christianity when it penetrated into Rome. Not those who were convinced of its spirituality but those miserable poor and oppressed people for whom porridge distributed free of cost, served as a meal. People who worked as slaves and serfs for their Roman masters. The poor and the oppressed became converts to Christianity. Mr. Gibbon, the renowned historian and author of the 'Rise and Fall of the Roman Empire' scornfully branded Christianity as a religion of the poor and the beggars. Mr. Gibbon is not alive today. He would have been shocked to see the whole of Europe engulfed by Christianity.

Some people, here in India, will no doubt say that this Buddhism is the religion of the Untouchables. They will malign and pass disparaging remarks. Brahmins in his time, did not spare even Bhagawan Buddha. Irreverently they addressed him as 'O Gautama' or 'Bho-Gautama'. They wanted to show disrespect towards him. They wanted to insult him.

In spite of all the vilification's and the abuses showered on this religion, Buddhism has cultivated better acquaintance in Europe and America than Hinduism. You will be surprised to know that if the images of Rama, Krishna, Shankara or any other Hindu deity are kept for sale or export, nobody would care to buy them. But instead if the images of Buddha are kept in the morning for sale none will be found in the evening.

If there is any name which is known outside India, which is popular and revered, it is not the name of Rama or Krishna, but it is the name of the Buddha. Very few people know Rama or Krishna outside India.

There is no reason why this religion of ours should not spread throughout the world. Much will depend on how we live it. We shall go ahead undauntedly on the path we have chosen. We have found a new way to life and we shall follow it. This path leads to progress.

In fact this is not something new nor have we imported it from outside. Buddhism is the religion of this country. It is more than two thousand years old. I feel sorry for the fact that I did not embrace this religion earlier.

The teachings of the Buddha are eternal but even then Buddha did not proclaim them to be infallible. The religion of Buddha has capacity to change according to times. A quality which no other religion can claim to have.

Main reason for the decline of Buddhism in India was the invasion of India by the Moselms. Thousands of images were mutilated and destroyed. Viharas were desecrated and thousands of Bhikkhus were massacred. Terrified by these ghastly events, the Bhikkhus fled to the adjoining countries. Some went to Tibet; some went to China; they spread throughout the world. The result was that the Bhikkhus disappeared from this country. The followers of Dhamma are required to protect the Dhamma in the times of crisis. When the Greek King Menander came to the North Western Province, he had established his reputation as an expert on the religious affairs. He had defeated the Brahmins many a time during the religious discussions and they could not satisfy the learned king. Attracted by the teachings of the Buddha, he invited the Bhikkhus and the scholars of Buddhism to his court, but nobody was prepared to cross swords with the King Menander. He instructed his courtiers to bring any Bhikkhu who preached the Dhamma. The Bhikkhus approached Nagsena, a learned and versatile Bhikkhu to discuss the religion of Buddha. He was a Bhikkhu of outstanding learning and ability. The catechistic discussions between the King Menander and Bhikkhu Nagsena were collected and have been preserved in the form of a book, known by the name of 'Milind Panha'. In this book a question is asked:

"What brings about the ruination of religion? Explaining the reason for the downfall of religion, Nagsena replied", There are three reasons for the downfall of religion: a religion is foredoomed to ruin, If (i) its basic principles are not cogent, that is, if its foundation is weak: (ii) if its preachers and missionaries are not learned enough to surpass the rival preachers and missionaries; and (iii) if the religion and its principles do not get translated into the temples and other modes of worship popular among the common people.

The religion which is not based on truth, on justice and on strong principles, does not last long. It has only a temporary existence. With the passage of time it goes on deteriorating and ultimately it withers away. Secondly if there is nobody to preach the Dhamma, it does not make any progress and ultimately becomes extinct. The intellectuals and the learned people must discuss religion in their every day life. If there are no scholars well read in the scriptures of the Dhamma to answer the critics or the opponents of Dhamma, even in that case the religion dies away. Dhamma and its principles are for the learned to expound while the laymen or the 'Upaskas' can go to the temples and Viharas where they can learn the teaching of Dhamma and worship.

You must bear in mind the following four facts in respect of Buddhism .You must never think that the teachings of Buddhism are of temporary value and are not likely to last longer. Even after a lapse of 2500 years the world respects the teachings of Buddha. There are as many as 2000 institutions of the followers of Buddhism in the United States of America. In England a Buddha temple has been built at a cost of Rs.3,00,000. There are some 3000 or 4000 institutions founded in the name of Buddha in Germany.

The principles and teachings of Bhagwan Buddha are Eternal but in spite of this fact Buddha did not claim any status for himself, nor did he claim his principles to be infallible. He never claimed divinity for himself or for his religion. Buddha did not say that he was the Son of God or the last prophet-messenger of God. On the contrary he said 'My Father and my mother are ordinary mortals'.

Now what is the basis of Buddhism? If you study carefully, you will see that Buddhism is based on reason. There is an element of flexibility inherent in it, which is not to be found in any other religion.

Only those people should embrace this religion who earnestly believe in it. If they do not believe in it or it does not appeal to them, they should not embrace it. For such high principles are not to be found in any other religion. There is a world of difference between this religion and other religions of the world. Main principles of Buddhism form no part of theistic religions. According to other religions God created the world, this earth and thereafter he created heaven, air, moon and other planets. That means he has created, also the stone in the bladder. God has done all that was required to be done and now there remains nothing for us to do. All that we are required to do is, just to sing the praises of Almighty God. This does not appeal to rational man today.

Buddhism denies the existence of God and soul. The real

basis of Buddhism is rational way to eradicate suffering. "There is", Buddha said, 'suffering in the world-suffering wide-spread'. 90 percent people are afflicted with suffering or misery of some kind or the other. The main object of Buddhism is to emancipate the suffering humanity. The question arises, then what is the use of Das Kapital? I believe that Karl Marx was far behind Buddha, for he did not say anything that had not, been brought to light by the Buddha himself, some two thousand and four hundred years before Marx was born.

I see so many Communist friends here. I see one amongst the reporters. I ask them, in what way was Buddha's aim different from that of Marx. Whatever Buddha said was simple and the path he showed was straight. Buddhism is an all-comprehensive religion.

With the education, intelligence, knowledge and experience that I have, it is not difficult for me to oppose or fight against any evil. But there is a mountain-collossal mountain of caste hierarchy; Vaishyas, Brahmins, Kshatriyas sitting on our heads. The question before us is, how to topple it down and blast it. It is for this reason that I wanted to acquaint you fully with the religion of Buddha. I owe it as a duty too.

Some people say that Buddhism is on its death-bed or practically dead. If it is so, it is our duty to raise it to better status. We should act in a manner so as to enthuse, inspire respect among other people. We may have a garden or a temple and arrange for discourses there.

I will do my best by writing books or by removing your doubts. All I wish today is that you should have faith in me and follow me. The trust you depose in me will not be used for personal gain and I shall endeavour to satisfy all your doubts.

A great responsibility has fallen on your shoulders too. You should do nothing that will bring bad name. You must lead such a life that you may command respect. Don't think that this religion is like the dog collar tied round your neck.

So far as Buddhism is concerned this country of ours has become a desert. Now it has fallen on you that you should endeavour to follow this religion sincerely and always keep in view the position it had once attained. If you do not do so, people will laugh at this conversion.

This religion can serve not only this country but the whole world. At this juncture in the world affairs, Buddhism is, indispensable for world peace. You must pledge today that you the followers of Buddha, will not only work to liberate yourself, but will try to elevate your country and the world in general.

This task which you have taken in hand is of immense responsibility. You have to labour hard. This thing you will have to bear in mind. Hitherto most of us have been interested only in our bread and butter. Don't be self-centered. Don't be selfish in your outlook.

We need money for the propagation of this great religion. I have no mind to ask for any monetary help from any foreign country.

You must resolve to contribute at least 1/20th of your income for the propagation of the Dhamma. I am to carry you all with me. Bhagwan Buddha used to carry on initiation ceremony himself. When it became unmanageable for one person, he allowed that work to be shared by other competent persons among his followers. You might have heard the name of one 'Yasha'. He was the scion of a rich family. Yasha became his disciple and there were forty more men who followed him. Bhagwan told them, "My religion is for the good of many; for in the good of many lies the happiness for many. This is good in the beginning; this is good in the middle and this is good at the end". So, Brothers and Sisters, this is my religion.

Buddha adopted the method, which was most suitable in the circumstances obtaining then, for the propagation of His religion. Accordingly, we, too, should adopt the method, which is most suitable in the existing circumstances. There are no Bhikkhus in this country to do this work. So every one of you has to take 'Deeksha'. A Buddhist has the right to convert others to his faith. If a disruption comes at a later stage, we must have a provision in our sleeves to meet the situation. We must organise a huge machinery for the propagation of Dhamma. Every Buddhist has the right to initiate others. I make this announcement today. Go forth with the message of the Buddha. Go forth to liberate people.

Appendix - XIII

Buddhism and Communism

"President, Your Reverences, and Gentlemen:

I am sorry that, having come to Nepal to attend the Conference, I have not been able to participate in its proceedings in the way in which a delegate ought to participate. But I am sure, most of the delegates are aware that although I am here, I am physically a very ill man, and I am quite unable to bear the stress and strain of the Conference Proceedings. It is, therefore not out of any disrespect for the Conference that I have been usually absent, it is because of my personal condition that I could not do justice to the task of the Conference. It is perhaps because of my absence from the Conference that I was asked by way of compensation to address you this afternoon. I consented to do that, but even here there have been surprises flung on me. I had not enough notice that I was to speak here. And when I was asked what subject I would speak on, I mentioned the subject of, Ahimsa in Buddhism. But I find that a large majority of the people attending this Conference are desirous that I should speak on "Buddhism and Communism," a subject to which I, in a very passing sentence, referred at the first General Meeting. I am quite prepared to agree to the suggestion of the change of subject, although, I must say that I am not quite on the spur of the moment prepared to deal with such a large, enormous, and if I may say so, a very massive subject. It is a subject which has had half the world in grips, and I find that it has held also in its grip a large number of the student population even of the Buddhist countries. I look upon the latter aspect of the matter with grave concern. If the younger generations of the Buddhist countries are not able to appreciate that Buddhism

---

Report of the 4th World Buddhist Conference of The World Fellowship of Buddhists 15 -21 Nov. 1956, The Dharmodaya Sabha, Kathmandu, Nepal.

supplies a way of life which is better than what is supplied by the Communist way of life, Buddhism is doomed. It cannot last beyond a generation or two. It is, therefore, quite necessary for those who, believe in Buddhism to tackle the younger generation, and to tell them whether Buddhism can be a substitute for Communism. It is then only that Buddhism can hope to survive. We must all remember that today a large majority of the people in Europe and a large majority of the youngsters in Asia look upon Karl Marx as the only prophet who could be worshipped. And they regard, the largest part of the Buddhist Sangha as nothing but the yellow peril. That is an indication which the Bhikkhus must take up, must understand, to reform themselves in order that they could be compared with Karl Marx; and Buddhism could compete with it.

Now with this introduction; I propose to give you a few salient points in Buddhism and in Marxism or Communism in order to show you where the similarity of ideals lies and where the differences arise between Buddhism and Marxism. And thirdly, whether the Buddhist way of life of reaching the goal which communism has is a lasting one or whether the Communist way of bringing about the goal is the lasting one. Because there is no use in pursuing a certain path, if that path is not going to be a lasting path, if it is going to lead you to the jungle, if it is going to lead you to anarchy, there is no use pursuing it. But, if you are assured that the path you are asked to follow is slow, may be devious, may be with long detours, yet if it ultimately makes you reach a safe, sound ground so that the ideals you are pursuing are there to help you, to mould your life permanently, it is much better, in my judgement, to follow the slower path, and the devious path rather than to rush up and to take what we call short-cuts. Short cuts in life are always dangerous, very dangerous.

Now let me go to the subject. What is the theory of communism? What does it start with? Communism starts with the theory that there is exploitation in the world, that the poor are exploited by the rich because of the property that they hold, and they enslave the masses that enslavement results in suffering, sorrow, in poverty. This is the starting point of Karl Marx. He uses the word 'exploitation.' What is the remedy that Karl Marx, provides? The remedy that Karl Marx provides is that in order to prevent poverty and the suffering of one class it is necessary to remove private property. Nobody should possess private property because it is the private owner who appropriates or misappropriates. To use the technical language of Karl Marx the surplus value which the workers produce, the worker does not get the surplus value which he produces, it is appropriated by the owner. Karl Marx asked the question why should the owner misappropriate the surplus value, which is produced by the efforts of the working man? His answer is that the only owner is the State. And it is because of this that Marx propounded the theory that there must be the dictatorship of the proletariat. That is the third proposition that Marx enunciated. That government must be by the exploited classes and not by the exploiting classes, which is what is meant by dictatorship of the proletariat. These are fundamental propositions in Karl Marx, which have the basis of Communism in Russia. They have undoubtedly been expanded, it has been added too, and so on. But these are the fundamental propositions.

Now let me, for a moment, go to Buddhism and see what the Buddha has to say about the points made out by Karl Marx. As I told you, Karl Marx begins with what is called exploitation of the poor. What does the Buddha say? How does He begin? What is the foundation on which he has raised the structure of His religion? The Buddha, too, 2000 or at any rate 2400 years ago, said exactly the same thing, He said, "There is 'Dukkha' in the world." He did not use the word 'exploitation' but He did lay the foundation of His religion on what He called 'Dukkha'. There is 'Dukkha' in the world. The word 'Dukkha' no doubt has been interpreted in various ways. It has been interpreted to mean rebirth , the round of life, that is 'Dukkha'. I do not agree with that. I think there are lots of places in the Buddhist literature where the Buddha has used the word 'Dukkha' in the sense of poverty. Therefore, so far as the foundation is concerned, there is really no difference at all.

It is unnecessary for the Buddhist people to go to Karl Marx to get the foundation. That foundation is already there, well laid. It is where the Buddha begins His first sermon- the Dhamma-chakra Pravartana Sutta. Therefore to those who are attracted by Karl Marx, I say, study the Dharmachakra Pravartana Sutta and find out what the Buddha says. And you will find sufficient satisfaction on his question. The Buddha did not lay the foundation of His religion either on god, or on soul, or anything super-natural like these. He laid His finger on the fact of life - people are living in suffering. Therefore so far as Marxism or Communism is concerned, Buddhism has enough of it. And the Buddha has said it 2000 years before Marx was born.

With regard to the question of property, you will again find some very close affinity to the doctrine of the Buddha and the doctrine preached by Karl Marx. Karl Marx said that in order to prevent exploitation, the State must own the instrument of production, that is, property. Land must belong to the State, industry must belong to the state, so that no private owner might intervene and rob the worker of the profits of his labour. That is what Marx said.

Now let us go to the Sangha, the Buddhist Sangha, and examine the rules of life that the Buddha laid down for the monks. What are the rules that the Buddha laid down? Well, the Buddha said that no monk shall have private property. Ideally speaking, no monk can own property. And although there might be a few lapses here and there, and I have noticed that in some countries the monks own some property, yet in the large majority of the cases the monks have no property at all. In fact, the Buddhist rules for the Sangha are far more severe than any rule that the Communists have made in Russia. I take it as a mute subject, nobody has yet discussed it and come to any conclusion.

What object did the Buddha have in forming the Sangha? Why did he do it? Going back a little into the history, when the Buddha was engaged in propagating His religion, those we today call the" Parivrajakas" were existing there long before the Buddha was there. The word "Parivrajaka" means a displaced person, a person who has lost his home. Probably during the Aryan period the different tribes of the Aryans were warring against one another as all tribal people do. Some broken tribes lost their moorings and they were wandering about. And it is those wanderers that were called Parivrajakas. The great service that the Buddha did to these Parivrajakas was to organise them into a body, to give them rules of life-those that are contained in the 'Vinayapitaka' In these rules, the Bhikkhu is not allowed to have property. The Bhikkhu is allowed to have only seven things - a razor, a lota for getting water, a Bhikshyapatra and three Chivaras, and the needle for sewing things. Well, I want to know if the essence of Communism is to deny the private property, can there be any greater and more severe rule as regards private property than is found in the 'Vinaya Pitika? I do not find one. Therefore, if any people or any youngsters are attracted by the rule contained in the Communist system of rules that there shall be no private property, they can find it here. The only question is, to what extent can this rule of denial of private property be applied to society as a whole. That is a matter of expediency, time, circumstances, development of human society. But, so far as theory is concerned whether there is anything wrong in abolishing private property, Buddhism will not stand in the way of anybody who wants to do it because it has already made this concession in the organisation of the Buddhist Sangha.

Now we come to another aspect of the matter, and that aspect is- what is the way and means which Karl Marx or the Communists wish to adopt in order to bring about Communism? This is the important question. The means that the Communists wish to adopt in order to bring about Communism (by which I mean the recognition of Dukkha, and abolition of property) is violence and killing of the opposed. There lies the fundamental difference between the Buddha and Karl Marx. The Buddha's means of persuading people to adopt the principles is by persuasion, by moral teaching, by love. He wants to conquer the opponent by inculcating in him the doctrine that love and not power can conquer anything. That is where the fundamental difference lies-that the Buddha would not allow violence, and the Communists do. No doubt the Communists get quick results; Because when you adopt the means of annihilating men, they do not remain to oppose you.

You go on with your ideology, you go on with your ways of doing things. The Buddha's way, as I said, is a long way, perhaps some people may say, a tedious way. But I have no doubt about it that it is the surest way.

There are two or three questions, which I have always asked my Communist friends to answer and which, I must frankly say, they have not been able to answer. They establish by means of violence what they call the dictatorship of the proletariat. They deprive all people who have property of political rights. They cannot have representation in the legislation. They cannot have right to vote they must remain what they call second grade subjects of the State, the ruled not sharing authority or power. When I asked them. "Do you agree that dictatorship is a good method of governing people?" they say, "No, we don't, we don't like dictatorship." But they say, "This is an interim period in which dictatorship must be there." You proceed further and ask them "what is the duration of this interim period? How long? Twenty years? Forty years? Fifty years?" No answer, they only repeat that the proletarian dictatorship will vanish, somehow automatically.

Very well, let us take the thing as it is that dictatorship will vanish. Well, I ask a question, "What will happen when dictatorship disappears? What will take its place? Will man not need Government of some sort?" They have no answer.

Then we go back to the Buddha and ask this question in relation to His Dhamma. What does He say? The greatest thing that the Buddha has done is to tell the world that the world cannot be reformed except by the reformation of the mind of the man, and the mind of the world. If the mind is changed, if the mind accepts the Communist system and loves it loyally and carries it out it is a permanent thing, it does not require a soldier or a police officer to keep a man in order. Why? The answer is: The Buddha has energised your conscience itself that is acting as a sentinel in order to keep you on your path. There is no trouble when the mind is converted, the thing is permanent.

The Communist system is based on force. Supposing tomorrow the dictatorship in Russia fail and we see signs of its failure, what would happen? I really like to know what would happen to the Communist system. As I see it there would be bloody warfare among the Russian people for appropriating the property of the state. That would be the consequence of it. Why? Because they have not accepted the Communist system voluntarily. They are obeying it because they are afraid of being hanged. Such a system can take no root, and therefore in my judgement unless the Communists are able to answer these questions, what would happen to their system? When force disappears there is no use pursuing it. Because, if the mind is not converted, force will always be necessary, and this is what I want to say in conclusion that one of the greatest things I find in Buddhism is that its system is a democratic system. The Buddha told the Vajjis when the Prime Minister of Ajata Satru went to conquer the Vajjis, He said the king won't be able to do it as long as the Vajjis follow their ways of their age-old system. The Buddha for unknown reasons did not explain in plain terms what He meant. But there is no doubt that what He was referring to was the democratic and the republican form of government, which the Vajjis had. He said: so long as the Vajjis were following their system, they would be unconquered. The Buddha, of course, was a great democrat.

Therefore, I say, and may I say so if the President will allow me, I have been a student of politics; I have been a student of economics, I was a Professor of Economics and I have spent a great deal of time in studying Karl Marx, Communism and all that and have also spent good deal of time in studying the Buddha's Dhamma.

After comparing the two I came to the conclusion that Buddha's advice with regard to the great problem of the world, namely, that there is Dukkha, that Dukkha must be removed, and that the Buddha's method was the safest and the soundest.

Thus do I advise the younger generation of the Buddhist countries to pay more attention to the actual teachings of the Buddha.

If I may say so in conclusion if any peril arises to the Dhamma, in a Buddhist country the blame shall have to be cast upon the Bhikkhus, because I personally think that they are not wholly discharging the duty which devolves on them, Where is the preaching? The Bhikkhu is living in his cloister taking his meal, one meal no doubt and sitting quietly: probably he is reading, and most probably I find them sleeping, and in the evening having a little music. That is not the way of propagating religion.

My friends, I want to tell you, I do not want to criticise anybody; but religion, if it is to be a moral force for the regeneration of society, you must constantly din it into the ears of the people. How many years has a child to spend in school? You do not send the child to school on a day and then withdraw the child home and expect the child to grow into learning, to get education. The child has to go to school every day, sit there for five hours and study constantly. It is then, and then alone that the child gets somewhat saturated with what is called knowledge and what is called learning. Here the monastery is not a state. The Bhikkhus do not call the people to the monasteries on any single day and deliver sermon to them on some subject or moral education. I have never seen it.

I went to Ceylon and I told some people that I was particularly anxious to see how the Bhikkhus preach. They told me that they have got 'Bana', 'Bana' some word they use which, I subsequently learnt meant, 'vanaka'. They took me at 11 o'clock to one place, to small little square thing as big as this, a table and I sat on the ground. A Bhikkhu was brought in. Several men and women brought water and washed his feet and he came up and sat there. He had a fan with him, you see, gods only know what he said. Of course he must have preached in Sinhalese, It was not more than two minutes, and after two minutes he departed.

You go to Christian Church. What happens? Every week people assemble there. They worship, and some priest delivers a sermon on some subject from the Bible in order to remind the people what Jesus told them that they should do. You will be probably surprised, most of us are that 90 percent of Christianity is copied from Buddhism both in substance and in form. You go to Rome, see the main Church and you will be reminded of the big temple which is known as 'Viswa karma' at Bharut.

Vishabigne, who wrote a book on Buddhism, and was a missionary in China, had expressed his great surprise as to how this similarity occurs between Buddhism and Christianity. So far as the outlook, he dared not say that the Buddhist copied Christian, but he would not admit that the Christians copied Buddhism. There is so much of it, I think time has turned and we must now copy some of the ways of the Christians in order to propagate our religion among the Buddhist people. They must be made aware, every day and all time, that the Buddha's Dhamma is there, standing by them like a policeman to guard lest they should go the wrong way. Without that this religion will remain probably in a very decadent state. Even now I find that in the Buddhist countries, its condition is very decadent. But its influence is there. No doubt about it.

I wanted to tell you one very interesting epilogue, which I saw in Burma. I went to Burma. I was called for the Conference and they took me to show how they were going to reconstruct the villages. I was very happy. I went with them and the Committee had planned to reform the village. Their streets as usual were crooked, bent here, and there, nothing systematic. So the Committee put down iron pillars and lined ropes that this street must go this way. In good many cases I found that the lines drawn by the committee went across a portion of the house of some one or across a piece of land which was owned by a private individual. When I went and saw and I asked them. "How are they going to manage? Have you got money to pay for the property that you are going to take?" They said, "No body wants money". Everybody said, "if you want it, take it." Why is this? Why in my country there would have been bloodshed if you take a little piece of land from somebody without giving his compensation. But there it is, why? Why were the Burmese so free with their property? Why did they not care for it? It is because the Buddha has taught "Sarvam Anityam." Everything you see is impermanent. Why fight for impermanent things? It is all right if you want the land, take it.

Now ladies and gentlemen, I do not think I can continue any further, nor is it necessary for me to do that.

I just wanted to give you a point of view from which to look at. Do not be allured by Communist successes. I am quite confident that if we all become one tenth as enlightened as the Buddha was, we can bring about the same result by the methods of love, of justice and good will. Thank you very much.

Soon after the historic event of mass conversion ceremony at Nagpur, Ambedkar visited Nepal to participate in the Fourth Conference of the World Fellowship of Buddhists held at Kathmandu in November 1956. This was the first appearance of Ambedkar as a formal Buddhist at an international Buddhist gathering. The World Buddhist Community was eager to hear his views on the present day problems of Buddhism, particularly the challenge of Communism. Responding to their request Ambedkar addressed the Conference on 20 November 1956.

Bibliography

PRIMARY SOURCES

Ambedkar B.R., *Who were the Shudras? And How they came to fourth Varna in Indo-Aryan Society* (Bombay: Thacker & Co., 1946).

———, *The Untouchables: Who were they and why they became Untouchables* (New Delhi: Amrit Book Co., Connaught Circus, 1948).

———, *Mr. Gandhi and Emancipation of the Untouchables* (Bombay: Thacker & Co., 1943).

———, *The Buddha And His Dhamma* (Bombay: Siddartha, 1957).

———, *Buddha and Karl Marx, 4th Conference of World Fellowship of Buddism* (Kathmandu, 1956; reprinting by M.D. Panchabhai, Nagpur, 1964).

———, *The Rise and Fall of Hindu Women: Who is Responsible for It? Mahabodhi* (Calcutta, May-June, 1951).

———, *The Buddha and the Future of his Religion, Mahabodhi* (Calcutta, Viasha Number, Vol. 58, April-May 1950).

———, Address: *Annihilation of Caste with a Reply to Mahatma Gandhi*, 3rd ed., (Ambedkar School of Thoughts, Katra Jaman Singh, Amritsar, 1944). Ist Published by Thacker & Co., Bombay, 1937. (Undelivered speech before the Annual Conference of Jat-Pat-Todak Mandal, Lahore, 1935).

———, Unpublished Works.

———, Marathi Weekly the Mook Nayak (Bombay), 1920.

———, The Bahishkrit Bharat (Bombay), 1927, 1929.

———, The Prabuddha Bharat (Bombay), 1955 to 1968.

Dalai Lama XIV, *An Introduction to Buddhism* (New Delhi: Tibet House, 1965).

———, *The Key to Madhyamika* (Dharamsala: Tibetan Works & Archives, 1976).

Dalai Lama XIV, *Ocean of Wisdom: Guideline for Living* (New Mexico: Clearlight Publishers, 1981).

———, *Kindness, Clarity and Insight* (New York: Snow Lion Publications, 1988).

———, *The World of Tibetan Buddhism* (Boston: Wisdom Publication, 1995).

———, *The Buddhism of Tibet and the Key to the Middle Way* (London: George Allen & Unwin Ltd. 1975).

———, *The Way to Freedom: Core Teachings of Tibetan Buddhism* (New York: Harper Collins Publishers, 1994).

———, *Worlds in Harmony: Dialogues on Compassionate Action* (California: Parallax Press, 1992).

———, *Tibet's Contribution to the Future* (London: The Office Of Tibet, 1991).

———, *Compassion and the Individual* (Boston: Wisdom Publications, 1991).

———, *Universal Responsibility and the Good Heart* (Dharamsala, Tibetan Works & Archives, 1980).

———, *A Human Approach to World Peace* (London: Wisdom Publications, 1984).

———, *Freedom in Exile* (London, A John Curtis Book, 1990).

———, *Cultivating a Daily Meditation* (Dharmsala: Library of Tibetan Works and Articles, 1991).

———, *The Kalachakra Initiation, the Full Six Session Yoga* (London: George Allen & Unwin, 1976).

———, *Path to Bliss, A Practical Guide to Stages of Meditation* (New York: Snow Lion Publications, 1991).

———, *The Opening of Wisdom Eye* (Madras: the Theosophical Publishing House, 1971).

———, *Compassion in Exile* (Birmingham: External Affairs, Central Broadcasting Limited, 1992).

———, *My Land and My People* (New York: Potala Corporation, 1977).

———, *Tantrian Tibet, The Great Exposition of Secret Mantras* (London, George Allen & Unwin, 1977).

———, *Statements, Interviews & Articles* (Dharamsala: Information office, 1982).

Gobeazon, Jose Ignacio, ed. *The Bodhgaya Interviews: His Holiness Dalai Lama* (New York: Snow Lion Publications, 1988).

Other works

Moon, Vasant, ed., *Dr. Babasaheb Ambedkar Writings and Speeches* (Bombay: Education Department , Government of Maharashtra, 1989), Vol. 1,3,4,5,7 & 11.

Document of Government of Tibet (in exile): *Tibetans in Exile* (Dharamsala: Information Office, 1981).

Proceedings of the X International Buddhist Conference: *Buddhism and World Peace* (Bodh Gaya: Editorial Board, International Buddhist Conference, 1984).

SECONDARY SOURCES

Books

Ahir, D.C., *Buddhism in Modern India* (Nagpur: Bhikkunivas Prakashan, 1972).

———, *Buddhism and Ambedkar*, (New Delhi: Ajay Prakashan, 1968).

———, *Buddhism in North India* (Delhi: Classics India Publications, 1989).

Ahluwalia, B.K. and Ahluwalia, Shashi, ed., *B.R. Ambedkar and Human Rights* (New Delhi: Vivek Publishers, 1981).

Balwant, Damodar, *Dr. B.R. Ambedkar and Revolutionary Thoughts* (Bangalore: K. Shanta, 1989).

Bapat, P.V., ed., *2500 Years of Buddhism* (New Delhi: Government of India, 1956).

Bell, Sir Charles, *The Religion of Tibet* (London: Oxford University Press, 1970).

Benz, Ernst, *Buddhism or Communism* (New York: Double Day & Company Inc., 1995).

Bhagwan Das ed., *Thus Spoke Ambedkar* (Jullunder: Bhim Patrika, 1983), Vol. I & II.

Brown, Emily C., ed., *Hindu Revolutionary and Rationalist* (Arizona: Arizona Press, 1975).

Burnell, A.C., *Manu Sastra* (Ludhiana: Kalyani Publishers, 1972).

Chand, Attar, *Tibet, past & Present (1960-1981)* (New Delhi: Sterling Publishers, 1982).

Chatterjee, Satischandra, Dutta Dhirendra Mohan, *An Introduction to Indian Philosophy* (Calcutta: University of Calcutta, 1984).

Chattopadhyaya, Debi Prasad, ed., *Taranatha's History of Buddhism in India,* Translated by Lama Chimpa and Alok Chattopadhyaya (Simla: Indian Institute of Advanced Study, 1970).

Conze, Edward, *Buddhism: Its Essence and Development* (New York: Harper Torch Books, 1951).

Davids, Rhys T.W., tr., *Dialogues of the Buddha* (London: Lizac & Co. Ltd., 1950), Parts I & II.

Davids, Rhys. T.W., *Buddhist India* (Delhi: Motilal Banarsidass, 1971).

Denwood, Phillip and Piati Grosky, Alexander, ed., *Buddhist Studies: Ancient and Modern* (London: Curzon, 1983).

Derret, J.D.M., *Religion, Law and the State in India* (New York: Free Press, 1968).

Dutt, R.C., *Buddhism and Buddhist Civilisation in India* Delhi: Seema Publications, 1983).

Eisenstadt, S.N., *Modernisation: Protest and Change* (New Delhi: Prentice-Hall of India, 1969).

Elliot, T.S., *Hinduism and Buddhism* (London: Routledge and Kegan Paul Ltd., 1957).

Eppsteiner, Fred, ed., *The Path of Compassion: Writings on Socially Engaged Buddhism* (California: Parallax Press, 1988).

Ernst Benz, *Buddhism or Communism* (New Delhi: Doubleday & Co., 1965).

Gerth, Hans H. and Martindale, Don, tr. & ed., *Maxweber's Religion of India: The Sociology of Hinduism and Buddhism* (New York: Free Press, 1968).

Ginsberg, H., *Dhurkheim's Theory of Religion, on the discovery of Morals* (New York: Macmilan, 1957).

Goleman, Daniel & Thurman, Robert A.F., ed., *Mind Science: An East-West dialogue (The Dalai Lama with others)* Boston: Wisdom Publications, 1991).

Gonda, J., *Change and Continuity in Indian Religion* (London: Mounton, 1965).

Grenard. F., *Tibet, The Country and its Inhabitants* (Delhi: Cosmo Publications, 1974).

Guruge, Ananda W.P., and Ahir, D.C., ed., *Buddhism's Contribution to the World Culture and civilization* (New Delhi: The Maha Bodhi Society of India, 1977).

Hayward, Jeremy W. & Varela, Fransisco J., *Gentle Bridges: Conversations with the Dalai Lama on the Sciences of Mind* (Boston: Shambala Publications Inc., 1992).

Hazara, Kanailal, *Buddhism in India as Described by the Chinese Piligrims A.D. 399-689* (New Delhi: Munshiram Manoharlal, 1983).

Hopkins, Jeffrey, *The Dalai Lama at Harvard: Lecturers on the Buddhist Perspective* (New York: Snow Lion Publications, 1988).

———,tr., ed., Dalai Lama XIV's *The Meaning of life from a Buddhist Perspective*(Boston: Wisdom Publications, 1993).

Humphreys, Christmas, *Buddhism* (London: Penguin Books, 1951).

———, *Buddhist Way of life* (London: George Allen and Unwin, 1969).

Jinpa, Geshe Thupten, tr., ed., Dalai Lama XIV's *The World of Tibetan Buddhism – An Overview of its Philosophy and Practice* (Boston: Wisdom Publications, 1995).

Joshi, Lal Muni, *Studies in the Buddhist Culture of India* (Delhi: Motilal Banarsidas, 1977).

Karve, Iravati, *Hindu Society an Interpretation* (Poona:Deccan College, 1961).

Kenadi, L., *Revival of Buddhism in Modern India: The Role of B.R. Ambedkar and the Dalai Lama XIV* (New Delhi: Ashish Publishing House, 1995).

Keer, Dhananjaya, *Dr. B.R.Ambedkar-Life and Mission* (Bombay: Popular, 1962).

Ketkar S.V., *History of Caste in India* (London : Luzac & Co.., 1911), Vol. II.

Krishnan, S. Radha, *Indian Philosophy* (London: George Allen & Unwin Ltd., 1959), Vol. I

———, tr. *The Dhammapada* (Bombay: Oxford University Press, 1950).

Kuber, W.N., *Ambedker: A Critical Study* (Bombay: Popular Publishers, 1973).

———, *Builders of Modern India: B.R.Ambedkar* (New Delhi: Publication Division, Government of India, 1978).

Levenson B., tr., Stephen Cox, *The Dalai Lama, A Biography* (Bombay:Oxford University Press, 1989).

Ling, Trevor, *Buddhist Revival in India* (Hongkong: Macmillan, 1980).

Lohiya, Ram Manohar, *The Caste System* (Hyderabad: Navahind, 1964).

Lokhande, G.S., *Bhim Rao Ramji Ambedkar* (New Delhi: Sterling Publishers, 1977).

Lope, Donald S. tr., Dalai Lama's *Opening the eye of New Awareness* (London: Wisdom Publication, 1985).

Madan T.N., ed., *Religion in India* (Delhi: Oxford University Press, 1991).

Mahar, J. Michael, *The Untouchables in Contemporary India* (Arizona: University of Arizona Press, 1972).

Majumdar R.C., *Ancient India* (Delhi: Motilal Banarsidas, 1964).

Malik, Inder, *Dalai Lama's of Tiebet* (New Delhi: Uppal Publishing House, 1984).

Mandel Baum, David C., *Society in India* (Berkeley: The University of California Press,1970), 2 Vols.

Marion H. Duncon, *Harvest Festival Dramas of Tibet* (Hongkong: Orient Publishing Company, 1964).

Max Weber, tr., *The Religion of India: The Sociology of Hinduism and Buddhism,* Free Press of Glencoe, 1958.

Michel Peissel, *A Lost Tibetan Kingdom* (London: Collins and Harwell Press, 1968).

Pardue, Peter A., *Buddhism: A Historical Introduction to Buddhist Values and the Social and Political forms they have assumed in Asia* (New York: Macmillan Company, 1968).

Phadke Y.D., *Social Reformer of Maharashtra* (New Delhi: MIC, 1975).

Piatigorsky, Alexander, *Buddhist Philosophy of Thought: Essays in Interpretation* (London: Curzon, 1984).

Prabhu, Pandharinath H., *Hindu Social Organisation: A study in Socio-Psychological and Ideological Foundations* (Bombay: Popular, 1969).

Rahul, Ram, *The Dalai Lama: The Institution* (New Delhi: Vikas Publishing House Pvt. Ltd., 1995).

Rajgopalachari C., *Ambedkar Refuted* (Bombay: Hind Kitabs, 1946).

Rakshita, Sangha, *A Survey of Buddhism* (Bangalore: Indian Institute of World Culture, 1976).

———, *Ambedkar and Buddhism* (Glasgow: Windhorse Publications, 1989).

Rao, Padma K., *Women and caste in India* (Nidubrolu, A.P., Lokayata Publications, 1983).

Rhys Davids T.W., tr., *Dialogues of the Buddha* (London: Sacred Books of the Buddhists Series, Luzac & Co., Ltd., 1950) Parts I & II.

Rinchen Dakpa & Rooke B.A., *In Haste from Tibet* (London: Robert Hale, 1971).

Romikhosla, Buddhist , *Monasteries in the Western Himalaya* (Kathmandu: Ratna Pustak Bhandar, 1979).

Roy, Pratap Chandra, tr., *Mahabharata* (Delhi: Munshiram Manoharlal, 1970).

Saklanie, Girija, *The Uprooted Tibetans in India* (New Delhi: Cosmo Publications, 1984).

Samanta, Dipak Kumar, *The Dominant Weak: A Case Study of the Nava Bouddha of Maharashtra* (Calcutta: Anthropologcal Survey of India, 1991).

Sankrityayan Rahul, ed., *Buddhism: The Marxist Approach* (Delhi: P.P.House, 1970).

Sarkar, Anil Kumar, *Changing Phase of Buddhist Thought* (New Delhi: South Asian Publishers Pvt. Ltd., 1983).

Shakabpa, Tsepon W.D., *Tibet A Political History* (London: Yale University Press, 1967).

Shikhase D.N., *Dr.Ambedkar* (Poona: Jayant & Co., 1963).

Shiromany, A.A., *The Spirit of Tibet: Universal Heritage, Selected Speeches and Writtings of H H Dalai Lama XIV* (New Delhi: Allied Publishers, 1995).

Singh,Harijinder, *Caste Among Non-Hindus in India* (New Delhi: National Publishing House, 1977).

Singh, Sanghasen, ed., *Ambedkar on Buddhist conversion and Its Impact* (Delhi: Eastern Book Linkers, 1990).

Sircar D.C., *Studies in the Religious Life of Ancient and Medieval India* (Delhi: Motilal Banarsidas, 1971).

Snelling, John, *The Elements of Buddhism* (London: Element Books, 1990).

Sogen, Yamakami, *Systems of Buddhistic Thought* (Calcutta: Calcutta University, 1912).

Stcherbatsky, *The Central Conception of Buddhism* (London: Royal Asiatic Society, 1923).

———, *Buddhist Logic* (New Delhi: Orient, 1984).

Stein, A.,tr., Stapleton Driver J.E.,*Tibetan Civilisation* (London: Febar and Febar Ltd., 1992).

Steward, Whitney, *To the Lion Throne, the Story of XIV Dalai Lama* (New York: Snow Lion Publications, 1990).

Stewart, Tanka B. and Datta, Karubaki, *Religion and Society in the Himalayas* (New Delhi: Gyan Publishing House, 1991).

Suvandhana Maha Tera, *Selected Articles on Buddhism* (Bangkok: Chuan Printing Press Ltd., 1989).

Suzuki D.T., *Outlines of Mahayana Buddhism* (London: Luzac & Co., 1907).

Suzuki L. Beatrice, *Mahayana Buddhism* (London: George Allen & Unwin, 1959).

Swami Sankaranand, *The Western Buddhism or Christianity* (Calcutta: Nilmony Maharaj, 1956).

Taka Kusu Junjiro, *The Essentials of Buddhist Philosophy* (Hawaii: University of Hawaii, 1949).

Tambian S.J., *World Conqueror and World Renouncer* (Cambridge University Press, 1976).

Thapar, Romila, *Ancient Indian Social History: Some Interpretations* (New Delhi: Orient Longman Ltd., 1978).

———, *A History of India* (New Delhi: Penguin Books, 1990).

Thomas E.J., *History of Buddhist Thought* (London: Kegan Paul, 1953).

Vasu N.N., *Modern Buddhism and the Followers in Orissa* (Delhi: Gyan Publishing House, 1986).

Waddell, Austine L., *Buddhism & Lamaism of Tibet* (New Delhi: Heritage Publishers, 1974).

Wallace, B., Alan, tr. ed., *Dalai Lama XIV's Transcendent Wisdom* (New York: Snow Lion Publications, 1988).

Warder A.R. *Indian Buddhism* (Delhi: Motilal Benarsidas, 1970).

Warren H.C., *Buddhism in Translations* (Harward: Harward University Press, 1922).

Yamakami Sogen, *Systems & Buddhistic Thought* (Calcutta: Calcutta University, 1912).

Yogiraja, Swami Maharaja, (ed.), *The Buddha-Mimansa: The Buddha Relation to Vedic Religion* (Delhi: Sri Staguru Publications, 1912).

Zelliot, Eleanor, *From Untouchable to Dalit* (New Delhi: Manohar Publications, 1992).

ARTICLES

Ahir, D.C., "Dr. Ambedkar A Modern Bodhisattva", *Papers Presented in the National Seminar on the Life, Mission, Contribution and Relevance of Babasaheb Dr. B.R. Ambedkar* (New Delhi), 14 April 1991, pp. 1-12.

Baisantry, D.K., "Ambedkar and Conversions", *Mainstream* (New Delhi), 31 October, 1981, p. 9.

Barua B.R., "Revival of Buddhism in India", *Maha Bodhi Society* (Calcutta), Nov.-Dec. 1968, pp. 20-23.

Caroe, Olaf, "Tibet and the Dalai Lama", *Tibet Journal* (Dharmasala), Winter 1977, pp. 3-12.

Chandra, Pratap, "Buddhism as an Instrument of Social Change", *Current Biography* (USA), Vol. 476.

Chaudhary, S., "Renaissance of Buddhism", *Maha Bodhi society* (Calcutta), 1979, pp. 12-15.

Dalai Lama XIV, "Universal Responsibility", *Tibetan Review* (New Delhi), April 1976, p.21.

———, "India and Tibet", *Tibetan Review* (New Delhi), January/ February 1969, p. 14.

Das, Bhagwan,"Ambedkar journey to mass conversion", *Manthan* (New Delhi), Vol. 5, No.1, May 1983, pp. 51-67.

Davis, Grania, "Some Problems of Refugees Life and Inside Look", *Tibetan Review* (New Delhi), January 1978, p. 12.

Dhammaratana V., "The reason for Anti-Buddhist Propaganda in Brahmanical Literature", *Maha Bodhi Society* (Calcutta) , Vol. 62, pp. 4-6.

Dhondup, K., "What is Tibetan Culture?", Tibetan Review(New Delhi), April 1977, p. 22.

Duncan, Nancy, "Tibet's Dalai Lama Remains Powerful Force During Exile", *Tibetan Review* (New Delhi),January 1972, pp.14-15.

Dutta N., "Kerala Buddhism" *Maha Bodhi Society* (Calcutta), Souvenir, pp. 15-18.

———, "Hinduism and Buddhism", *Souvenir*, pp. 8-11.

———, "Dravidian Buddhist Children", *Souvenir*, pp. 20-30.

Ganguli, Dilip, "I Believe in Communism: An Interview with Dalai Lama ", *On Looker* (Bombay), 16-31 March 1979, p.36.

Gokhale, Jay Shree B., "Socio-Plitical Effects of Ideological Change: The Buddhist Conversion Maharashtrian Untouchables".

Journal of Asian Studies (Michigan), Vol. 45, No. 2, February pp.2690-92.

Goldstein, Melvync, "Tibetan Buddhist Monasticism: Social, Psychological and Cultural Implications" *Paper Presented in the National Seminar on the Life, Mission, Contributions and Relevance of Babasaheb, B.R.Ambedkar* (New Delhi), 14 April 1991, pp. 22-30.

Jatav D.R., "Dr. Ambedkar's Philosophy of Religion" *Papers Presented in the National Seminar on the Life, Mission, Contributions and Relevance of Babasaheb, B.R.Ambedkar* (New Delhi), 14 April 1991, pp. 22-30.

Kananaikil, Jose, "The State used to Promote Hindu Religion", *Dalit Voice* (Bangalore), Vol. 6, No. 20, September 1-15, 1987, pp. 1-6.

Krishnamurti, B.B., "Buddhist' Dhamma", *Papers Presented in the National Seminar on the life Mission, Contributions and Relevance of Babasaheb, B.R.Ambedkar* (New Delhi), 14 April 1991, pp. 34-40.

Kvarne, Per, "Genesis of the Tibetan Buddhist Tradition", *Tibetan Review* (New Delhi), March 1976, pp. 9-15.

Macy, Joanna Rogers and Zelliot, "Tradition and Innovation in Contemporary Indian Buddhism", *Studies in the History of Buddhism* (Delhi), 1980, p.134.

Mullin, Glenn H., "Tibetan Buddhism and the Dalai Lama Office", *Tibetan Review*(New Delhi), Vol. 20, April 1985, p.13.

Narayan, K.R., "Remembering Ambedkar", *Mainstream* (New Delhi), 28 January 1984, p. 64.

Norbu Dawa, "Tibetan's Tibet", *Tibetan Review* (New Delhi), May-June 1973, pp.16-17.

———, "Tibetan Refugees and Tibetan Culture", *Tibetan Review* (New Delhi), April 1978, pp. 15-16.

———, "What Tibet did in 2100 years", *Tibetan Review* (New Delhi), July 1973, p. 8.

———, " The Democratic Dạlai Lama ",*Tibetan Review* (New Delhi), July 1973, p.13.

Palkhivala, Nani, "The Messaiah and the Testament", *The Illustrated Weekly of India* (Bombay), 23-24 February, 1991, p.6.

Raju, K.S., "Dr. Ambedkar's Life and Philosophy", *Paper Presented in the National Seminar on the Life, Mission, Contributions and Relevance of Babasaheb, B.R. Ambedkar* (New Delhi), 14 April 1991, pp. 48-53.

Rakshita, Sangha, "My Life and Mission and the teaching of Dr. Ambedkar", *Dhamma Megha* (Pune), No. 17 July 1984, pp. 1-22.

———, "Progress and Religion", *Dhamma Megha* (Pune), No. 21, July 1985, pp.1-10

———, "Dr. Ambedkar's True greatness", *Dhamma Megha* (Pune), No. 23, January 1986, pp. 1-29.

———, "A Modern View of Buddhism", *Dhamma Megha* (Pune), No. 26, October 1986, pp. 1-17.

———, "Buddhism, World Peace and nuclear War", *Dhamma Megha* (Pune), No. 30, October 1987,pp. 1-25.

Ramakrishna, H.A., "Hinduism and Dr. B.R. Ambedkar: A Study in Paradox", *Papers Presented in the National Seminar on the Life, Mission, Contributions and Relevance of Babasaheb, B.R. Ambedkar* (New Delhi), 14 April 1991, pp. 31-33.

Rimpoche, Jamyang Khentse, "The Diversity and Unity of Four Sects", *Tibetan Review* (New Delhi), September 1976, p.12.

Sattar, Abdul, "Dr. Ambedkar Contribution and Buddhism", *Papers Presented in the National Seminar on the Life, Mission, Contributions and Relevance of Babasaheb, B.R. Ambedkar* (New Delhi), 14 April 1991, pp. 41-47.

Shekawat, Prahlad Singh, "Mc Leod Ganj – A Foreign Town in India", *Tibetan Review* (New Delhi), July 1985, pp. 16-18.

Sinha, Nirmal Chandra, "Indic Elements in Tibetan Culture: Polity", *Tibetan Review* (New Delhi), May 1969, pp. 8-9, 13.

Somphel, Norbu, "Notes on Sects: The Tree and the Branches", *Tibetan Review* (New Delhi), September 1976, pp. 28-29.

Tagyal, "Lamaism", *Tibetan Review* (New Delhi), December 1973, p. 19.

Tethong, Tsewang C., "A Tibetan View", *Tibetan Review* (New Delhi), January 1979, pp. 20-21.

Theiner, George, "Culture in Exile", *Tibetan Review* (New Delhi), May 1984, pp. 10-11 & 19.

JOURNALS

Dalit Voice (Bangalore)

Mainstream (New Delhi).

Maha Bodhi Society (Calcutta)

The Illustrated Weekly of India (Bombay)
Tibetan Bulletin (Dharamsala)
Tibet Journal (Dharamsala)
Tibetan Review (New Delhi)

Index